SMART GROWTH

From sprawl to sustainability

SMART GROWTH
From sprawl to sustainability

Jon Reeds

green books

First published in the UK in 2011 by

Green Books
Foxhole, Dartington,
Totnes, Devon TQ9 6EB

Design by Jayne Jones
Cover design by Jim Banting

ISBN 978 1 900322 82 9

Printed on Corona Natural 100% recycled paper by
TJ International Ltd, Padstow, Cornwall, UK

Contents

Introduction   9

Part I – How we got here

1   A squandered land   21
2   The germination of a bad idea   35
3   Decline and sprawl – a century of spatial planning   55
4   The death and life of great British cities   80
5   Travelling hopelessly – a century of unsustainable transport   103

Part II – Where we are

6   An unsustainable communities plan   120
7   Climate change and other future challenges   138
8   America – land of dreams   147

Part III – Where we need to be

9   Care and maintenance for a small country –
    Smart Growth planning   172
10 Care and maintenance of the countryside   197
11 Smart Growth transport   213
12 From consumers to citizens   230
13 News from Somewhere: a Smart Growth vision   250
14 Conclusions: urban rides   265

References   281
Index   289

Acknowledgements

I would like to thank all those many individuals and organisations who have helped with the writing of this book, especially those involved with the Smart Growth UK Steering Group.

My particular thanks for their encouragement, support, inspiration and practical assistance are due to Kaid Benfield, Keith Buchan, Elizabeth Cox, Allan Dare, Chris Gent, Kate Gordon, Jim Harkins, Fiona Howie, Bridget Leach, Brian Lomas, Gail Mayhew, Paul Miner, Marina Pacheco, Henry Oliver, Paul Squires, John Whitelegg, Rebecca Willis, Glynn Wilton and, of course, to everyone at Green Books.

I have had a great deal of wise advice and input from a range of organisations and individuals, both those involved with the Steering Group and others, but while this book reflects much of their advice and wisdom, I would stress that the views and conclusions contained in it, and any mistakes, are mine and mine alone.

Finally I would like to thank Kathy, for putting up with me while I was writing it – and even when I was cursing an empty screen and not writing it.

*For Chris, whose generation will have to cope
with the mess we made.*

Introduction

It hardly needs pointing out that at this moment we are in a very serious mess, so serious that even the dullest witted people find it difficult to remain unaware of it.

George Orwell, *The Road to Wigan Pier*

These are challenging times for environmentalists. While the gloomy prognostications of the last 40 years are starting to come true and governments are, at long last, paying at least lip-service to the problems, opposition is mounting too, and some long-standing beliefs are proving, in all senses of the word, unsustainable.

Take urban sprawl, for instance. Fought by conservationists since the nineteenth century, we in the UK have nevertheless spent the last 100 years pursuing it relentlessly, spurred on by a fuzzy nostalgia for our ancestors' rural past, by a desire to live in the countryside the sprawl destroys, by a widely held belief that low-density garden city or garden suburb living is good for us, and by a retreat from community into individualism. Meanwhile, across the Atlantic in the country of hypersprawl, robust principles for turning back the tide have been developed.

Or take car dependency, fought by environmentalists since the 1960s. We have nevertheless spent the last 100 years pursuing this too, spurred on by an illusory 'freedom of the open road', by the self-inflicted destruction of our public transport, by the demands of low-density living and by the same retreat from community into individualism. Curiously, one of the places pursuing the 'transit-oriented development' philosophy long practised in some European countries and effectively trashed here is, once again, the United States – the land of 18-lane freeways and heroic individualism. One shouldn't knock individualism, of course, but we have come to practise it at the expense of the community, and its blind pursuit has left us with some strangely contradictory beliefs about the environment.

The US is certainly not the first country most people in the UK seeking answers to the problems of urban sprawl or car dependency would look to for inspiration. Haven't we had the world's finest planning system for more than 60 years? Haven't we recently elected 'the greenest government ever'? Isn't our right to drive anyway seriously curtailed by congestion, by speed limits, by narrow roads, by speed cameras? Surely there's nothing the Americans can teach us? But, as we shall see, there is.

Invitation to join the government of Britain?

The Conservatives so entitled their manifesto for the general election in May 2010, but the election was a strange affair, overshadowed by a two-year financial nightmare. Few other issues really made it on to the political radar and, while there was a lot of hot air about global warming, there was little debate on environmental and social issues such as urban regeneration or even New Labour's long-neglected urban renaissance. Car dependency and urban sprawl hardly registered with politicians determined not to upset the voters or their newspapers with such hostages to fortune.

Labour's reticence was understandable – with John Prescott managing domestic policy it had spent three years pursuing an urban renaissance, brownfield-first policy and an emphasis on transit; it then spent ten more under Gordon Brown dismantling them. But, almost uniquely among the major parties, it did mention urban regeneration and reiterated its long-standing (and long-exceeded) target of building 60 per cent of new homes in England on brownfield sites. The Conservatives promised councils and local people the sort of 'knit your own' planning system foreshadowed in a paper called 'Open Source Planning' in February 2010. They promised to replace detailed national planning guidance with a simple statement of national policy and to scrap regional strategies on the grounds that their destructive top-down house-building targets had exacerbated urban sprawl. But the reality was that sprawl would, instead, be promoted by allowing local authorities money if they allowed new development and leaving them hopelessly impoverished if they didn't. All three main parties promised protection for 'the green belt' (in a country which actually has lots of green belts) and there were promises to improve the protected area system, while the Greens went further and promised landscape-scale conservation.

Policies to tackle our 'great car economy' offered little more grounds for optimism. There was a great deal of talk about high-speed rail links that we probably can't afford and, while Labour was sticking to its doomed plans to expand Heathrow and other airports, the other parties wanted these scrapped, although there was vague talk of pursuing alternatives elsewhere. There was vague talk too about electric cars but little about urban public transport, apart from Labour having the audacity to promise tram systems in major cities, after spending six years derailing such schemes. Both Labour and the Conservatives were almost silent over whether they intended to go on spending billions on building roads, although the Liberal Democrats did at least promise to reopen railway lines and divert money from the roads budget to rail investment – perhaps the only radical transport policy pursued by the major parties, but one that never made it into the coalition agreement. The Green Party also proposed to reallocate the road-building budget to public transport. Virtually alone among the political parties, it did voice some urban transit policy too, with a proposal to "plan for mixed-use developments where shops, housing and businesses are closely located and connected by pavements and cycleways" and to invest in light rail.

Attention grabbing

One brownfield issue did become an election issue, however, and it demonstrated how far debate needs to go in the UK if we are to start really taking across-the-board sustainability seriously. The issue was the product of a couple of years of largely manufactured outrage among the opposition parties about a subject that began life as 'back-garden development' and metamorphosed into the catchier 'garden grabbing'. According to this theory, the brownfield-first and urban-densification policies pursued since the late 1990s had been encouraging developers to knock down beautiful suburban villas and replace them with flats (destroying most of their gardens) or even just to build flats in the gardens around them.

It does happen, of course – sometimes – though only occasionally. But opposition politicians, even some happy to rail about urban sprawl, found it was a good way to get their names in the local paper or even the national press. And so, as the 2010 election approached, politicians queued up to claim that their constituents' gardens were being 'grabbed', while one Sunday newspaper claimed that government figures showed 180,000 domestic gardens had been concreted over in five years and even that, in some areas, "up to 94 per cent of residential development was on gardens".[1]

In the end, an embattled Labour government commissioned Kingston University to study the problem.[2] Of 127 local authority areas studied, only 50 noted garden grabbing as an issue and, while 1,739 such new homes had been approved in 2007-8, 6,892 had been refused. The study noted that existing guidance actually gave councils powers to formulate local plans to eliminate the issue if they wished but that few had found it necessary, and it referred to a Brentwood Borough Council supplementary document that had done so effectively. It was noted too that the changes to planning guidance alleged to have created the problem had been introduced by a Conservative government in 1992; curiously, Conservative-supporting papers omitted to mention this. Instead they kept up the onslaught and, although the problem was mostly bogus, powers existed to control it and it wasn't actually the government's fault, a general election was approaching and the New Labour government announced changes to planning guidance to make clear that there was no presumption that previously developed land was suitable for development or that all of it should be developed.[3] This was quite enough to prevent any further problems, yet both Conservatives and Liberal Democrats included this largely bogus concern in their manifestos.

The trouble is that, once you promise something specific and get elected, you may even be expected to deliver. Within a month of the election, planning guidance had been changed to rate gardens as 'greenfield sites'. That would have had little effect in practice, but somewhere along the line the house builders had persuaded the Conservatives to confuse the issue with another cause dear to the hearts of both – an end to minimum housing density standards, which they claimed were causing 'town cramming' and construction of insufficient 'family homes'.

As we shall see in Chapter 6, minimum density standards had been imposed for the first time in 1999 as part of a brief but commendable 'urban renaissance' pursued by the New Labour government for its first three or four years before Gordon Brown gained full control over domestic policy. Its 30-homes-per-hectare standard was pretty low by historical standards, but it followed 90 years of *maximum* density standards. Victorian builders could build houses with amenity space at 70 to the hectare or more, but today the last thing house

There are many ways of grabbing gardens.

builders want is to do is cram lots of houses on a site. Believe it or not, it's much more commercial to build as few houses as possible on a given plot, as large houses are much more profitable than small ones. They waste land on a grand scale, and one of the factors that helped the new government get elected was the partially accurate view that Labour had spent nearly a decade pursuing urban sprawl. Yet, in its first five weeks, the new coalition had introduced a major measure to increase sprawl and had the Campaign to Protect Rural England accusing it of threatening the country with environmental disaster.[4]

The distant roots of sprawl

Environmental disaster? Surely protecting our gardens and building family homes have nothing to do with environmental disaster? Don't be so sure.

You could, of course, be forgiven for thinking that the change in planning guidance introduced by the new coalition government in June 2010[5] was a real green advance, as it was supported by impeccably environmental bodies. It drew immediate support from the Town & Country Planning Association, the Royal Horticultural Society and the Royal Society for the Protection of Birds, with the latter two organisations even quoted in the government's press release. The Joseph Rowntree Foundation (JRF), whose century of philanthropy and dedication to social and environmental causes is beyond question, issued a paper shortly afterwards which lauded the decision.[6]

And herein lies the root of this tale. The JRF report went very much further than merely joining in the garden-grabbing campaign for, despite admitting that a decade of England's 'brownfield-first' policies had helped deprived areas' population and housing market recover and reduced deprivation there, and had done so at the expense of greenfield sprawl (which had heightened the plight of deprived urban areas), it called for an end to the national brownfield residential target, which stipulated that 60 per cent of all new homes in England be built on brownfield sites. This apparently contrary policy was justified on the basis that areas with little brownfield land supply should have more greenfield land released for development (which already happens), that the economic downturn could reduce interest in brownfield land, so reducing overall house building, and that "the move towards high-density, compact urban development raises concerns over town-cramming and garden-grabbing as well as the compatibility of new development with the character of the built environment in some mature residential neighbourhoods." It also claimed that the policy had prompted house builders to build too many flats (true) and claimed that the Environment Agency was worried at the effect on flooding of brownfield reuse (in fact the Agency spends a lot of time shouting itself hoarse over greenfield development in floodplains).

The Foundation's conclusion was that brownfield policy needs to be "more nuanced and contextualised", and if I knew what that meant I might agree, but there was evidently a full-scale onslaught on urban densification and brownfield-first policies buried here.

Why should this be? What was such an august and impeccably philanthropic body doing attacking a policy introduced to protect undeveloped land and reduce our dependence on remote, car-dependent development? To find the answer we must look back more than 100 years to the roots of our present disorder.

In 1900, the sweet manufacturer and philanthropist Sir Joseph Rowntree became alarmed by work by his son Seebohm Rowntree, which revealed poor housing conditions in the city of York where his factory stood.

Contact with his business rival, fellow Quaker and friend George Cadbury convinced Rowntree that a model village on the lines of Bournville, or W. H. Lever's Port Sunlight, was the solution. Rowntree met two young architects called Raymond Unwin and Barry Parker, became impressed by their book *The Art of Building a Home*[7] and Unwin's pamphlet *Cottage Plans and Common Sense*,[8] and commissioned them to design a new model village at New Earswick outside York.

The building standards of the time emphasised high-density house building which made highly efficient use of land while still allowing residents sunlight and fresh air and providing at least a small amount of amenity space for each house. Unwin and Parker, products of the Arts and Crafts movement, tossed all that aside in favour of low-density groups of 'cottages' in short blocks with large front and back gardens and enclosing a large area at the rear away from the road. A large (too large as it turned out) village green was supplied in the centre of the new suburb.

New Earswick grew slowly but proved seminal in the reaction against the traditional, land-efficient town building and led to more than 100 years of low-density urban development in the UK, which was widely imitated abroad. It entered the DNA of the planning profession, for reasons described in Chapter 2, and it obviously took firm hold at the Joseph Rowntree Foundation. A century after New Earswick, the Joseph Rowntree Housing Trust was supporting another low-density greenfield suburb outside York called Derwenthorpe.

Why this matters

The United Kingdom is a most overcrowded country. I know that just saying this will put many people on alert, for such thoughts can play midwife to some really unpleasant and dangerous political beliefs. So, unless you're one of those strange people whose historical heroes strutted their stuff in plus-fours and jackboots, we need to find a peaceful way of coping with this challenge. For overcrowded it is, even though large parts of the island of Great Britain and small parts of Northern Ireland have relatively low population densities by European standards (though why an overcrowded continent like Europe should be taken as the standard is unclear).

In fact the existence of remote areas such as the mountains and moors of these islands is part of the problem, for most of the country's population is squeezed into its limited lowland areas. The trouble is that these areas are also supposed to provide us with our food, our workspace, much of our water, our transport system and our amenity. The problem is particularly acute in England, where the Pennines, moors and downland take up a significant percentage of a small country and tens of millions of people are squeezed into the rest.

Until 2008, the Netherlands had the dubious distinction of being the mostly densely populated country in Europe (apart from the crowded island of Malta), with a density of 393 people in every square kilometre. But in that year it was overtaken by England, whose population was growing rapidly on the back of an unsustainable economic bubble, with 395 people packed into every square kilometre. Even taken as a whole, with its large areas of mountains and moorland, the UK was still accommodating 253 people per square kilometre.

But most of that is packed into England's lowlands. England's 395/km^2 makes its population density 70 per cent higher than Germany's, more than twice Italy's and more still than France's. Worldwide, only a small handful of acutely overcrowded countries, such as Bangladesh and South Korea, have higher population densities than England.

Now, a rational person might conclude that a country with a really high population density, unable to feed itself in an uncertain world, short of water, with an environment scarred by two or three hundred years of industrial development, would be intensely protective of its land resource. As Mark Twain said, "buy land because they aren't making it any more." But we actually build our homes at pretty much the lowest density of any country in western Europe, and we have been doing this for 100 years. And although our endlessly sprawling suburbs are linked by a transport system heavily dependent on fossil fuels and which is destroying more of our precious land, we persist in building roads and neglecting alternatives.

We need to look at why we do this. Why does such a crowded country build at such low densities? Why are we building so many 'family homes' when the growth in households is single people and the elderly? Why was New Labour's urban renaissance derailed by New Labour itself? How has the roads lobby kept transport spending concentrated on roads? Why was the light railway programme killed? What happened to our community values and how can we get them back? How should we fashion our country to cope with climate

We've spent 100 years building at ruinously low densities.
Image: Leeds Library and Information Service

change? How will we feed ourselves in an overcrowded world increasingly short of food, and how will we get around and keep warm in a world where the oil and gas are running out?

I know the British have always been proud to be potty, and to some extent I admire that, but there comes a time to admit that we smell a rat. No doubt we have all been complicit in some way – we are all (author not excepted) seduced by the idea of a house in the country, a house with a garden, the freedom of the open road, etc. But for most of us, most of the time, these dreams are just that: dreams. When we buy a new home in the country, it's no longer the country, it's part of an expanding suburb. When we buy a house with a garden, our time-poor lifestyles prevent us from enjoying it. When we take our cars out we don't enjoy the freedom of the open road, we struggle from one traffic jam to the next. Suburban sprawl has become a monster destroying our environment, not the answer to our dreams. We have to change, whether we like it or not.

We have to, because this matters. It matters because that change will get harder every year this sprawl continues. It matters because people are getting rich out of this orgy of environmental destruction and paying for extremely successful lobbies to keep it going. And it matters because a whole range of environmental factors – climate change, soil degradation, peak oil, peak food, peak water (more about these in Chapter 7) – mean there's no rational alternative to change. It is time to change not only because we want to but because we have to. It is time to recognise too that there are ways of changing that will bring us great benefits and which can be achieved without the usual millions of casualties that tend to accompany really radical change. The change could be made across two, three, four decades without real pain – and with real gain.

Disasters and what to do about them

This book begins with the story of an environmental disaster and ends with a very positive alternative.

Like most of the biggest environmental disasters, the one we're concerned with took place over such a long timescale that no one recognises it as a single disaster and many influential people would still rate it a success.

The disaster was sustained by two very powerful lobbies. The existence of a 'roads lobby' is well enough recognised by environmentalists, but I believe there has also been a 'sprawl lobby' at work, composed of a similar mixture of idealism and vested interest. The two seldom seem to cooperate, but together they have wrought this disaster.

Its time frame was a very long one – roughly the whole twentieth century – quite slow enough for any sort of disaster to be overlooked. But it has still been a disaster, for all of that. And it matters in more than the abstract way that most history matters. For it is a disaster that continues to wreak havoc on our environment on every single day of every single year. It is a disaster that powerful vested interests are fighting very, very hard, and very successfully, to make worse. Some are doing it because they still believe it to be right, while others are doing it for the very rational reason that they stand to make a lot of money from it. And in an epoch that regards profitable commerce as one of the highest human callings, that is a challenge that needs to be taken very seriously indeed.

A smarter approach

All too often, environmental books make you miserable (admit it, there is much to be miserable about). But we must try not to be too miserable as we look at this history and its legacy – not because this is some kind of green 'truth and reconciliation' commission, but because tackling the problem requires us to recognise that these forces hold sway today and are still wreaking havoc, sometimes even in the name of environmental protection.

Tackling them will necessitate learning some lessons from, of all places, the United States of America, for the country that made these mistakes the most enthusiastically is now tackling them the most energetically. The UK and the USA are very different countries with very different needs – but the principles developed by the 'Smart Growth' movement in the US over the last two decades are ones we can learn from, adapt and apply if we are to retrofit our cramped and beleaguered country to face the very real environmental challenges to come.

Smart Growth rejects urban sprawl and car dependency and promotes compact, functional towns and cities, the regrowth of communities and an emphasis on rail-based transit systems. It has grown out of decades of opposition to the sprawl and highway development that have so damaged America and out of the work of urbanists and conservationists. But America is a much bigger and less densely populated country than the UK, so if it matters a lot there, it matters much, much more here. Work has already begun in bringing these ideas to our shores. Now it's time to look at ways they might be adapted and developed.

Smart Growth UK

Some effort has already been made to create a UK Smart Growth initiative. In the autumn of 2006, with environmental NGOs watching with horror as Gordon Brown stripped away the gains made by the urban renaissance and the UK's tentative environmental approaches to transport planning, proposals were discussed to hold a conference on bringing the Smart Growth philosophy to the UK. Speakers were provisionally identified, a programme put together and marketing began.

It didn't get very far. Planners in particular quickly revealed that most had never heard of Smart Growth; when it was explained to them what it was, most responded 'We do that anyway.' Amidst much dismal evidence that Britain believed itself to be at the forefront of the world's sustainability movement, one particularly common response was 'There's nothing the Yanks can teach us about planning and transportation.'

As will become clear in this book, this isn't the case, but, sadly, it was enough to get the conference abandoned. Yet out of the wreckage came an initiative by a group of green NGOs to set up a Smart Growth UK initiative. A steering group held a series of meetings in 2007-8, which sought ways of promoting the Smart Growth principles and objectives, a more comprehensible approach to planning sustainable communities, a counterbalance to the excessive emphasis on the economy in UK policy, etc. It was agreed to formulate a set of principles for Smart Growth in the UK and to set up a new body, to act as a coalition, from the participating groups and other bodies that might wish to join. The principles were agreed (see box, right) and recommendations about launching an initiative were put to the participating groups.

Despite agreement on the principles, however, the initiative didn't go ahead at the time, although the Smart Growth UK Steering Group has continued to meet sporadically and none of the participating groups has, at the time of

The Smart Growth UK principles

- **Plan compact communities**
  Smart Growth promotes well-designed, compact, functional communities and rejects land-hungry sprawl and wastage of greenfield land.

- **Strengthen and direct development towards existing communities**
  Smart Growth emphasises use of communities' existing infrastructure and resources and conserves open space and urban fringes.

- **Provide sustainable transport choices**
  Smart Growth reduces dependence on road transport and increases opportunities for walking, cycling and public transport. Towns, cities and villages should be pedestrian-friendly and rail-accessible.

- **Protect the unbuilt environment**
  Smart Growth believes our countryside and open space is a precious environmental, social and economic resource. It should be protected and husbanded if we are to move towards a more sustainable society. Squandering it will create, not solve, problems for our towns and will do nothing for our national economy.

- **Foster distinctive, attractive communities with a strong sense of place**
  Smart Growth encourages communities to develop their own identity and vision, respecting their cultural and architectural heritage. It supports human-scale development and opposes large, monolithic developments, out-of-town retailing and 'big box' architecture.

- **Mix land uses**
  Smart Growth supports a sensible mix of land uses to suit communities, which meets their daily needs.

- **Encourage communities to flourish and grow**
  Smart Growth supports mixed-income, mixed-age, inclusive communities that take responsibility for their own development. Local economies should be developed to make them more self-supporting.

- **Create a range of housing opportunities and choice**
  Smart Growth supports quality living for people of all income groups, ages and needs. We want human-scale development at appropriate densities to support sustainable transportation and local facilities.

- **Make development decisions fair and economically inclusive**
  For communities to successfully implement Smart Growth they must ensure all three sectors of the economy – public, private and community – function successfully and sustainably.

writing, formally withdrawn. The reason given for halting progress put forward by two of the groups was that they intended to concentrate their immediate efforts on research into integration of transport and land use planning to reduce journey lengths, and to compare the transport emissions of high- and low-density communities. In the event, this research went ahead (eventually supported by only one of the groups) and the following year an excellent report was issued. It has certainly informed that group's work in a number of areas and has been cited in evidence to inquiries, etc., but is a long way from forming part of a coherent national movement, which was the objective of Smart Growth UK.

But we do need to look beyond the 'dumb growth' world we're still creating. For a Smart Growth nation would be a very different nation a few decades from now, and it's worth seeing how. We have much to gain even if we have to give up a few long-cherished dreams, for these dreams have become nightmares.

How did we get in this mess? Where are we now? And what can we do to make things better?

PART I

How we got here

Chapter 1

A squandered land

*The preparations for this work have been suitable to the author's
earnest concern for its usefulness.*

Daniel Defoe, *A Tour Thro' the Whole Island of Great Britain*

Man and boy

One bright February morning in 1885, a stout, bearded man took a walk
around the historic streets of Oxford before heading for Wadham College and
the Holywell Music Room where he was to address a political meeting. It's just
possible that his walk was witnessed by one of the city's younger citizens – a
seven-year-old boy – although in fact he was probably attending the Church
School in Cowley, close to where his father worked as a clerk. Our bearded
man, a graduate of Exeter College, made several visits to the city at this period,
and while it's possible that his and the boy's paths could have crossed, their very
different social circumstances make it unlikely. Which is a pity, for here were
two people whose ideas and activities profoundly influenced the way we lived
throughout the twentieth century and into the twenty-first, and the thought of
them occupying the same stretch of pavement is a curiously seductive one.

But the comings and goings of well-to-do gentlemen connected with the
University probably occupied few of the younger man's thoughts as he grew
up, for he was of a mechanical bent and in 1891 was apprenticed to a bicycle
repairer. Yet their two paths may have crossed one last time, one wet October
day in 1896, when the older man's funeral cortège paused at Oxford station to
allow local people to pay their respects. No one from the University attended,

for the deceased man had shocked its sensibilities a few years earlier with a harangue about his political beliefs. Once again, our young bicycle repairer, now four days short of his fourteenth birthday, might still have shown little interest in the eccentric and obviously artistic mourners or the beautifully carved coffin in the train's guard's van laid out like a chapel, unless someone had mentioned the name of the man within, for the name was his own.

It's easy to read too much into coincidence, but these two namesakes, despite their very different backgrounds, really did mould the physical shape of our country today. Although both men were philanthropists, both believed strongly in improving the lot of the poor and both were lovers of the country-side and historic buildings, they were very different. Yet their ideas and activities contributed so hugely to creating the car-dependent urban sprawl that passes for environment in the UK today that even such a coincidence is impossible to ignore. The name they shared was William Morris.

Mention of the name William Morris today is likely to bring to most people's minds the founder of the Arts and Crafts movement; the passionate guild socialist; the inspired designer of fabrics, furnishings and furniture; the poet; the writer; the building conservationist and much else besides. Born in 1834, William Morris I (as I shall call him) was an extraordinary man, rightly revered today for his skill as a designer, his advocacy of handicrafts, his role in founding the Society for the Protection of Ancient Buildings, his influence in developing Britain's socialism along a very different path from the one in those countries where Marx was revered, for his poetry, for his close association with the Pre-Raphaelite Brotherhood and for much else.

Yet Victorian aesthetic values underwent a long eclipse in the mid-twentieth century, and mention of the name William Morris in that period would have brought to most people's minds an equally famous, but wholly different individual. William Morris II (1877-1963) was an engineering colossus who once stood at the peak of British manufacturing, earning him the title by which he's better remembered: Lord Nuffield. William II was responsible for introducing mass production methods to the British car industry and, within a couple of decades of his founding it, Morris Motors was by far the largest car manufacturer in the land. So successful was it that Morris was dubbed 'the British Henry Ford' and generations of motorists enjoyed their cheap but reliable 'bull-nosed' Morris, Morris 8, Morris Minor and Morris Oxford cars.

The differences between the two are marked. William I came from a well-to-do background and enjoyed a comfortable lifestyle, despite which he became a passionate socialist. William II came from a humble background and became a hugely successful and wealthy industrialist and, although he liked to describe himself as 'apolitical', he flirted with fascism in the early 1930s (to his subsequent regret – he later gave generously to charities helping Jewish refugees from Europe). Both, as befits men with a good Oxfordshire surname, were associated with Oxford for part or much of their lives, but although William I was a graduate he fell out with the University after delivering his tub-thumping socialist polemic to its worthies. William II wasn't a graduate, but held the University in such high regard that he endowed Nuffield College, which he intended should become predominantly an undergraduate engineering college. The University was so grateful it made it a postgraduate social science college.

Both men loved Oxford's historic buildings and both owned substantial homes in the Oxfordshire countryside, but their influence took very different forms. William I inspired a new generation of architects and planners with a view of simple rural idylls for all, which led to an explosion of suburbia that he would no doubt have deplored. William II brought cheap mass motoring to the people at large, enabling them to pursue this rural/suburban dream. The result of a century of practising these ideals is a ruined environment and a country hopelessly ill-equipped to deal with the challenge of climate change.

If that seems harsh, particularly on William I, then bear with me. This will be a tale of idealism gone wrong and greed got right, of the things we craved and the things we continue to crave. It will describe where we went wrong and how we continue to get things wrong. It will look at how we can challenge these failings with ideas from the country where they were most enthusiastically, successfully and damagingly embraced. It will try – and fail – to avoid the seductive trap that most environmental books fall into, of saying 'we need to do things differently', because we do, and urgently. But worry not: a great

The Morrises' Oxford. *Image: National Tramway Museum*

deal of what we need to do is rediscover old ways of doing things, and in seeking inspiration we will merely need to do what we frequently do but may be reluctant to admit. We will have to look for inspiration across the Atlantic.

Travelling hopefully

This book is partly about history, partly about the present and partly about the future, but even I haven't been around for much of the history I cover. Luckily

William Morris   1834-1896

William Morris.

Designer, poet, reformer, socialist, writer, artist, architect, environmental campaigner, craftsman – the range of William Morris's achievements in his lifetime is huge. Today he is probably best remembered for being the key figure in creation of the Arts and Crafts movement, but the sheer range of his life's work is much broader, and hard to encompass in a few paragraphs.

Morris was born into a well-to-do London family, grew up in modest affluence and studied at Oxford. At the University he met Edward Burne-Jones and other artists influenced by the Pre-Raphaelites. His life encompassed spells as an architect and painter before he founded Morris, Marshall, Faulkner & Co., which produced a range of wallpaper, fabrics, carpets, decoration and much else with a firm ethos of hand-made craftsmanship at a time when industrial production was increasingly mechanised.

Much of Morris's life's energy went into politics, where his passionate brand of socialism was an important thread in developing the philosophy along non-Marxist lines in the UK. He was one of the first people in Britain who could be called an environmental campaigner; he founded the Society for the Protection of Ancient Buildings and was active in the Commons Society, which fought to protect open space from development, and the Kyrle Society, which campaigned to bring beauty into people's lives. He owned Kelmscott Manor in Oxfordshire but was never a great ruralist, although he campaigned for open space use for areas threatened with development.

He was such a polymath that it is hard to categorise him, but his ideas were certainly used by Ebenezer Howard, Raymond Unwin, etc. to promote sprawl. What Morris would have made of the result is anybody's guess. His fantasy novel **News from Nowhere** foresees a future very different from the way the twentieth century actually developed.

I have a string of volunteers to help describe these changes from a first-person viewpoint, and it was extremely good of Britain's domestic travel writers over the last 800 years to cooperate in this way. For, among our many eccentricities as a nation, we are spectacularly prone to blunder our way around our islands and publish an account of our travels. Some of these are insightful, some obscure and some completely lunatic, but many give us first-hand views of

William Richard Morris
1st Viscount Nuffield   1877-1963

William Richard Morris grew up in humble circumstances in Oxford, left school at 15 and was apprenticed to a bicycle repairer, but his mechanical flair and business acumen was to turn him into one of twentieth-century Britain's most successful industrialists. Morris Motors, at one stage the largest UK car manufacturer, earned Morris the title of 'the British Henry Ford'.

He began manufacturing the 'bullnose Morris' car at Cowley before the First World War and later introduced Ford's mass production techniques. By the outbreak of the Second World War Morris Motors was one of the four main UK manufacturers and Morris's smaller cars brought the era of mass motoring to the nation. His company merged with Austin in 1952 to form the British Motor Corporation, which dominated the British motor industry for the rest of his life and after, until its long decline as British Leyland.

Morris was a great philanthropist and gave to many good causes, including Oxford University, hospitals, depressed areas, sports, medical and armed forces charities and Nuffield College, which he endowed and is named after him. He gave away more than £30 million during his lifetime – estimated to be the equivalent of more than £11 billion today.

He was a man of simple tastes and was never happier than when he had his hands on automotive machinery, and even later in life he would stop his car if he saw a broken-down motor and try to help.

He represented the last generation that assumed Britain could be the workshop of the world, and would no doubt have been astonished to see industry pass into foreign ownership and move to the Far East. He saw his low-cost but reliable cars as a force for democracy. Probably more than any other single figure he was responsible for turning a country of public transport users into a nation of motorists.

Morris's simple and reliable cars helped revolutionise British motoring.

what went on, what's going on and, in a few amazing cases (including one by William Morris I), what's going to go on. This is especially useful, as my publishers have turned down my entirely reasonable request for an enormously expensive but state-of-the-art time machine, as a luxury an environmental writer should learn to do without.

And it really is over 800 years since the Welsh monk Giraldus Cambrensis – 'Gerald of Wales' – mounted his horse to produce his *Topographia Hibernica* (1188), *Itinerarirum Cambriae* (1191) and *Descriptio Cambriae* (1194). Giraldus became chaplain to Henry II, a hazardous occupation if you remember what happened to Thomas Beckett, and accompanied Prince John and the Archbishop of Canterbury on tours of Ireland and Wales.

Giraldus lived at a time when the population was expanding rapidly, and no doubt urban sprawl was too. Scholars still argue about medieval demographics, but it seems likely the population of England was around a million in 1066 but had grown to anything between four and six million by 1300. But early in the fourteenth century Europe was hit by famine and then by the Black Death and subsequent plagues, though the population may have been already in decline before these events, and although historians argue over the reasons – overpopulation, increasing wealth inequality and poverty, food shortages and consequent reduced resistance to disease – the period provides a salutary reminder that we ignore our impact on the environment at our peril.

Plagues were to trouble us for another four centuries and population probably continued to decline into the fifteenth century and didn't begin to grow again until the early sixteenth, but even pestilence, the awful standard of the inns and the state of the nation's roads (no change there) failed to deter the Renaissance, or even the renaissance of UK travel writing. The Tudor period saw populations starting to grow again and travel writers saddling up and sharpening their quills. During the sixteenth century the population of England grew rapidly from a little more than two million to almost four, and in Queen Elizabeth I's reign a statute was passed to prevent London spreading into the productive horticultural land around it, as food security was as concerning then as it was until the Common Agricultural Policy made us worried about surpluses – for a while.

The Tudor travel writers such as John Leland, William Camden, Edward Chamberlain and Edward Blome were concerned with topography, in its broadest sense, with Camden setting himself the colossal task, given the communications of his time, of describing the entire island from the Scillies to the Shetlands. Had he succeeded he would have been able to describe a country with a rapidly rising population.

The seventeenth century saw the growth of interest in antiquities, but this was the beginning of the Age of Enlightenment and even the antiquarian writers of the day showed a keen interest in science and technology. Many travelled to the Fens, where drainage was hitting its stride and helping to feed an English population grown to perhaps five million, despite the onset of the 'Little Ice Age'. Climate change, whether man-made or natural, is something we ignore at extreme risk; we assume that the comfortable temperate weather we've enjoyed for the last couple of centuries or so will continue.

At the end of the seventeenth and the beginning of the eighteenth centuries two of our greatest travel writers dismounted from their horses and reached for their quills. Celia Fiennes spent 20 years recording her impressions of a country where population growth had been stalled by civil war, religious conflict and climate problems. A little later the 'hack journalist' Daniel Defoe (nothing wrong with hack journalists thank you very much) made his own journeys. Both shed a great deal of ink recording the way people grew their corn or earned it and how they lived.

By the early eighteenth century the English population had grown to around six million, and antiquarian writers such as William Stukeley and wealthy men like the Hon. John Byng left accounts of their travels and their stays with the local aristocracy, who seemed to offer a sort of hostel service for the rich.

As the century went on and the agrarian revolution gathered pace, writers such as Arthur Young took particular interest in farming, and by the time the nineteenth century arrived, with the population of Great Britain swollen beyond 10 million and people flocking to industrial towns, it was still possible for the great William Cobbett to record his passionate interest in the working of the land, in rare intervals between raging about his age's social and economic injustices. How we use the land – one way or another – is what this book is about.

In the two centuries that followed Cobbett there was an initial eclipse in travel writing while the birth of the railways shrank Britain's size drastically, even as its population exploded. By 1841 the population had grown to 15.9 million, by 1851 it was 17.9 million, in 1861 it passed 20 million, in 1871 it was 22.7 million, in 1881 25.9 million, in 1891 29 million and in 1901 it was 32.5 million, more than triple what it had been a century earlier. The growth was driven by advances in public health, the beginnings of mechanisation in agriculture and the ability to buy in food, thanks to the wealth created by the industrial revolution. This period also saw people flocking to the industrial cities. It took a world war and a depression to see the reflowering of travel writing. H. V. Morton harked back to a time in the eighteenth century when topography and antiquarianism was in vogue and sparked a rebirth of the travel book about nice places. And in the inter-war period two other writers of genius, George Orwell and J. B. Priestley, opened the eyes of their compatriots to the misery and squalor of the poverty in their midst, which rekindled the travel writing genre about not-so-nice places that has also seen a recent reflowering. By 1931 the UK population was still rising, but the growth was concentrated into southern England and the Midlands; the older industrial areas were stagnant or beginning long periods of decline. In the inter-war period another UK travel genre emerged – the traveller using a strange form of transport. D. H. Lawrence described Walter Wilkinson's first book *The Peep Show*[1] as revealing "England better than 20 novels by clever young ladies and gentlemen". This was no mean achievement given that Wilkinson's chosen mode of travel around the hazardous motor roads of the 1920s and 1930s was a hand-cart carrying his own Punch & Judy show.

After the Second World War came another hiatus in travel writing, but from the 1960s, with the UK population up to 50 million, writers such as John Hillaby and Roger Higham began to revive the genre. Since then the literature has, like the population, just grown and grown, with writers anxious to share their accounts of travels on foot, by bike, on horseback, by punt or, for all I know, by wheelbarrow or pogo stick. A more recent development since the mid-1990s has been explorations of our growing social dystopia. By the end of the century, with the UK population past 60 million, these were coming thick and fast, as were accounts of travel by train, car and even, in more than one case, in the footsteps of H. V. Morton. Today, travelogues are pouring out at a huge rate.

Decline and sprawl

One of the very gloomiest travelogues of the last 800 years is Iain Sinclair's *London Orbital*,[2] an account of how he and his friends walked around London's M25 country, and it proved to be every bit as horrifying as you might imagine. The book would be a strong contender for Most Depressing Environmental Book of the Year Award, if you could create such a thing. Bizarrely, in the book's blurb, one reviewer describes it as "a hoot".

But the only real hoots within pages describing our ruined, dysfunctional Home Counties are the ones coming from motor horns. One of the book's most demoralising chapters describes that slice of south Hertfordshire where so many trunk-roads wipe the filth off their feet before diving across the M25 into the capital.

At the poor old village of South Mimms, now totally surrounded by trunk-roads, Sinclair picked his way through the "interlinked spirals, under and over, the multi-choice channels at Junction 23 of the M25" and achieved the not-inconsiderable feat of arriving at the Forte Posthouse Motel on foot.

"Before it was a service station, South Mimms (Myms) was a hilltop village with church and notable funerary monument for the Austen family," notes Sinclair.

And within the dust of its churchyard lie one or two of my own very distant ancestors, their sleep disturbed by the incessant conversion of fossil carbon into CO_2. Poor old South Mimms: half a century ago it was just squeezed between the A6 and A1; now it's had London's concrete garrotte, the M25, applied and the A1 has become a motorway.

Sinclair pressed on, to Shenley. "The village of Shenley is green belt, South Mimms is not," he noted. But green belt designation has not saved Shenley. Its former psychiatric hospital, closed after 'care in the community' began life as 'neglect in the neighbourhood', was being turned into a housing estate – 'the Pavilions, Shenley' – at the time of Sinclair's visit.

"Nice title, 'the Pavilions', with its suggestion of John Major's reworking of Orwell, the England of warm beer, bicycling spinsters, the sound of willow thwacking leather," wrote Sinclair. "*The Far Pavilions*. A retreat to the hills. A mock Surrey, Guildford or Dorking, Abinger Hammer, with lawns and trees and cricket squares. An escape from the heat and dirt of the city. 800 yards from the M25." He notes the developers' brochure promising that "the historic village of Shenley combines excellent local interest with outstanding travel convenience" and "fine views northwards over the historic city of St Albans."

How much of our land, in the last 100 years or so, has been covered with this sprawl of bogus country living? A great deal, as we shall see. Hertfordshire has been a particular victim: not only was it near London and well served with

A house builder's rural rhapsody. *Image: Henry Oliver*

commuter railways and, later, roads, but it was also where the garden cities movement first pursued its ideals, with the first garden city, then the second, then the first new town and other new towns, and finally part of a massive growth area stretching all the way from Corby in Northamptonshire to Faversham in Kent. The isolation of South Mimms by motorways and the expansion of Shenley by suburban housing development didn't occur simply because we were lax in our planning. As we British never cease to remind ourselves, the idea of spatial planning was something we gave to the world, but this environmental wreck was the result of planning – and indeed transport planning, its symbiotic twin. Both professions offer us the possibility of making our environment function sustainably, but both have dark shadow personalities of their own: urban sprawl and motoring. These have left our overcrowded island much more damaged than it needed to be, by a population overload grown to serve an industrial base that has mostly now died. Most of us could have lived very well in the type of tight, compact and functional cities, towns and villages our ancestors created and loved. But, as we shall see in the next four chapters, we didn't, for a whole series of very bad reasons.

Dumb growth nation

This dumb approach to planning and transport policy matters. Most people have some vague idea about traffic management (basically a plot to use speed cameras to extort money from them), road building (reduces congestion – doesn't it?), trains (late, crowded and expensive but there's nothing we can do about it without putting up taxes, which would be worse still) and airports (don't want to live near one but expect ever-cheaper flights). Many people see planning just as a tiresome tier of bureaucracy, except for green belts (erroneously believed to protect most of the countryside) and sprawl.

Well, what would this 'dumb growth nation' look like in, say, 30 years' time given a continuation of current policies? It's difficult to predict confidently at a time when things are so uncertain, but some things seldom change, whoever's in power, despite the rhetoric. This is the 'age of aspiration', but often that just means an aspiration to own your own home well before you are 30 – a goal that has gained near-mystical status. So, on those rare occasions when politicians try to stand up to demands from house builders for greenfield land, the builders win every time.

The 2007 housing Green Paper set out plans to build two million new homes in England by 2016 and three million by 2020. This would have raised the 2007 level of house building (205,000) substantially to 240,000 homes a year by 2016 and it was decided that level of building would continue through the 2020s. So, even allowing for the fact that within two years of the Green Paper appearing, English house building had actually dropped by half, it's safe to say that the then government would have liked to build perhaps five million new homes in England alone by 2030. It sort-of thought that the 60 per cent brownfield target for them might be maintained, so probably at least two million homes would have had to be built on land that had not been previously developed. At the 30-to-the-hectare specified until 2010 on greenfield sites, those houses alone would have consumed nearly 70,000 hectares or 700 square kilometres of countryside. You can add half as much again to accommodate the roads and other services such houses require, so you could say that Whitehall was looking to bury 1,000 square kilometres of English countryside under housing in the next 20 years. Add to that an unidentifiable but substantial area for employment and retail use (neither of which has ever had a brownfield target) and you can see that's a lot of sprawl. Concentrate much of it in the south and east of England, add on further large dollops of building for Scotland, Wales and Northern Ireland and you can see that many towns would have run into one another if they weren't separated by sad, pathetic 'green wedges' designed to sustain the semblance of separation. Much of the lowlands of Britain would essentially have become huge, endless, sprawling low-density suburbs.

The new coalition government in 2010 ditched the regional planning powers that would have directed where the sprawl went, but not, apparently, the aspiration to build lots of homes, preferring to leave the issue of where to others. But wherever sprawl occurs, it essentially depends on the private car, so whatever the rhetoric about public expenditure restrictions, sustaining greenfield housing growth means we will need to sustain something like the roads-oriented transport policies of recent times. This would be mad, because we urgently need to reduce our transport carbon footprint, because petrol is going to get much more scarce and expensive over the next few decades, and because the alternatives don't stack up. But if you're going to pursue low-density sprawl as your default development mode, you need a substantial roads programme and must accept either spending a massively increased proportion of our national wealth fuelling our vehicles or becoming dependent on low-quality bus services for getting around.

Meanwhile, our dependence on lorries to move our goods around – often just between one distribution depot situated near a motorway interchange and the next – would continue. Large retailers like the just-in-time system that enables them to call up the goods they need and minimise storage at shops. This may involve vast amounts of unnecessary fossil fuel consumption, but who's worrying about that when there's the last halfpenny of profit to be squeezed out of the punters? Rail freight is recovering from decades of destruction and is likely to continue to do so over the next 20 years even with the minimal help it gets, but, if things go on as they are, we will still be critically dependent on a land-hungry, fossil-fuel-hungry road haulage system for most of our freight transport needs.

So how will our low-density suburbs fare if motoring becomes more restricted or terminally expensive? How are people going to get to work, to the shops, to distant schools or hospitals without their cars? It's a good question to ask yourself – could you sustain your current lifestyle if your car(s) were taken away entirely? If the answer is 'no' or 'only with great difficulty', it's probably a good moment to start reconsidering your situation. Yet for millions of people in the UK the answer probably is 'no', and this is by no means true only for those who live in remote country districts.

The future for low-density suburbs, especially those remote from town centres, must be a slow decline. It's already happening in the US, where property prices dropped much faster in distant sprawl areas as gasoline prices shot up and long-distance commuting became more expensive. Don't imagine this decline won't happen here – it would mirror the decline of some 'outer estates' (low-density council estates built on garden city principles around once-prosperous industrial towns). Given our neurotic obsession with house prices, this ought to give us pause for thought.

What future, then, for our traditional towns and cities, whose economies depend on our tottering financial services economy or our shattered industrial base? Well, surprisingly perhaps, they're better placed than the suburbs. It will still be possible to move around them, as their high density ensures they will have at least a good bus service and, despite a continuation of 'dumb growth' policies, some at least enjoy light rail systems or metros. For the others, waiting for buses would once again become a major part of people's lives.

And what about our sense of community? A pervasive sense of anxiety seems to permeate our society – fear of crime, fear of antisocial behaviour, fear of regulation, fear of our neighbours, fear of a hostile world. It was those fears that prompted us to spend 100 years running to the suburbs, but that's what it is – running away. Long ago people dreamed of returning to their ancestors' countryside, but running to a suburb, however remote from the nearest town, brings us no nearer the countryside, it just destroys another bit of it. Meanwhile, the suburban exodus stripped the towns of their youngest and brightest people, so beginning the long decline that culminated in the 'inner city' problems of the 1980s and deeply damaged our sense of community.

Community grows in cities, towns and villages, but it seldom takes root in low-density suburbs and when it does, it's weak. It's easy for those who dwell in comfortable, if boring, outer suburbia to blame city-dwellers for all society's ills, and while I'm not remotely suggesting that anyone should try to evade moral responsibility for his or her lifestyle, the process of destroying communities and putting people on the road to crime and antisocial behaviour began when our great-grandparents, our grandparents, our parents and we ourselves chose an escape to the suburbs, leaving the blighters to it.

We need to stop being consumers and become citizens again, but it won't happen if we crawl into suburban bunkers and leave the rest to fester.

Meanwhile, across the pond

In February 2010, 1,700 delegates assembled for a conference in Seattle: an annual gathering of planners, local authority officials, campaigners etc. that had been growing for some years. But it was a conference that had obviously achieved a degree of national political importance, for attending it were three senior ministers from the Administration in Washington: the secretary of housing and urban development, the secretary of transportation and the deputy administrator of the Environmental Protection Agency. And, unusually for ministerial speeches at conferences, they left the delegates enraptured.

Part of the reason for the delegates' satisfaction was, no doubt, hearing that three federal government departments would actually try to coordinate their policies – a pretty radical idea in Washington. But the Administration officials also had progress to report on the Administration's attempts to roll back decades of policies that brought about urban sprawl and car dependency far beyond our worst nightmares.

The conference was called New Partners for Smart Growth. 'Smart Growth' is a term with which few people in the UK are familiar, even the planners and transport planners who ought to be. Indeed, there have been some attempts to hijack the term by economic development agencies, in their efforts to introduce new electronic methods of communication into our everyday lives, or even just their efforts to revive our sagging regional economies. But Smart Growth in the US is very different. It's a holistic philosophy of spatial, transport and community planning that has been adopted by many cities and states and has now taken hold of Washington itself.

"Communities must have what they need to grow sustainably," said the three ministers in a column in *The Seattle Times*[3] to coincide with the conference. "We need communities where residents have easy access to jobs; where there are clean, reliable options for transportation to work and school; where housing is affordable and energy-efficient; and where clean and renewable energy is abundant. For the first time, the federal government has embraced these principles of Smart Growth. The Obama Administration recognises that making urban, suburban and rural communities more liveable is essential to our nation's shared economic future."

Sure, this is the sort of thing ministers say in the UK too. But Smart Growth policies are making a huge difference on the ground right across the US, despite the recession. In the UK, meanwhile, our politicians are trying to persuade people how to accept more urban sprawl, and still show no recognition of the need for urban rail-transit expansion.

In the United States, the last 15 years or so have seen a huge explosion in planning for compact development, opposition to sprawl, (rail-)transit-oriented development, urban development that is permeable to walking and cycling, protection of traditional urban areas, rebuilding of communities, etc. As one British observer noted, it sounds like motherhood and apple pie, and perhaps it is, but failure to unite spatial, transport and community planning has been at least as obvious in the UK as in the States.

Across the US, federal, state and local governments are trying to put an end to sprawl, to densify their town centres or areas around transit stops, to build rail-based urban transit, to revive communities, to build inter-urban rail and even to close urban freeways and turn them into parks or whatever. In the UK, meanwhile, we've spent years trying to implement a mishmash of policies with a bit of urban regeneration combined with fresh dollops of sprawl. The dark hand of the Treasury has worked with some vested interests to promote sprawl and to undermine the sustainable development that is supposed to be the common aim of all our political parties.

This hasn't come about by accident. It came about thanks to a 100-year process that began with the very highest environmental ideals, entered the commercial and governmental mainstream, took hold of us and left most of us unable to even imagine there was a better alternative, as we shall see in Chapters 2 to 6.

Chapter 2

The germination of a bad idea

*Why Ebenezer Howard should have emerged as something of
a hero out of this soup is a mystery.*

A. A. Gill, *The Angry Island*

A sprawl lobby is born

One June day in 1899, a group of men met in a City of London solicitor's office, but they weren't there to discuss business or litigation; they had higher ideals to pursue. They had come to found the Garden City Association.

We think of the urban sprawl of the twentieth century as a product of the commercial spread of housing and our obsession with home ownership, together with the need for post-war reconstruction and housing a population following the economy relentlessly south-eastwards. But before either of these processes turned a century of change into a century of sprawl came the idealism that judged sprawl a good thing.

The most influential figure at the meeting at 70 Finsbury Pavement was not the usual aristocrat, business magnate or senior clergyman one associates with Victorian philanthropy (although there was a clergyman among their number), but a 49-year-old Parliamentary shorthand clerk called Ebenezer Howard. The previous year he had published a book called *To-morrow: A Peaceful Path to Real Reform*,[1] which advocated a utopian way of organising society in cooperative municipalities living in entirely new townships built on greenfield sites surrounded by belts of countryside. Howard believed their inhabitants would not only enjoy a lifestyle freed from the economic constraints of late-nineteenth-century capitalism but would also enjoy the benefits of town and country living, without the drawbacks of either.

To get the book published at all he'd had to borrow £50 from an American friend, and there is little doubt that our environment today would be in much better shape to face the challenges to come if his friend had found something better to do with his money. For mighty oaks grow from such acorns, although this acorn was ultimately to be responsible for clearing thousands of oaks and other trees from our countryside. So, 10 June 1899 deserves to be remembered as one of those dates when the disaster that engulfed the British environment throughout the twentieth century and beyond began. Despite the presence of the clergyman, no one noticed there were thirteen at the table, but from this ill-omened meeting grew not just a couple of early-twentieth-century garden cities or the post-war new towns and overspill estates; what it also spawned was the sprawling suburbs the century wreaked across our landscape in endless profusion, the decay of our cities as the century grew old, the apparently limit- less growth of gridlocked highways and many of the environmental problems that benight us today and leave us woefully ill-prepared to tackle the challenges to come.

About the only kind thing one could say about that meeting was that it was also seminal in creating the modern planning system that has mitigated this harm and holds the potential to create something better. The garden city Pan- dora may have unleashed all these evils on our landscape, but it did leave us this element of hope. But Howard and his chums nevertheless bequeathed the planning profession some darkly recessive genes.

A hundred years after Howard helped found the Garden City Association, he is still revered by many in the profession as its patron saint. The planner and geographer Peter Hall has described Howard as the first, and without doubt the most influential of a number of figures in Britain and North America who set the whole tenor of urban planning between 1880 and 1945.

Howard's fundamental idea was to separate where we lived from where we worked. In Victorian cities, dirty and polluting industry lived in the same street as the workers' houses; the labour went where the industry went. While the more affluent might gather their homes together (often on the south-west of major cities, where the wind took the smell away), you seldom had to go far to find industry; the poor couldn't afford to ride and lived within walking distance of their work.

Howard lived at a time of huge debate that puts our present torpid consen- sus to shame, and radical ideas of all kinds were attracting ready audiences. The last four decades of the nineteenth century had seen massive social reform and many people were projecting further change; Howard found influential people ready to listen.

Some myths are buried with those who spawn them; others linger. One great myth that admirers of Oliver Cromwell and V. I. Lenin have successfully propagated, for instance, was that they were great champions of the people who overthrew tyrannical monarchs and established democracy. In reality, however, both were military dictators who overthrew their countries' first-ever democratically elected governments and installed themselves as despots.

An equally misleading myth has grown up around the garden city pioneers, which paints nineteenth-century Britain as a filthy, unplanned, industrial sink in which most people lived in disgusting slums riven by poverty, disease and squalor, tackled only when the garden cities movement and its successors started building sunlit, airy and spacious alternatives. The picture of British cities as dirty, overcrowded, insanitary and ramshackle has much to support it if we look at 1850, but the half-century of radical reform that preceded the First World War was one of the most remarkable periods of social change Britain has ever seen, and many of these problems were being radically addressed well before 1900. A 100-year assault on that legacy by the sprawl lobby has left that achievement largely forgotten, but I believe it offers us clear lessons for our present disorder.

The last four decades of Queen Victoria's reign brought a remarkable string of legislative and social reforms and bequeathed us many advantages we enjoy today: public health, universal education and literacy, urban public transport, waste management, public works and housing standards. We have forgotten they also brought us compact, sustainable, mobile, well-serviced, community-friendly towns and cities.

The sprawl lobby has planted another myth too: that the pre-industrial-revolution town or village was a sprawling, low-density affair where nearly everyone had gardens and we all lived in cheerful, vegetable-growing harmony, bathed in sunshine and lacking only modern conveniences. In fact, of course, housing in both towns and villages was compact; land was expensive and mostly used for agriculture. People were poor, mighty few owned property and

By the early twentieth century, social reform had made our cities into compact, sustainable communities. *Image: National Tramway Museum*

few could afford the rent on big houses that were expensive to build, heat, light and maintain; gardens were a luxury for rich folk and for those country folk with a small patch of land for some vegetables and a pigsty.

Until the industrial revolution, of course, most people lived in the country, but from the mid-eighteenth century (and earlier in some places), the movement to the towns began to accelerate. Travelling through Lancashire in 1792 and recording, as was his wont, the awful state of English roads and inns, the Hon. John Byng also noted the destruction that industrialisation was wreaking on the rural workforce.[2] Padiham had "numberless coal pits"; Accrington had row upon row of houses while "every vale swarms with cotton mills". While Byng wished the cotton industry well, he feared the mills would end up as workhouses and bemoaned the damage to the rural economy.

"No corn is raised where cotton mills abound, for no hands could be found for agriculture," he noted. Still, it could have been worse: in Rochdale his Sunday stroll was interrupted by "naked-legged boys and impudent wenches".

The industrial poverty to come was to leave many boys naked-legged and girls forcing themselves to look impudent to wealthy gentlemen as a way of feeding their families. The well-to-do communist Friedrich Engels visited several English cities in the 1840s and left a particularly vivid account of Manchester.

> Slums are pretty equally arranged in all the great towns of England, the worst houses in the worst quarters of the towns; usually one- or two-storied cottages in long rows, perhaps with cellars used as dwellings, almost always irregularly built. These houses of three or four rooms and a kitchen form, throughout England, some parts of London excepted, the general dwellings of the working-class. The streets are generally unpaved, rough, dirty, filled with vegetable and animal refuse, without sewers or gutters, but supplied with foul, stagnant pools instead. Moreover, ventilation is impeded by the bad, confused method of building of the whole quarter, and since many human beings here live crowded into a small space, the atmosphere that prevails in these working-men's quarters may readily be imagined.[3]

Imagined indeed, and, thanks to many of the family myths created by the new middle classes in the early twentieth century to 'improve' their heritage, we forget that most of us had ancestors who lived thus in the mid-nineteenth century. But 'Victorian values' included a strong onslaught on this poverty, overcrowding and squalor through redistribution of wealth, huge public works, social reform and much else that would surprise those who came to believe these values were all about self-help. But a free market untrammelled by public works or interventions was a Georgian value, not a Victorian one.

Still, the horror of mid-nineteenth century city life was real enough, although it spawned a vigorous response which Engels noted as early as the 1840s. Victorian writers such as Charles Dickens or Elizabeth Gaskell painted such vivid pictures of these early Victorian horrors that they have come to stand for the whole nineteenth century; meanwhile, the new urban proletariat was busy telling its children and grandchildren of the rural utopias they had left behind, forgetting perhaps that they had left behind the extreme poverty brought about by mechanisation of agriculture, a fast-growing population, common land enclosure and free trade initiatives to flee to towns that may have seemed horrific but at least offered employment, food and shelter of some kind. When Queen Victoria ascended the throne in 1837, most of her subjects were country folk; when she died in 1901, most were town dwellers. The change had sparked decades of vigorous reform of health, education and town and city building, so when Edwardian idealists spun the ideas of Victorian seers such as John Ruskin and William Morris I into their vision of low-density sprawl, they were attacking a problem already in sharp decline with a solution that would eventually do far more harm than good.

Sustainable towns and cities – Victorian style

It is true to say that in 1899 significant areas of Victorian slums still stood, and some were to stand for several decades more thanks to world wars and economic

Towns a century ago were vibrant communities. *Image: National Tramway Museum*

depression. But the garden city boys were to launch their attack indiscriminately on all that had gone before, good as well as bad, even though a very radically different form of urban development was already advancing across our towns and cities.

Their key failure – and one that still affects twenty-first-century policymakers – was a failure to realise that the compact, well-administered, well-serviced towns created in the half-century before the First World War, far from being 'slums', were actually one of the best and most sustainable urban development models this country has ever seen.

The late-Victorian terraces that became so terribly unfashionable between the two world wars – even the smaller ones, the 'bye-law' homes built to house the working classes in tolerable conditions – have proved to be well-built and adaptable and were built at densities that made superb use of the scarce land supply in an overcrowded island. Typically, the bye-law houses – the 'Coronation Street'-type terraces – could be built at over 100 to the hectare or sometimes even more densely. Even up-market terraces of the time could be built at far higher densities than many socially rented houses today. The government was fiercely opposed by house builders in 1999 when it imposed a minimum density of 30 to the hectare and, although brownfield densities crawled up to the mid-40s-to-the-hectare over the next ten years, greenfield densities took nearly a decade even to comply with the new policy. Builders complained that anything higher would mean only flats, something the Victorians had effortlessly disproved more than 100 years before.

The high density of the Victorian city meant most of its citizens could live within walking distance of their work and, when they didn't, they could use a bicycle or one of the highly sustainable modes available to them – railways or electric trams. Their homes had running water and sanitation and they had corner shops, shopping centres and schools nearby. It was compact because it had to be compact, a healthy and sustainable urban format that the twentieth century miserably failed to emulate and which we seem unable to re-attain. Of course, the towns of that era had their imperfections: they were a product of coal-fired technology and lacked refinements that a century of innovation could have given them. But, so flexible were they, such improvements are possible.

It is hard to escape the conclusion that no model of urban development proposed in the last 100 years has come anywhere near being as sustainable as that evolved in the late nineteenth century. Despite this, the late-Victorian model has seen 100 years of insult and deprecation as 'slums' and we continue to try to replace it with something far less sustainable. We are even still tearing such areas down, no longer in the name of 'slum clearance' but of 'market renewal'. We are seeking models of 'new urbanism' when an old one is staring us in the face. We have spent a century destroying these sustainable cities and replacing them with unsustainable sprawl.

These sustainable cities were the product of legislation. A few local building acts in the 1820s were followed by the 1844 Metropolitan Building Act, which controlled the size of underground rooms and the natural light they received and which set limits to the size of buildings in relation to the space around them. As early as the 1840s, legislators were tackling the narrow, dark alleys of the slums by requiring streets to be 40 feet wide and limiting buildings' height according to the width of the street. The 1847 Town Improvement Clauses Act and the 1848 Health of Towns Act began the process of allowing local health boards to set 'bye-laws' which so changed the face of Victorian homes. The 1858 Local Government Act introduced requirements for how bye-law homes were built – there had to be 150 square feet of space behind a building, two-storey buildings had to be 15 feet apart, single-storey buildings 10 feet apart and roads 36 feet across. All major towns began issuing such bye-laws and the 1875 Public Health Act brought national standards to the process. Model bye-laws issued in 1877 imposed requirements including all homes being self-contained for water supply and sanitation, together with huge investment in water mains and sewerage. The huge destruction of life by cholera, typhoid and other diseases suddenly began to fall sharply.

The bye-laws were rigidly enforced and created the ranks of late-Victorian terraces which are still a feature of most towns and cities, despite a century of sprawl lobby prejudice and endless attempts to destroy them. Different kinds could be built to house the poor, the emerging middle-class or even the

Bye-law homes were compact and accessible. *Image: National Tramway Museum*

moderately well-off. Even the simplest have a symmetry of proportion, and the better ones have a style and elegance that nothing built since the First World War comes anywhere near.

Bye-law homes were one of Victorian Britain's finest creations; for the first time the urban poor had homes fit to live in, and overcrowding, lack of sanitation, lack of facilities, etc. were vigorously addressed. A terraced house with an outdoor toilet, cold running water, a kitchen range to cook on and two or three bedrooms for a large Victorian family may seem primitive by today's standards, but to a poor nineteenth-century family rehoused from a single room (or even a shared single room) in an unsanitary courtyard with a shared earth closet and a pump at the end of a dark and stinking alleyway, it must have seemed like paradise.

The communities these buildings housed were the heart of industrial Britain for 100 years, and we still have nostalgia for the 'Coronation Street' type of terrace, even though most of them in the Salford the series was based on have been swept away. The hatred bye-law homes engendered (often among those who had never lived in them) is one of the twentieth and twenty-first centuries' enduring curiosities. But it's been a destructive curiosity, as we shall see.

Infancy of the garden city idea

When Queen Victoria died in 1901, it marked more than the end of a royal era. The country had been in a ferment of new ideas for years and some were starting to take root. Pressure for reform had brought the urban reforms such as bye-law homes, bringing the more fortunate poor well-built, relatively spacious houses with modern amenities like gas lighting, mains water and sewerage. These people travelled to work on foot, by electric tram or by a suburban train, which might even then be electrically powered. They could shop at a corner store or take a tram to the centre. Their children could walk to a local school. They enjoyed a high level of social cohesion and a strong sense of community and civic duty and pride. The widespread drunkenness that marked the early and mid-nineteenth century had largely died away. Most of the goods the population consumed came by rail or waterway close to their homes and were delivered by horse and cart. They consumed low levels of energy compared with our present habits and, if that energy hadn't been provided by coal, the lifestyle would have been quite remarkably sustainable.

Any ferment of new ideas will throw up bad as well as good ones, and some very bad ideas germinated at the end of the nineteenth century and took root in the 1900s. Ebenezer Howard was a key figure at this period; he had returned from an unsuccessful spell in America in 1876 and "listened to all the preachers and the prophets, the reformers and the revolutionaries"[4] for some years.

It seems inevitable he attended meetings involving William Morris I and later said his inspirations included Morris, Ruskin, Thomas More, Moses and the anarchist Peter Kropotkin; they had failed "by a hair's breadth" to give expression to his own great garden city idea, he claimed.

When Howard published *To-morrow* in 1898, he was by no means the first to have proposed a new model settlement, but his complex garden city ideal was planned to the nth degree, powered by windmills and managed by a benevolent communal enterprise on behalf of its citizens, and seems to have engendered more immediate support. He proposed a cluster of settlements housing 250,000 people, with a central city of 58,000 on 2,000 acres, surrounded by a circle of garden cities each with 30,000 people, all set in an agricultural belt. This planned, low-density sprawl was to be replicated all over the country until everyone lived in paradise. Howard is best remembered today for these ideas, but his writings actually make clear his main preoccupation was land reform and community control.

Those ideas got nowhere, but the Garden City Association rapidly attracted support from a range of academics, philanthropists, architects, clergy and George Bernard Shaw, who dubbed Howard 'the Garden City Geyser'.

As the movement gathered momentum it attracted opposition too. Fabian Society secretary Edward Pease argued that what was needed was to make better use of existing cities and complained that Howard wanted "to pull them all down and substitute garden cities, each duly built according to pretty plans, nicely designed with a ruler and compass" and dubbed it 'utopian scheming'. But that utopian scheming and its blend of economic and physical elements was attracting a diverse range of radical Liberals, socialists, Fabians, anarchists, etc., many of whom had little interest in spatial planning. More practically, Howard's ideas also attracted a number of wealthy philanthropists including George Cadbury, W. H. Lever and Joseph Rowntree.

The infant grows

By 1902 the Association had attracted 1,300 members, and its first conference at Bournville that year attracted 300 delegates including George Bernard Shaw. The next year's conference at Port Sunlight attracted over 1,000 delegates, and a company was founded with Howard as managing director. More influential members were drawn in, including MPs, the novelist H. G. Wells, George Cadbury's brother Edward, soft drink manufacturer Thomas Idris and cotton king Franklin Thomasson. Howard's book was republished under the slightly more comprehensible title of *Garden Cities of Tomorrow*.[5]

With the sprawl ball firmly rolling, Howard and the Association's energetic young secretary Thomas Adams began the search for their first garden city.

Sites to be destroyed for Utopia were visited in Warwickshire, Essex and Nottinghamshire, and the Chartley Castle Estate in Staffordshire only narrowly escaped destruction when they found somewhere nearer London and its markets, which the wealthy industrialists evidently considered more suitable.

The First Garden City Ltd was registered on 1 September 1903 and planning began for the new site, at Letchworth in north Hertfordshire. At 4,000 acres it was considerably smaller than the 6,000 acres Howard considered the minimum, and raising the capital sparked a debate between the idealists and the realists, which was to result in both work beginning on the garden city and the decay of the Association's communitarian ideals. On 9 October 1903, over 1,000 guests gathered in a muddy Hertfordshire field to formally launch the scheme and, sadly, the pouring rain failed to cool their enthusiasm. So work went on to raise the purchase price (with the help of a mortgage), despite less enthusiasm from the industrialists than had been hoped.

Garden cities versus garden suburbs

But no sooner was the movement up and running than an issue was to seriously tax it – namely, whether sprawl was best delivered in garden cities or garden suburbs. Howard and the purists were firmly of the view that the entire urban fabric of the nation should be rebuilt in new garden cities, but the movement succeeded in riding two very different horses, by tapping into a trend that had been growing since the mid-nineteenth century: garden suburbs.

For the most part these had been commercial developments to lure the newly prosperous upper-middle classes out of the malodorous industrial cities to homes with gardens from which they could still access their central workplaces by train. Calthorpe in Birmingham and Merton Park near Wimbledon were early examples, although Bedford Park in West London is often (erroneously) dubbed 'the first' garden suburb. In fact what it represented was the site where the design values of the fast-growing Arts and Crafts movement and the Aesthetic movement first dictated architecture on any scale. Several Arts and Crafts architects of this period, including Norman Shaw, who designed much of Bedford Park, were designers of real genius, but their contempt for the classicism that had underpinned domestic architecture for 200 years was to leave a lamentable legacy.

While every Georgian or Victorian jobbing builder could, by following a few simple rules of proportion even in the humblest bye-law house, produce a good-looking and harmonious building that still pleases after more than a century, the Arts and Crafts legacy was to dump all this in the bin in favour of a demented eclecticism of vernacular styles. Local vernacular style is fine and dandy if done well; an architect of real talent can even, on a good day, mix some of the styles. But Arts and Crafts architects liked to mix vernacular styles in crazy profusion, and there were few geniuses of Norman Shaw's talent to make it work; leave it to your local jobbing builder and you create the ill-designed mess that has been British domestic 'architecture' for most of the twentieth century and beyond. Pandora had opened another box.

One of the Association's very first successes was not a garden city at all, but a garden suburb – Joseph Rowntree's New Earswick, on 60 hectares of innocent farmland two miles outside York – and it was here that the true model was set for twentieth-century urban sprawl – low-density 'cottages' with gardens (a twelfth of an acre each) and village greens, winding roads, cul-de-sacs, etc.

New Earswick was designed by two young architects, Raymond Unwin and Barry Parker, and Unwin provides one of the garden sprawl movement's indisputable links with William Morris I, with whom he had collaborated politically as a young man in the 1880s. Unwin became a key figure in both the sprawl movement and the nascent planning profession, to which he bequeathed his sprawl-friendly legacy.

Unwin and Parker were soon at work on an even better-known example of early twentieth-century spatial flatulence – Hampstead Garden Suburb. This was the brainchild of one of the Edwardian era's most formidable reformers, Dame Henrietta Barnett, and, as ever, the road to hell was paved with the best of intentions. Her plans for the new garden suburb were, bizarrely, the product of her desire to protect the countryside, as she feared the opening of Hampstead tube station would ruin the setting of the Heath with "rows of ugly villas such as disfigure Willesden and most of the suburbs of London". Unwin and Parker were commissioned to produce a type of villa that was pretty soon to disfigure most of the suburbs of Britain, and while Hampstead Garden Suburb's promoters' philanthropic ideals soon eroded, some very well-connected people were on board and it even obtained its own Act of Parliament, which freed it from the bye-law standards designed to prevent land being wasted in low-density sprawl. The garden suburb's houses were to be built at no more than eight to the acre – about twenty to the hectare – setting the pattern for a century of sprawl.

Roads were to be wide and homes to be separated by hedges, and so began the retreat into our suburban fortresses, safe behind privet, behind *Cupressus leylandii* or behind six-foot larch lap panels. The 1906 Hampstead Garden Suburb Act was the moment when community life in the UK entered its long decline.

It's tempting to wonder whether Dame Henrietta or her colleagues ever considered the implications of trying to house the population of Britain at this ruinously low density. Because that's pretty much what happened for the next 100 years – the Garden City Association added creation of garden suburbs to its objectives in 1906.

The first garden city

The ubiquitous Unwin and Parker were also commissioned to design the new Letchworth Garden City, and came up with a plan that wasn't exactly in line with Howard's ideal. It did contain a central park, but not one that was the focus of public buildings, and what public buildings were proposed were grouped rather more practically near the railway station. Howard's garden city would have had a ring of industry round it and a railway round that, but the Letchworth site was crossed by the Great Northern Railway's Hitchin–Cambridge line and the architects placed the town centre just south of it and the industrial estate to the north-east, on the sensible assumption that the wind would blow the smoke away. The vision of a 'smokeless, slumless city' powered by windmills pumping water into an elevated reservoir to generate hydro-electricity – beyond early twenty-first-century technology to deliver, let alone early twentieth – soon evaporated. Howard's Grand Avenue was omitted too, sparing modern Letchworth a traffic-choked inner ring road.

Manufacturers, in any case, took years to come to Letchworth in significant numbers, even though it eventually developed a reputation as a centre of corset manufacture. What kept the early idealism alive was that railway: it may not have been where Howard wanted it and the garden city was supposed to be self-supporting, but at least it enabled early residents to commute to Cambridge

Letchworth's cottages set the pattern for a generation of municipal housing.

or London or wherever, and many still do. From the start, the utopian sprawl of the twentieth century was commuter sprawl.

Letchworth grew slowly, although it soon gained a reputation for attracting eccentrics and national notoriety as 'the town with no pubs'. This wasn't strictly true: it had the Skittles Inn, designed to look like a pub or as much like a pub as Arts and Crafts architects could manage. Within its walls, the settlers could drown their sorrows in tea, Bournville drinking chocolate, an apple drink called Cydrax, or Sasparilla. Not surprisingly, this didn't last, and in 1923 it was turned into an adult education centre.

Howard dreamed that, as soon as the population of his first garden city reached 30,000, work would begin on the second and so on. He never gave up these dreams but the sprawl movement's other successes before the First World War were all garden suburbs.

By the time the war broke out, a significant number of garden suburbs were under way and the model was starting to be adopted for council housing. Very few council homes were built before the turn of the century even though powers had existed for some time, but the Edwardians realised that over-crowding still needed to be addressed. At first the extra housing was in con-ventional houses and flats, but soon the ideal of 'cottage homes for the poor' began to take root. In 1911, the London County Council began building its Old Oak Estate, heavily influenced by the design of Hampstead Garden Suburb, and other local authorities were pursuing the idea too.

The sprawl movement was up and running by the First World War, even if things hadn't turned out as the purists wanted. Meanwhile, however, another powerful force for environmental destruction was growing into a lusty infant too.

The roads lobby is born

Almost 18 months before the Garden City Association was formally incorpo-rated, another important body in the history of sprawl was inaugurated in London. On 8 December 1897 – another key date – the Automobile Club of Great Britain, today better known as the RAC, was incorporated, and from this we can trace the development of an even more successful lobby than the one promoting sprawl, for the foundation of the RAC marks the beginning of the roads lobby.

The previous year had seen the repeal of the 'red flag act', which, in theory, required a man with a red flag to walk in front of motor vehicles, although many local authorities were by that stage ignoring it. And even though the UK boasted fewer than 200 motor vehicles at that time, their drivers already packed a political punch and secured Parliamentary time for legislation for their rich men's toys. Despite these vehicles' very rudimentary brakes and steering systems, they managed to get the speed limit raised to 12mph and soon motorists were killing people.

Unlike their garden city counterparts, the Automobile Club had no need to go in search of the wealthy and influential, for its founders were mostly rich and well-connected young men with a passion for motor cars. With such wealthy backers, the Club expanded rapidly and the patronage of King Edward VII enabled it to become the Royal Automobile Club, which, by the First World War, had built its own vast premises in Pall Mall and owned a country club near Epsom.

The roads lobby grew fast. In 1903 William Rees Jeffreys, a former civil servant and secretary of the Roads Improvement Association (RIA), a body set up to campaign for better road maintenance for cyclists, became secretary of the Automobile Club, although he continued to work with the RIA, which soon changed from a pro-cycling organisation to a pro-motoring one.

Two of the RIA's new council members were Conservative MPs – Sir Arthur Stanley and John Scott Montagu, later the 2nd Lord Montagu of Beaulieu, and both were senior members of the Automobile Club. Later in 1903, Montagu helped steer the Motor Car Act through Parliament and, although it introduced tax and registration for motor vehicles and licences for drivers, it failed to require that the latter be qualified. It also repealed the 12mph speed limit, which drivers were ignoring anyway, and replaced it with one of 20mph. This waltzed through Parliament with the main opposition coming from early petrolheads who favoured 25mph or no limit at all. 1903 also saw the introduction of motor racing.

Right from the introduction of the 12mph limit in 1896, motorists waged war on police 'speed traps' as they were called, a battle that continues to this day. Although motorists were killing more and more people, they seemed to regard their freedom to drive as fast as they liked as some kind of human right. Hundreds of thousands of people have since had all human rights obliterated by speeding motorists in Britain, but still the campaign goes on.

1903 had been a remarkably successful year for the roads lobby, but it ended with major embarrassment when *The Times* obtained a letter sent by Rees Jeffreys to county councils pointing out the Club was receiving letters from members wondering in which county they should meet the new requirement to register their vehicles, as this could be done anywhere. So, his letter wondered, which counties would be the "most anxious to adapt their roads and their administration to modern requirements", and he warned the councils that his Club planned to list those it considered most suitable – who would then secure the bulk of this attractive new revenue stream. This was followed by a list of questions that left little doubt about what was meant by "modern requirements" – road improvement spending, refusal of police speed traps, etc.

Today we have become used to the roads lobby trying to blackmail public bodies over issues such as speed cameras, but in 1903 principles such as respect for public bodies, probity, the rule of law, etc. went unquestioned. The subsequent row enabled the Club to purge some of its old guard, and Rees Jeffreys, who had shown such public contempt for the law was moved – to become head of its legal department.

The roads lobby was really motoring by now; it soon had a public inquiry into the administration of roads set up and stuffed with figures sympathetic to it (a pattern that was to continue for the next 100 years). It recommended setting up a national roads board, the building of bypasses to speed traffic around towns and compulsory purchase powers for road schemes. This was in 1903, at which time there were only about 9,000 cars in the whole of the UK.

With such support for the unsustainable new technology, however, that figure rose fast, and it was pushing up towards the 30,000 mark by the end of 1905. Motorists continued to bleat about speed limits, and 1905 saw the creation of the Automobile Association to campaign against speed traps and, presumably, in favour of their right to kill more pedestrians.

Poop-poop!

What is it about road vehicles that just rots our whole moral fibre? Around the time the garden cities movement was creating the new planning profession to further its objectives, Kenneth Grahame's Mr Toad was nearly run over by a newfangled motor car.[6] Ever since Mole and Rat picked up their friend from the road where he had been dumped by a violent encounter with an early petrolhead and were astonished to find him staring besottedly after the departing car, we have had a love affair with road transport which has completely destroyed our sense of practical reality. "Poop, poop," said Mr Toad as he sat in the road "in a sort of trance, a happy smile on his face, his eyes still fixed on the dusty wake of their destroyer."

Vainly his friends tried to bring him to his senses, but Toad had been infected by a virulent and infectious disease which has contaminated tens of millions of us since.

"The poetry of motion! The *real* way to travel! The *only* way to travel! Here today – in next week tomorrow! Villages skipped, towns and cities jumped – always somebody else's horizon! Oh bliss! Oh poop-poop! Oh my! Oh my!"

What a vision of our nation over the next 100 years the far-seeing Mr Grahame had. Toad, of course, went straight out and ordered the large and very expensive motor car that was to be his undoing, but Grahame's vision of Toad enraptured by "that beautiful, that heavenly vision" was all too prophetic. In the century since, we have become a nation of Mr Toads.

Poop-poop! Mr Toad comes to town. *Image: Gateshead Council*

There's obviously something deeply seductive about the infernal combustion engine. Robbie Coltrane, for instance, eulogised about the vintage sports car the TV company provided for his travels in the series accompanying his book *B-Road Britain*[7]: "I still haven't got over the joy of cruising around in a darling like the XK150," about stunt aircraft: "a pair of biplanes buzz just feet over my head, their engines shattering the bucolic silence as they emit a dirty tail of stinky Avgas exhaust. I inhale greedily. Bliss," and power boats: "the 350hp boat can go from 30mph to 120mph in six seconds. *Ding dong!*"

The symbiotic twins

Although the sprawl lobby and roads lobby have maintained an apparent complete separation over the last 100 years, they are in reality symbiotic twins, wholly bound together since birth and, like all the most successful conspiracies, they seldom need to actually conspire.

Take the proposed £91 million Norwich Northern Distributor Road (yes, in case anyone was worrying about ways to reduce our national deficit, that *was* ninety-one million quid), explicitly intended to open up areas to the north and north-east of the city to sprawl developments on greenfield land. If anyone doubted this, the County Council's announcement[8] that the scheme had been accepted on to the government's conveyor belt for public funding (curiously, in the same week ministers were in Copenhagen telling the world how keen they were to tackle climate change) included a statement by leader Daniel Cox noting that the new road would mean "the greater Norwich area will be much better placed to cope with the major growth in housing and employment that is anticipated in the years ahead." Note those words 'greater Norwich' and be very afraid.

Back in the long Edwardian summer, however, the links between the two lobbies were harder to discern but they were there. One of the most obvious was the Harmsworth family.

Alfred Harmsworth (1865-1922), later Lord Northcliffe, is best remembered as a journalist of genius who dragged journalism out of its wordy Victorian mire into the punchy but informative style the best news writing still delivers today. But he also became one of the early twentieth century's most successful newspaper barons, owning, at various stages, the *Daily Mail*, the *Daily Mirror*, the London *Evening News*, *The Times*, the Glasgow *Daily Record* and the *Sunday Dispatch* and much else. He also launched the first motoring magazines and was a keen early motorist, and his newspapers helped see the 1903 legislation passed, yet even he could admit in a letter to his friend John Montagu that "road hogs" could have scuppered the Bill.[9]

"The considerable number of road hogs who are timed at 20 and 30 miles an hour through populous villages have rendered the task of those of us who set out to convert public opinion very difficult," he wrote – a letter that might surprise the current *Daily Mail* management with its campaigns against speed cameras. But Northcliffe and his papers remained enthusiastic supporters of the roads lobby, and he instructed them not to report road accidents in case this led to new restrictions.

No fewer than four of Northcliffe's brothers gained peerages or baronetcies, and one of these was Cecil Harmsworth, 1st Baron Harmsworth (1869-1948). He was involved with his brother's newspapers but pursued a career in politics, becoming a Liberal MP in 1906. As early as 1902 he had become one of the 101 distinguished or wealthy vice-presidents of the Garden City Association and was able to ensure the *Daily Mail* gave favourable publicity to the cause.[10] He evidently persuaded his elder brother to look favourably on the garden cities movement; the *Mail*'s editor was instructed to give Ebenezer Howard space to peddle his ideas.[11]

So, as early as 1903, the country's most popular newspaper was supporting moves to free up motorists from any restrictions, to build roads, to build houses at much lower densities than hitherto and to build them in new settlements on greenfield sites. That support hasn't wavered – Northcliffe knew how to tap into a deep seam of British insularity. The vision of a populace in its own castles, secure within its privet hedges or larch-lap panels, venturing out in a motor car and never rubbing shoulders with the rest of the population was alive, bawling lustily and having its birth announced in the paper before Queen Victoria had been three years in her tomb.

But Howard's ultimate legacy would be car-dependent sprawl.

The birth of the planning system

To attack the foundations of the sustainable Edwardian city, the garden sprawl movement had to repeal legislation and replace it with some of its own, so a planning system that could have cemented the sustainability gains of the late nineteenth century into the twentieth actually began life as an attempt to undermine those gains.

A key early figure in the process was Birmingham's housing chairman John Nettlefold, who visited Germany in 1905 to observe the new planning profession there. He reported back to his council that "The garden city idea, the garden suburb idea, have taken hold of the minds of Englishmen. We cannot hope to make Birmingham into a garden city, although something can be done towards that end, but we can, if we will, create garden suburbs around Birmingham." He went on to propose "healthy, wholesome surroundings for every Birmingham adult, give every Birmingham child light and fresh air which is so essential to its healthy development." Here, in essence, is the garden city myth – that all cities were smokeless, sunless slums. In fact, of course, city dwellers can enjoy health and light and were doing so in the new sustainable cities they were inhabiting – like, say, Birmingham at the time.

The Housing, Town Planning, etc., Act 1909 was the child of the Garden City Association, by now called the Garden Cities and Town Planning Association, and of the social housing pioneers with whom it had close links through a body called the National Housing Reform Council (NHRC), which also advocated sprawl. Significant political support was obtained from both Liberal and Labour politicians and the Bill was piloted through the Commons by local government board president John Burns, a former socialist firebrand turned Liberal who was advised by both the garden city enthusiasts and the NHRC.

Burns told the Commons the Act would secure "the home healthy, the house beautiful, the town pleasant, the city dignified and the suburb salubrious" and left no doubt that one of its targets was repeal of the bye-law standards which had done so much to create sustainable towns and cities over the previous four decades.

As a piece of planning legislation, the 1909 Act proved pretty useless, as indeed were most of its successors until the 1947 Act. But it gave impetus to formation of the new profession, and a Town Planning Institute was founded in 1914, the brainchild of garden sprawl enthusiasts, notably Thomas Adams, who had been inspired by Raymond Unwin's dismal but influential 1912 tract *Nothing Gained by Overcrowding!*[12] This launched an attack on high-density housing standards and set us on a 100-year path during which *Everything Has Been Wrecked by Sprawl!*

The worm in the bud

So what have the Edwardians ever done for us? Many of the things we take for granted today – old age pensions, social security payments, female suffrage – had their roots in the early years of the twentieth century, but the era spawned some bad things too – world wars, mass motoring and urban sprawl. One could say that 1903 was the pivotal year in which both the sprawl lobby and the roads lobby began to achieve real success and set them on the road to modifying our environment so disastrously.

There was, however, one precious pearl in the oyster of the garden cities movement, and that was the planning profession. It took another four decades to make real progress, but without it we would have become completely engulfed by sprawl and our crowded country would be close to ceasing to function. Yet within this profession's DNA is the darkly recessive sprawl gene, and even today there are many planners who not only see urban sprawl as a necessity to house an ever-more socially fragmented population, but who also see the establishment of new settlements or suburbs on greenfield land as a very positive virtue. The view of the profession as facilitators rather than regulators of development is alive and well thanks to developers' ability to convince most of our politicians that any restriction on development is a threat to prosperity. But this view has its origins in the garden cities movement and the 1909 Act.

Sprawl goes on, powered as ever by the internal combustion engine and by the ideas of Ebenezer Howard. It began with Edwardian idealism but later was seen as a necessity, before eventually becoming just another aspect of our apparently unstoppable acquisitiveness.

So *Tomorrow* we need to choose *A Path to Real Reform*, but not Ebenezer Howard's. Over the century since his time this path has been widely followed and certainly led to real reform; whether any of it was beneficial is another issue altogether.

1903 – A year that doomed our environment

The year 1903 was the year in which both the sprawl lobby and the roads lobby achieved the breakthroughs that enabled them to leave our land covered in low-density development and motor roads. It was the year the first of Unwin and Parker's low-density cottages at New Earswick were occupied, the year Dame Henrietta Barnett conceived the idea for Hampstead Garden Suburb and the year Letchworth was chosen for the first garden city.

27 March: Royal Assent for the Light Locomotives (Ireland) Act, which legalised motor racing on public roads in the UK.

23 April: Garden City Association Board discusses Letchworth as the site for the first garden city.

7 May: Ebenezer Howard reports his visit to the Chartley Castle Estate in Staffordshire to the Garden City Association Board, but it prefers Howard Pearsall's proposed site at Letchworth.

2 July: The Gordon Bennett road race held on a 90-mile public road circuit near Dublin.

23 July: The first Ford Model A car is sold, in Chicago.

August: Northern Art Workers' Guild exhibition 'Cottages Near A Town' in Manchester shows designs by Unwin and Parker.

8 August: Motor Car Bill raising speed limits passes the Commons and Lords.

1 September: The First Garden City Ltd registered.

October: Raymond Unwin moves to Letchworth village and begins planning the garden city with Barry Parker.

9 October: Garden City Association's formal opening of the Letchworth Estate.

3 December: William Rees Jeffreys' letter to local authorities suggesting they would raise more car registration revenue if they built roads and dropped 'speed traps' is exposed in *The Times*.

17 December: Wright Brothers' first flight at Kittyhawk, North Carolina.

1 January 1904: Royal Assent for the Motor Car Act.

Chapter 3

Decline and sprawl – a century of spatial planning

The progressive city planner can only visualize the concept of the mega-alopolis: the countryside entirely enveloped by an endless city.

Roger Higham, *The South Country*

Why stop for the war? Part 1

One Sunday in October 1918, three men left Hatfield railway station and set out northwards for a walk. Although the German spring offensive that had brought the *Wehrmacht* within sight of Amiens had petered out and the allied armies were now chasing them eastwards, the horrific toll of dead from the western front continued. But the three men were not interested in the war. One was too old to fight, another had been discharged from the army on medical grounds and the third was a conscientious objector evading conscription by hiding with his friends. They had come to identify a site for the second garden city.

The older man was, of course, Ebenezer Howard, who was continuing to push his purist garden city ideal despite the garden suburb backsliding of his colleagues. With him were two ardent young followers of his path to real reform: Charles Purdom, who had worked for the Garden City Pioneer Company prior to his spell in uniform and who had recently published an influential pamphlet entitled *The Garden City after the War*, and F. J. (Frederic) Osborn, who had been secretary of the Howard Cottage Society at Letchworth. Both were to remain steadfast keepers of the faith.

Purdom's pamphlet had (accurately) predicted that, after the war, a few model garden suburbs would be badly imitated by many speculative builders, and pushed for revival of the garden city ideal. Osborn, holed up in the British Museum Reading Room, had worked hard on the scheme and the two published a book[1] with Howard early in 1918, updating his earlier work and proposing 100 new towns.

Some of the movement's purists had warned that building just a second garden city would dilute their message that the government should build half a million homes in garden cities, but Howard was unshakeable. The three

Sir Ebenezer Howard   1850-1928

Sir Ebenezer Howard.
Image: © National Portrait Gallery, London

Though not the only figure who changed the way we build towns and cities at the end of the nineteenth century and the beginning of the twentieth and prompted us to plan rather than regulate, Ebenezer Howard stands head and shoulders above the others.

He was born into a London shop-keeping family and began his working life as a city clerk. At 21 he moved to America, where he tried farming before getting work through his shorthand skills in Chicago, where he watched urban rebuilding at work after the 1871 fire. He returned home to a recession in 1876 and saw country folk pouring into the already-overcrowded city, which evidently sparked his ideal of low-density living.

Work as a Parliamentary shorthand writer gave him first-hand experience of the politics of the day, and he threw himself into the ferment of non-conformist, socialist and anarchist debate which questioned accepted standards in every field.

He distilled his ideas in *Tomorrow: A Path to Real Reform* (1897), which set out his belief that carefully planned garden city dwellers would enjoy the advantages, but not the disadvantages, of both town and country. A competent public speaker, Howard soon attracted a substantial and influential following, and the Garden City Association was set up the following year.

As the movement grew, Howard became leader of a purist faction who saw the future as garden cities against those who supported garden suburbs. He was able to obtain funding from his wealthy industrialist friends to begin the first garden city at Letchworth and, eventually, the second at Welwyn. But his principal concern for his new settlements was that they should be exemplars of new forms of cooperative municipal control, and most of his writing is devoted to that end, although these ideas achieved little success.

Howard stood out against the urban industrial ethos of his day and created an idealistic vision of a move to a suburban, cooperative lifestyle that sometimes even frustrated his admirers. His legacy is an anti-urbanist ideal, even among environmentalists, and a century of low-density sprawl. His friend George Bernard Shaw described him as a "heroic simpleton"; he was certainly no simpleton, but whether you consider him a hero or not will probably depend on your view of low-density living.

Sir Frederic Osborn   1885-1978

F. J. Osborn was a disciple of Ebenezer Howard who kept the purity of the garden city ideal alive and kicking until his death in 1978.

Born into humble origins in London, he began his working life as a clerk and developed an interest in politics and socialism, joining the Fabians in 1905. But it was his successful application to become the secretary-manager of the Howard Cottage Society in Letchworth in 1912 that was to lead to him becoming one of the movement's leading tub-thumpers. His work as a housing manager in the town brought him into contact with Howard and his disciples such as Charles Purdom and W. G. Taylor, and the four of them formed the 'New Townsmen' during the Great War to rescue the garden cities movement from what they saw

Sir Frederic Osborn.
Image: © National Portrait Gallery, London

as the heresy of garden suburbs. Osborn accompanied Howard on the fateful day that some Hertfordshire countryside was designated as the site of the second garden city, and in 1918 published his first book, *New Towns After the War*, to keep the ideal alive.

Osborn became Welwyn's company secretary and estate manager and worked there until 1936 when one of the movement's fallings-out and major financial reconstruction led to his being expelled. Taking a job at a local radio manufacturer allowed him the time to proselytise for the movement, and he continued to press for a national garden cities programme through, and after, the Second World War. He later became secretary of the Garden Cities and Town Planning Association, which the original Garden City Association had by then become, and continued to pursue Howard's vision of low-density living in new settlements for the rest of his life.

He republished *New Towns After the War* during the Second World War to revive the flagging interest in garden cities, and it was one of the inspirations for the post-war new towns movement, for the new settlements of more recent decades and even the 'eco towns' programme. His role at the Town & Country Planning Association (TCPA) allowed him wide scope to disseminate his views throughout the planning profession, although he later complained they were being influenced by the 'Modern movement' to prefer rebuilding towns *in situ* rather than at remote, green-field sites.

The man who once described himself as "estate manager, publicist and industrial bagman" at Welwyn eventually became the garden sprawl movement's elder statesman and keeper of Ebenezer Howard's flame. He is widely honoured – the TCPA has an annual memorial lecture, while Welwyn has the Sir Frederic Osborn School and the Osborn Way long-stay car park.

strode north across land owned by a supporter, the Fourth Marquess of Salisbury, whose Hatfield House seat was nearby. Halfway between Hatfield and Welwyn, Howard had spotted from the train some beautiful countryside sloping down towards the River Lea. This, Howard ordered, should be destroyed. The three men retreated to Hatfield to plan its destruction over lunch.

Tudor Walters fires the starting gun

The infant planning profession was, meanwhile, also gearing up for the post-war world. Its powers may have been minimal and its numbers few, but it plainly meant business. In 1917, with the war finely balanced, the new profession launched another great assault of its own on compact, sustainable cities and their density in particular.

Lloyd George had promised "a fit country for heroes to live in", but the Local Government Board had already estimated there would be a shortage of at least 120,000 homes and that year commissioned a report under the chairmanship of Liberal MP Sir John Tudor Walters, who was active in the garden cities movement. Among the committee's other members was architect Raymond Unwin, perhaps by that time the movement's leading practitioner. Unwin convinced the committee to recommend a maximum density standard for house

Hundreds of suburbs imitated Welwyn's town centre.

building of 12 to the acre (about 30 to the hectare), around a third of what was being achieved under the bye-law system. It was, perhaps, one of the most radical (and radically destructive) pieces of planning the country has ever seen, and the committee recommended building half a million homes to this ruinously low density. Its 1918 report was as important in setting Britain on the path to unsustainable development as the founding of the Garden City Association or the 1909 Town Planning Act. Legislation was soon passed destroying the earlier, sustainable standards and requiring both cash-strapped local authorities and commercial builders to squander precious land on a grand scale.

Purdom's prediction that speculative builders would simply take the bits they wanted of the garden suburb ideal was to prove all too gloomily accurate over the 20 years between the wars. The equally gloomy prognostications of the '100 new towns' proponents that the second garden city would be the last also turned out to have a degree of truth. Welwyn Garden City grew slowly – by 1928 it had only 7,000 inhabitants – and it took some years to get its architecture, etc. fixed to its promoters' satisfaction. And Howard's ideal of a benevolent company managing the city's affairs and creating an instant community proved even more challenging than at Letchworth. After that, no one really bothered to try very hard.

Sprawl for all – the growth of municipal suburbs

The sprawl movement turned its attention to garden suburbs, but they were proving ever harder to distinguish from the huge tide of speculative sprawl unleashed by the Tudor Walters report. One area where the sprawl lobby's ideals still held some sway, however, was in municipal housing. Few council houses existed in 1900, and while the Edwardians began to build them, it was the inter-war period when the idea flowered. A great deal of idealism was involved, and who came forward to present themselves as guardians of the very highest idealism in planning and design? Go on, guess.

Inter-war councils were able to buy up farms that adjoined their cities and cover them with cottage homes, just like the garden village pioneers of 30 years before. They were decent little homes, but many were built on remote and windswept sites with rotten bus services, no tram or train services, few shops and miles from anywhere that anyone needed to be. Some are still popular, but quite a few are the hated 'outer estates' that have fallen into deprivation and decline, where those who exercised their 'right to buy' discovered the hard way that that doesn't include a right to sell. It's an interesting reflection on those who believed that moving people to 'suburbs salubrious' with front and back gardens, privet hedges and an endless walk to school or shops would turn everyone into model citizens.

The great British semi takes over

What the Tudor Walters committee had opened the door to was private sprawl on a grand scale, and, despite the idealism of the young planning movement, this was mostly unplanned. It wasn't socially inclusive either, or communitarian, but it was certainly popular. Every speculative builder in the country could knock up 'cottages', 'villas', 'semis', 'bungalows' or whatever for a few hundred quid and buyers could easily be conned into thinking they were moving to the country. All too often the new estates bore the name of the farm or other rural feature destroyed to accommodate them; 'Metroland', promoted by the railway companies north-west of London up to the Chilterns, is a much-cited example. It would be nice to quote the travel writers of this period on what they thought of this unchecked sprawl, but for the most part they avoided it like the plague it was.

One exception, however, was the writer Walter Wilkinson and his wife, who pushed their puppet show off the South Downs into Worthing.

> We looked down, with gypsy eyes, on all the new houses that scatter themselves out and up the Downs behind the town – a vast area, very civilized, with wild Sussex well subjugated by pavings and lamp-posts, and kerb-stones. After being familiar with the unconfined Downs for weeks, after growing used to the irregular masses of grass, and the gentle contours of the hills, it was a painful experience to come into this world of straight lines, and geometrically confined areas. The pretty, open country which, no doubt, had attracted the residences was lost beneath a pushing exploitation. All sensitiveness to anything that did not pay seemed to be absent, and, instead of Sussex, you got – well – anything you would get in the urbanization of any county.[2]

And by 1936, the urbanisation of any county was roaring ahead. Between 1918 and 1939, around 4.3 million new homes were built in Britain, with 69 per cent of them built privately. Although exact figures are hard to obtain, it's been estimated[3] that around 9,100 hectares of land were being converted from farmland to housing in England and Wales alone *every year* in the early-to-mid 1920s. By 1926-31 this had shot up to 21,000 hectares and between 1931 and 1939, despite the effects of the Depression, it reached an astonishing 25,100 hectares a year. That's almost 100 square miles of farmland (about the area of Birmingham) disappearing under sprawl every year and, even if that's a slight overestimation, it was close to madness in a country unable to feed itself in time of war. Most of this sprawl was housing development and much was being built at even lower densities than Tudor Walters' recommended maximum.

A string of planning legislation between the two world wars did next to nothing to curb the sprawl and little to improve its design. Speculative developers homed in on the arterial roads between towns because building houses there didn't even mean spending money on providing roads. By 1930 this was dubbed 'ribbon development', and Parliamentary time was devoted to fretting about it rather than tackling it. In the end a fairly ineffectual Restriction of Ribbon Development Act was passed in 1932 – and even this turned out to have been promoted by the roads lobby, which was scared that ribbon development folk would park their Austin 7s and Morris 8s along arterial roads, holding up the gleaming roadsters and lorries and causing trouble with demands for speed limits.

Bizarrely, one of the few measures to provide any limit on sprawl came directly from the garden sprawl movement. Neville Chamberlain is today remembered for the Munich Agreement and some ineffectual leadership at the start of the Second World War, but he was also a keen supporter of the sprawl movement. In 1927, as health minister, he created a Greater London Regional Planning Committee, suggesting at its first meeting that the fast-expanding metropolis needed an 'agricultural belt' to separate it from its satellites and provide open space.

A committee was set up to examine the idea with Raymond, by now Sir Raymond, Unwin as technical advisor, and in 1929 it recommended London should have a 'green belt'. London of course had always had a pretty impressive

Inter-war semis: a sort of architectural food fight.

Between the wars, low-density sprawl replaced compact development.
Image: National Tramway Museum

green belt called the Home Counties, and what this represented was pretty much Howard's garden city agricultural belt blown up to encompass the whole of London. Of course, protecting rural land outside the capital would do little to provide Londoners with the everyday open space they needed, but it ensured that, as London continued to grow, its development would leap the green belt to places like, er, Letchworth or Welwyn or perhaps some of the 100 new towns the purists wanted to build all over the Home Counties.

Green belts would have to wait for another war to pass, and while today the majority of major UK conurbations have one, development is leapfrogging them into remote areas. The garden cities never happened, but new towns and growth areas did, and today only 13 per cent of England (and far less of the rest of the UK) is protected as green belt. But the population at large believes that any undeveloped land is so protected, so although 2 per cent of England's new homes every year are built within green belts, it's easy to replace with farmland elsewhere, enabling cynical politicians to claim 'the green belt has actually grown'.

Why stop for the war? Part 2

The Second World War brought a temporary halt to urban sprawl, but once again it sparked a remarkable flowering of idealism about the future. The sprawl lobby was quick to exploit this and already had people in positions of

Sir Raymond Unwin   (1863-1940)

Raymond Unwin represents the most important link between William Morris I, the Arts & Crafts movement, the garden cities movement and the planning profession.

   He was born in Yorkshire to a high-minded academic family, grew up in Oxford and was influenced by Ruskin. As he grew up he came under Morris's influence and became a strong socialist. He began work in industry as an engineering draughts-man, but this led to an interest in architecture and in 1896 he formed a partnership with Barry Parker, another key Arts & Crafts figure in the garden cities movement, and also married Parker's sister.

   He was a key figure in the move away from classical architecture towards an idealised version of vernacular, cottage architecture. He was co-designer of New Earswick, Letchworth and Hampstead Garden Suburb and played an important role in creating the young planning profession before the First World War.

   He was also instrumental in promoting low-density sprawl through his pre-war pamphlet *Nothing Gained by Overcrowding!*, and was able to further his support for this through his influential membership of the Tudor Walters Committee and through the planning and architectural professions. From 1927 he joined the Greater London Regional Planning Committee, where he was able to advance the view that green belts and garden cities should be used to redistribute population and industry.

   Unwin achieved considerable recognition both in the UK and overseas, but he never abandoned his ascetic and unconventional demeanour. F. J. Osborn described him as "long-haired" and Lewis Mumford as "a bit of a Quaker", but his influence in creating a century of low-density sprawl was at least as important as Ebenezer Howard's.

influence as war broke out. A Royal Commission on the distribution of indus-try under Sir Anderson Montague-Barlow was set up in 1937 and reported early in 1940, as Hitler was fuelling his tanks to rip into Holland, Belgium and France. Inevitably it noted that prosperity was moving south, but a radical minority, including Patrick Abercrombie (who always managed to keep a foot in the garden sprawl and countryside protection camps), wanted decentralisa-tion from the cities. This began an attack on compact cities, which soon saw Lord Reith, patrician boss of the BBC, extreme family tyrant and sprawl enthu-siast, appointed to chair a committee on reconstruction.

   With bombs raining down there was certainly a need for reconstruction, but this wasn't about necessity, it was about idealism, and bomb damage was seen as an opportunity to replace our towns and cities with low-density sub-urbs. While most people were devoting themselves to the war effort, a string of reports emerged from Whitehall's garden sprawl enthusiasts setting out their vision. In 1942, with the U-boat campaign leaving the country just weeks from starvation, the Scott Committee on land utilisation recommended that only the most agriculturally productive 4 per cent of the British land mass needed protecting from development. A 1943 committee recommended that house building should precede the reconstruction of our factories – which might have paid for it – and pulling down a million existing homes and replacing them too. The Dudley Committee in 1944 recommended new house building standards, while the Ministry of Information produced a string of public information films promoting the idea of new towns and low-density suburbs.

Lord Reith, meanwhile, asked the London County Council to produce a plan for its future, and it responded with one by Patrick Abercrombie and J. H. Forshaw proposing moving people out to new settlements, while a successor, covering a much wider area of south-east England, proposed cutting London's population by a third and moving a million people out beyond the green belt.

Thus was created the problem that, by the 1970s in London and dozens of other cities, was known as the 'inner-city problem'.

New Jerusalem, new towns – post-war planning

Post-war Britain was rich in ideals and financially broke, but house building quickly became the symbol of political virility it has remained ever since. Labour wanted council houses, Conservatives owner-occupied ones, but for both the paradigm remained sprawl, and no one was to seriously question that for another 50 years.

As the war drew to a close, the sprawl lobby set out its strategy for domination via a new planning system in a book of essays called *Homes, Towns and Countryside*,[4] which took an overtly garden city line.

"The most significant efforts in positive planning in Britain in the present century have been the creation of two new towns, Letchworth and Welwyn," noted the editors in their introduction. "The creation of many new towns, first-class examples of modern town-building technique, must take a high place in any well-conceived plan for Britain after the war."

New Jerusalem was going to be dedensified and 'polynucleated' – Lewis Mumford's word for replacing a "badly organised mass city" with a cluster of small towns separated from one another – or, to put it another way, replacing a well-organised city that had thrived for centuries with some blob of characterless sprawl separated from some other blob of characterless sprawl by a pathetic strip of green space.

And this decentralisation was to be low-density and, nonsensically, destroying communities and building on the countryside was expected to, um, improve our sense of community and to protect the countryside.

"There is the loss of the community sense: whole areas are found to consist of mere slabs of housing without any social centre or, at any rate, facilities for social intercourse," wrote Patrick Abercrombie in his contribution.[5] "This defect is found no less in the recently built, sprawling suburbs than in the older close rows of bye-law building (though of course the former have the advantage of more spacious lay-out)."

And the latter of course had the advantage of pubs or shops on every corner, schools and other facilities a short walk away, and a short walk or tram ride to the town or city centre where a large range of community activities was available. But garden sprawl enthusiasts were never ones to let the facts interrupt their narrative.

The book gave Frederic Osborn a chance to restate the garden city gospel that homes should be built at no more than 12 to the acre (about 30 to the hectare) lest a huge range of plagues be unleashed, and the book's editors underlined the need for dedensifying both our residential and industrial areas.

"Such an approach does not conflict with the desire to preserve the countryside," they wrote in the introduction. "The countryside will be preserved not by shutting up our industrial populations in cities and towns too crowded to hold them but by seeing to it that the overspill of population is guided into grouped development by the creation of new towns and the expansion of existing towns and villages."

Hope that's clear: the way to protect the countryside is to build on it. But in case anyone disagreed, higher powers were invoked and the book concluded with a postscript by Archbishop of York Cyril Garbett bemoaning the lack of community sense in large cities and the destruction of our countryside by sprawl and proposing reductions in the size of cities to allow citizens "to take some intelligent part of the community".[6]

In the fevered atmosphere of the time there was virtually no-one to challenge this, and even the countryside protection movement seemed mollified when someone like Abercrombie told them his planned sprawl would save a countryside that the inter-war period had seen destroyed at an abominable rate. No sooner was the war over than Lord Reith was appointed to head a committee to look at new towns, and the sprawl lobby had both people to sit on his committee[7] and ideas for sprawl towns. Soon it was recommending new settlements of 30,000-50,000 people surrounded by agricultural belts straight out of Ebenezer Howard's *Big Book of Songs for Garden City Chaps*. But while Howard favoured community control of his cities, Reith wasn't even prepared to allow municipal control; his New Jerusalems were to be nationalised and run by corporations funded by, and controlled from, Whitehall. Within months legislation was on the statute book, within a year new towns had been designated at Stevenage, Newton Aycliffe, Crawley, Harlow, Hemel

Planned sprawl was supposed to save the countryside.
Image: Leeds Library and Information Service

Hempstead and East Kilbride, within three years more were designated at Corby, Peterlee, Cwmbran and Glenrothes (together with expanded towns at Basildon, Bracknell, Hatfield and Welwyn), and within five years the new towns programme had actually built some houses – 20 of them at Stevenage.

During the Attlee years, however, nearly a million homes were built in Great Britain, 80 per cent of them council homes – a remarkable achievement given the era's economic problems. But the rate of building couldn't be sustained and fell to 170,000 in 1951, Labour's last year in office, becoming a key political battlefield. Winston Churchill's promise to the electorate of 300,000 homes a year was to reap electoral success.

Private passions – post-war sprawl

The new Conservative government reversed the passion for council houses but had the wit to realise that not everyone could afford to buy a home and, if the raw numbers of houses it had promised were to be achieved, many of them would have to be municipal (a simple truth forgotten in the 1980s and painfully being relearned today). Council house building grew to 248,000 in 1953 and thereafter declined slowly.

Private sector building grew slowly until the rising star Harold Macmillan became housing minister, charged with achieving the 300,000 target.

"Every humble home will bless you if you succeed," Churchill told him, and he quickly did, with the post-war record of 348,000 homes in all tenures achieved in 1954. But where were all these homes to go?

The new towns were never going to provide the sort of space needed to rehouse city dwellers at low densities, even before 'moving to the country' once again became a national passion. And HM Treasury was as passionate as ever about spending as little as possible, so 1952 saw the Town Development Act, which allowed 'exporting authorities' (i.e. cities) to enter agreements with 'receiving authorities' (i.e. towns) to provide housing for the 'relief of congestion and overpopulation'. People thus became exports, like cattle, and were duly exported. Receiving authorities could build houses with government grants and contributions from the exporting authority. It may not have been what the garden city purists wanted, but at least it was greenfield sprawl, even if it was in uncomfortable proximity to existing towns.

Macmillan was, in any case, against designating any new towns[8] and 1953 saw 100 local authorities meet at Leamington to discuss government plans for dispersal. But even more was needed, and cities began planning vast 'overspill estates' like London's New Addington and Boreham Wood – two of the thirteen built around the capital between 1945 and 1956 despite the nascent green belt.

By this time, of course, we had the beginnings of the modern planning system thanks to the 1947 Act, but the profession at this stage regarded sprawl as its paradigm, and if there was an opposition it came from the modernists who, as we shall see in Chapter 4, had their own plans for destroying the cities. So six post-war decades of planned sprawl have seen the waistlines of towns, cities and villages expanding even faster than those of their inhabitants.

Following designation of London's green belt, the green belt idea was to languish until a rare intervention by a politician rather than a civil servant or lobbyist. The new explosion of house building in the 1950s revived fears about destruction of the countryside, and local Conservatives were often at the forefront of such concerns. Housing and local government minister Duncan Sandys told the Commons further unrestricted sprawl needed to be tackled and stood up to his civil servants, who warned it would upset local authorities and that developers would simply seek sites beyond the green belts.[9] A circular was issued asking other local authorities to consider green belts wherever needed, to check the physical growth of built-up areas, to prevent neighbouring towns merging and to preserve towns' special character.

Few local authorities at that time, however, were prepared to suffer the unpopularity engendered by proposals for new greenfield settlements, although some attempted it: for example, Birmingham's plan for a new town at Wythall in Worcestershire or Manchester's at Lymm and Mobberley in Cheshire. Most were seen off by public inquiries. But the London County Council made

Post-war house building became a sign of political virility.
Image: Leeds Library and Information Service

strenuous efforts to use the Town Development Act to export citizens to towns
up to 100 miles away and the process was to continue into the 1980s.

By the end of the 1950s things were moving the sprawl lobby's way, however, often thanks to massive programmes of demolition for bye-law homes in
the name of 'slum clearance'. Designation of the first new town for ten years
at Skelmersdale in 1961 followed Liverpool's over-enthusiastic demolition
programme. The post-war baby boom also saw a sharp rise in the population,
especially in south-east England, despite politicians of all parties in that era
recognising the need for regional planning. The 1961 census showed that
decentralisation and the green belt had added 800,000 people to what was
becoming a 'ring city' around the capital, most in the suburban sprawl estates
typical of the post-war period, rather than in new or expanded towns.

It should have been a wake-up call, but it wasn't. Population projections
were rising – the 1960 projection of the national population in 2000 was 64
million; by 1965 that projection had risen to 75 million. In the event it was
58 million, but the projections were used to frighten governments into
approving more sprawl.

"Where, in this small island, in the next 45 years, are we going to find accommodation for a further 20 million people, or even more?" wondered Sir Colin Buchanan in his 1963 *Traffic in Towns* report.[10] In fact, the population rose by about eight million in that period.

The birth of regional planning

One positive result of these events was the birth of regional planning in the 1960s. It had been tried between the wars but the feeble planning laws of the time prevented it achieving much. It is, of course, open to abuse, and in 2010 it was summarily and arbitrarily ended in England, ostensibly because it had been used to force crazy house-building targets on local authorities. But it does offer huge scope for preventing urban sprawl and promoting Smart Growth.

Its first real fruit was the 1964 *South East Study*, by the Ministry for Housing and Local Government, which assumed the region would have to accommodate 3.5 million more people by 1981. It accurately predicted that growth of the ring city would promote long-distance commuting (sprawl promoters having concentrated on housing rather than employment, as usual) and proposed big increases in population around Northampton, Southampton, Portsmouth and Peterborough, all of which remain, half a century later, beset by sprawl.

Labour was elected in 1964 promising to put an end to all of this, just as it was promising to put an end to the Beeching rail closures and it didn't do that either. The new Cabinet included Town & Country Planning Association (TCPA) Executive member Michael Stewart, and several other TCPA supporters also joined the government[11] – which, instead of dumping the *South East Study*, was soon adding plans for the west Midlands and north-west England. New towns were proposed at Dawley, Redditch and Runcorn and major expansion at Warrington and in central Lancashire. Even north-east England, where the population was in sharp decline, was judged to require a new town at Washington. Soon another new town was being added – at the tiny village of Milton Keynes – on the obviously sensible grounds it happened to be halfway between London and Birmingham.

And in case anyone doubted the symbiotic relationship between roads and sprawl, the South East Planning Council in 1967 recommended major development along the new or proposed M1, M2, M3, M4 and A1(M) motorways radiating from London. Local authorities had the temerity to disagree, so a joint central/local government team eventually produced the *Strategic Plan for the South East* in 1970.

The cuckoo's egg laid by the garden cities movement six decades earlier had hatched and its product was now devouring everything in sight. Garden sprawl schemes had grown from Howard's 30,000 resident garden cities to the 60,000

The 1950s saw the sprawl lobby fully in charge.
Image: Leeds Library and Information Service

resident post-war new towns to 250,000 resident new towns in the *South East Study* and now to growth areas of 500,000-1,500,000 people.[12] For despite the sprawl lobby's fuss about them, new and expanded towns had delivered only about 3 per cent of the total housing programme, and 67 town expansion schemes in England and Wales had delivered just 68,000 homes by 1970.[13]

The *Strategic Plan for the South East* (SPSE) proposed five growth areas: south Wessex, south Hampshire, Milton-Keynes-Northampton-Wellingborough, Area 8 – a toilet-shaped area of innocent heathland and small towns between Reading, Bracknell and Aldershot, and Crawley. Significant growth was also proposed at Harlow, Bishop's Stortford, Chelmsford, the Medway towns, Maidstone, Ashford, Hastings, Eastbourne, Bournemouth, Poole and Aylesbury. Similar joint plans emerged for the west Midlands and north-west England.

Naturally, all the growth areas were served by new motorways or much-improved trunk-roads, for this was the 'motorway age' when the cosy ideals of the garden cities movement and the egalitarian optimism of new town promoters became engulfed by consumerism. Growth area sprawl was far from the cosy little garden cities sought six decades earlier, but its genetic inheritance was the same.

Walking across *The South Country*[14] in 1972, the writer Roger Higham found the countryside literally disappearing before his eyes. A morning walk across what was supposed to be rural Hampshire brought him to a footpath that was supposed to go to Lovedean, but it soon petered out and became overgrown.

> Its tenuous course, after negotiating a series of sloughs in a wood, col-lapsed and died in the face of vast depredations by building contractors, who were permanently ruining yet another tract of woodland in order to spread still further the featureless brick boxes of Cowplain. I made a dusty way through to an existing street, and had to consult my compass merely to find out which way I ought to go. To waste precious land in building wide streets of single-storey houses or bungalows seems wanton and criminal, but that is what had been done in this place; nor was there any indication whether I was in Lovedean, Cowplain or an up platform at Clapham Junction.

Higham had unwittingly wandered into one of the SPSE growth areas – south Hampshire – and he struggled on through "the wasteland of ill-conceived and unplanned housing that stretches from Havant to Southampton" (ill-con-ceived it might have been, but unplanned it was not) until faced with the ultimate horror.

> Standing in a field, as if they had just been unloaded from some giant wheelbarrow, there stood a number of tall, oblong, detached flat-blocks, and some long rows of terraced houses; from that point over another mile to the old coast road at Bedhampton, there stretched row upon row of these potential Gorbals. There appeared to have been no effort whatever to create the least impression of a community, no centre, no shops, no square, nothing for those unfortunate souls obliged to live there but the long trek into the middle of Havant itself, nothing but the endless, featureless, cheerless streets of mediocre houses, and those ugly, sore-thumb flat-blocks plonked stupidly in the middle of nowhere.

It's a perfect demolition of the legacy wrought by Ebenezer Howard and his gang. Of course this isn't what they sought – they wanted planned settlements of communitarian folk with village greens and cul-de-sacs and idealised town centres in perfect harmony. But Britain in the twentieth century didn't develop like that, it developed around the motor car, and the folk somewhere north of Havant, or wherever it was Higham had become enmeshed, did not and do not consider themselves "unfortunate souls" because they have to drive into

Little of the post-war sprawl was built in new settlements.

Havant or many miles beyond for their work, their shops or their schools. Few if any are likely to give a fig for Howard's communitarian ideals and probably consider themselves to be successful consumers, lucky to own their own property and their own cars. But unfortunate they are, as they will eventually discover when the era of cheap, unfettered motoring draws to a close. South Hampshire, meanwhile, became a 'growth point' once again in 2006, even if the then transport secretary Alistair Darling had just decided to prevent it having sustainable transit by cancelling the well-developed and ready-to-go plans for a light rail system linking Portsmouth to Havant.

The year 1968 brought more planning legislation and, curiously, marks the point where a relatively left-wing Labour government introduced a note of market influence into the planning system. Planning had previously been largely a matter of physically allocating land, but a new 'process planning' required councils to respond to economic and social indicators in their local plans.[15] As the century wore on, the all-too-visible hand of the market fastened ever more tightly around the neck of planning, whatever the environmental imperative, and politicians across the spectrum are now loath to loosen it.

The triumph of consumerism

The 1970s were to bring economic problems and a downgrading of the growth assumptions that underpinned planning for sprawl, and it was perhaps the last decade when party politics mattered very much, in any respect. Once our economic neuroses had brought Margaret Thatcher to power, her government was able to eviscerate the institutions that pursued change and it all became the market after that, whoever was in power. Out went council housing, out went the public sector, out (oops, oh, never mind) went British industry and out went government support for the planning system (to the despair of local Conservative associations). But any optimists hoping the eclipse of public housing would reduce residential sprawl were to be disappointed, and sprawl ran away merrily in the 1980s on the back of local plans and local planning committees endlessly having to nibble, nibble away at the land around our towns. Most larger conurbations, of course, by now had green belts, so the nibbling went on beyond them.

County structure plans, introduced in 1968, had been supposed to bring order to this process, but only 24 had been submitted to the government for approval by 1977 and only seven had been approved. In 1985 the government published a White Paper ominously called *Lifting the Burden*. It might more accurately, perhaps, have been called *Ramping Up the Burden of Whitehall Domination to Prevent You Lot Protecting Your Environment*, but such candour from Whitehall is not to be expected.

Lifting the Burden proposed "simplifying and improving" the system with some sketchy proposals for complicating and enfeebling it by abolishing structure plans in England and Wales and keeping them in Scotland, where the Thatcher government was starting to realise its writ hardly ran. The new world order would include statements of county planning policies on a limited range of issues, while districts would produce their own single-tier plans. The idea was to end developers' "uncertainty" about the outcome of their applications, but local authorities, many of them Conservative-controlled, got increasingly fed up with Whitehall telling them to approve things and overturning their opposition to developments.[16]

The row rumbled on through a new White Paper in 1989, which again proposed abolishing structure plans. But by the time *Planning Policy Guidance Note 15* appeared in 1990, structure plans were safe and county councils were urged to get on with reviewing them, although the government tried to legislate to require their approval by the Secretary of State. This was a crucial period in Whitehall's growing control over the planning system. A key change was making plans the primary consideration in development control, which was fine in theory, of course, as it meant councils could be reined in when making bizarre or irrational decisions, and it would give everyone an element of predictability. But the way the appeal system is set up, only applicants can appeal against refusals of planning permission; objectors have no such right to appeal when bad proposals are approved. All three main political parties have, at one

Endlessly nibbling at the land around our towns.

time or another, proposed to introduce such a system, and all three have failed to deliver.

Today's 'plans-led' system has its origins in this period, and even though ministers didn't get their absolute power over structure plans at that time, they did get powers to intervene and set up an examination in a public system through which they can introduce vast amounts of influence.

An unexpected consequence, however, was allowing amenity groups to participate more fully in the process – turning public inquiries into structure plans, and, later, inquiries into regional spatial strategies, into long-drawn-out affairs. Yet the public still remains astonished to discover, when a major planning application threatens their local environment, that the pass was sold several years earlier when a statutory plan was agreed. Amenity societies too are finding their ever-diminishing resources ground down by inquiries in a world where people have less time – and less inclination – to involve themselves in the health of their communities.

Protecting the countryside

People have been worrying about the destruction of our countryside since the nineteenth century, and a nascent protection movement was one of the many useful things born in late-Victorian times. The Commons Preservation Society, later the Commons and Footpaths Preservation Society, was set up in 1865 and survives to this day, and fought to protect a great deal of countryside. William

Morris I was an active member for ten years and by the First World War this body could claim it had saved and extended Hampstead Heath and Epping Forest and protected Ashdown Forest, the Malvern Hills, Wimbledon and Wandsworth Commons and much else.

But the garden sprawl movement has always regarded countryside protection with suspicion, and the 1909 planning legislation it promoted tried to give local authorities powers to sell or utilise for building purposes any land, including commons, open spaces or recreation grounds, notwithstanding any restrictions imposed by statute or deed of gift. The Society fought this but found itself fighting the Local Government Board, by this time firmly in the sprawl camp. In the end the Society had to mobilise some fairly heavyweight parliamentarians and the minister, John Burns, eventually had to agree to an amendment requiring that no common land, open space or allotment be acquired under the Act without either Parliament agreeing or the Board of Agriculture agreeing an equivalent area be given in exchange.[17]

1909 also saw the roads lobby having its three ha'p'orth, with a Development and Road Improvement Funds Act, which would have allowed industrial forestry on commons and open spaces (the Society got this one amended) and would also have allowed development commissioners to set back boundaries on either side of roads constructed under the Act. So, as early as 1909, the roads lobby had already persuaded Parliament that main roads could be widened into people's front gardens and so on.

But the Edwardian period also saw the beginnings of an insidious propaganda claiming that countryside protection and the garden sprawl movement had common aims. A history of the Commons Preservation Society by its chairman Lord Eversley in 1910 included a foreword by two of its prominent members, Sir Robert Hunter and Sir Edward Buxton, both doughty fighters for preserving open land, claiming that the Society's influences included the formation of garden cities and suburbs.

"It may even be questioned whether garden city and garden suburb – Letchworth, Bournville, Port Sunlight, Hampstead – would have yet been seen so soon, or would have attracted the same notice, had not Wimbledon Common and Epping Forest been fought for and rescued some 30 years ago," they wrote.[18]

This strange conflictual belief lasted for decades. In 1926, with sprawl running riot, Patrick Abercrombie, later to be known for proposing new towns in the countryside of the outer home counties, published *The Preservation of Rural England*,[19] calling for a national joint committee to protect the countryside, which helped lead to the foundation of the Council for the Preservation of Rural England (now the Campaign to Protect Rural England – CPRE). It was soon followed by an Association for the Protection of Rural Scotland, in 1926, and a Council for the Protection of Rural Wales, in 1928.

Soon CPRE and the others were actively fighting ribbon development and unsympathetic rural architecture and supporting national parks, but although the campaign attracted many of the brightest and best, several were still seduced by the silky propaganda of the sprawl movement. A well-known early CPRE supporter was the architect Clough Williams-Ellis, probably best remembered for Portmeirion village in north Wales. In 1928 he published a seminal and much-admired book on countryside protection – but what's this it's saying?

> What, then, is this Welwyn, this paragon of a place, this town unique – or almost unique – in all England? It is an humiliating admission, but it is just plain common-sense, foresight and good management, and nothing else. And so it is unique, and so it is becoming a by-word and a wonder, and so it is comely and spacious, prosperous and healthy. Perhaps the best definition that can be given of the idea of the garden city or village is that it is functional. The object of its founders is not to make a profit, but to provide for certain recognised human needs."[20]

So here was one of the countryside's biggest defenders seduced by one of its most serious threats. To be fair to Williams-Ellis, uncontrolled development was defacing huge areas of English countryside in 1928, and maybe a small and isolated example of planned development might have seemed a good idea to an architect, but good architecture in twentieth-century sprawl was already a lost cause.

In 1937 Williams-Ellis edited another book of countryside protection essays, *Britain and the Beast*,[21] which finally included one writer, Geoffrey Boumphrey, who attacked the garden cities movement for planning an "imitation arcadia" and, while saying he thought garden cities had much to say for them, judged the results unhappy. But in the same book Abercrombie popped up calling for new planning restrictions and a defence of the "garden suburb standard of twelve houses per acre". This would, he claimed, enable the whole population of England and Wales to be housed in a 20-mile radius and, while he called for compact towns reusing brownfield land, he also commended Raymond Unwin's support for pepper-potting new towns on greenfield sites outside cities. An ability to ride several horses running in different directions is a remarkable one; perhaps it's what got him put in charge of so much later on.

A great deal of the countryside protection work in the last three-quarters of the twentieth century concentrated on access to the countryside, as interest in walking exploded after the First World War. The Kinder Scout mass trespass in 1932 coincided with the start of a long campaign to establish national parks and, as early as 1931, a government committee noted that rural areas around towns were suffering disfigurement and improvements in road transport were putting even remote rural areas under threat. Although it pointed out that the UK had no large wilderness areas such as those that formed the basis of other countries' national parks, it recommended national reserve areas to safeguard areas of exceptional natural interest and to improve access – "by pedestrians". Eventually the National Parks and Access to the Countryside Act was passed in 1949 and ten national parks were created in England and Wales over the next few years. But they have always experienced a conflict between protection and access, although this is less evident in their poor relations – areas of outstanding natural beauty (AONBs) – which were never required to promote leisure. For their first 50 years AONBs lacked their own authorities and were often simply ignored.

Shopping and trucking

Margaret Thatcher's 'great car economy' of the 1980s didn't just generate housing sprawl and ever-more commuting by car, it also prompted an explosion in out-of-town shopping, a sort of 'great car environmental disaster'.

Introduction of a 'plan-led' planning system in the 1990s, however, did offer councils their first opportunity to stem the flesh-eating retail dinosaurs that major supermarkets and shopping centres were becoming, or at least to divert them to less damaging places where they could be served by public transport. But controls were weak and patchy at first and the retail outlets went on being approved in the 1990s as if we actually needed more of them. Slowly, painfully, controls were introduced, with *Planning Policy Guidance Note 6* in 1996 bringing in a 'sequential test' under which major town centre retail should be approved before edge-of-centre, and edge-of-centre before out-of-town. But, as we shall see in Chapter 6, Whitehall and the retail industry found ways to undermine this and a great deal of unsustainable retail space gets approved to this day.

The history of the UK's industrial and employment location over the last 100 years or so, meanwhile, is a complex one and largely beyond the scope of this book. Most of that period was marked by a gradual (and later not so gradual) decline of traditional industry and decreasingly successful attempts to replace it. One major piece of sprawl, however, was the attempt before and during the Second World War to move industry to remote sites that were less vulnerable to bombing. Today, many of those sites look like towns, but were countryside within living memory.

One of the main changes has been in the way we move goods around. Once, every factory, workshop, warehouse, mine or quarry had its own railway siding or wharf. By 1970, very few did, only those shipping large quantities of material and sited beside a railway, port or major waterway. For the rest it was the motor lorry – noisy, intrusive, polluting and wholly unsustainable

We embraced shopping, but not as we know it.

but great for those who want to see us eventually all having our own one-person businesses. (The 2000 fuel protest came as a major shock to ministers, who discovered that big companies had spent 20 years replacing their own-account lorry fleets with owner-driver vehicles. When the oil companies were told to order their drivers back to work it just produced blank looks.)

As the UK economy has become ever-more dependent on imported goods and as distribution and retailing have become ever-more pared down and just-in-time in outlook, planning for employment has increasingly become a process of finding greenfield sites near motorway interchanges for distribution depots, many of which are now vast, energy-hungry monsters cleverly disguised as huge tin sheds. Localism it is not, and nor does it provide much in the way of employment.

But it is a good way of releasing more greenfield land for development. There is a brownfield target for housing, but not for anything else. So, as the brownfield land is used up for housing, it increases the pressure to locate other activities on greenfield land.

Ebenezer and the ghost of sprawl yet to come

If the ghosts of Messrs Howard, Purdom and Osborn ever take a stroll north from Hatfield station today, they will find a landscape utterly transformed from the beautiful rural idyll Howard saw from the train in 1918. Where once they were soon out of Hatfield and on to Lord Salisbury's land, today they would find that Hatfield has grown. Their paths would be blocked by major roads, like the dual carriageway A414 across their path. To their left their companion would be the parallel A6129 and A1(M) dual carriageways, altogether providing ten lanes of incessant traffic noise to interrupt their beautiful thoughts. Instead of the broad sweep of countryside that Howard imagined could form an agricultural belt, they would find a narrow, pathetic green wedge of countryside a few hundred metres wide in the Lea valley before they reached their utopia of Welwyn Garden City, swollen hugely from the dreams of the 1920s to a goliath three miles across and mostly consisting of highway-dependent suburbia. Our walkers would find walking it difficult; with its many cul-de-sacs beloved of the garden city boys it really isn't designed for walking. They might find some remnants of the garden city design, together with post-war new town architecture and run-of-the-mill modern suburban sprawl, but it's a long way from the communitarian paradise of which Howard dreamed.

But, in one respect, Howard's plans have come to fruition – north Hertfordshire and its surroundings have become a national focus for sprawl. Stevenage is still expanding, with 3,600 sprawl homes approved in 2009 in the imaginatively named 'West of Stevenage' development, pushing sprawl beyond the A1(M) for the first time. At the same time, plans were being laid for 5,500 homes in the green belt east of Luton, or what was now poetically known as the Luton-Dunstable-Houghton Regis-Linslade conurbation (sprawl now threatening to join these once widely separated towns). The whole area lies within the London-Stansted-Cambridge-Peterborough Growth Area defined by the 2003 'sustainable communities plan' and, in case you thought that was a large enough area of England to grow in, it's adjoined by the almost-as-large Milton Keynes and South Midlands Growth Area to the west and the Thames Gateway Growth Area to the south-east. And in case people weren't sufficiently intimidated by the growth area designation, 'key growth location areas' within them were also identified, including Welwyn Garden City, St Albans, Luton, Stevenage, Hemel Hempstead and Harlow.

These towns long ago ceased to bear any relation to Howard's group of smokeless cities of around 30,000 souls. They are vast, sprawling towns largely dependent on cars, not pretty and certainly not sustainable. Hertfordshire and Bedfordshire form part of the East of England region, which during the 2000s received government instructions to accommodate more than three-quarters of a million new homes between 2009 and 2031, with vast sprawl around Cambridge, Norwich and Chelmsford, major sprawl around Ipswich, Colchester and Bury St Edmunds, significant sprawl around all the towns in the region, and six new settlements to keep garden city enthusiasts in their comfort zone.

It's difficult to imagine – and harder to care – what Ebenezer Howard's shade would make of the vast sprawl of suburbia his ideas detonated. But another side of his plan was the decay of traditional cities, and that too wrought destruction on a grand scale.

Chapter 4

The death and life of great British cities

There are whole neighbourhoods that look like bombsites. We'll be walking up a terraced street, perfectly normal. Then we turn a corner, and find ourselves in no-man's land. Nothing but mud and shattered brickwork, holes in the ground where the houses used to be.

Nik Cohn, *Yes We Have No*

Nothing but mud and shattered brickwork. *Image: Gateshead Council*

The garden cities' view of cities

Ebenezer Howard's enthusiasm for destroying our cities is quite clear from the ominously numbered Chapter 13 in *Garden Cities of Tomorrow*, where he sets out to trace the fate of London once garden cities are "springing up all over the country on sites owned by the municipalities".[1] First, he argues, land values would fall once people were "de-magnetised" and went and lived in his cocoa-glugging utopias. As the population of London fell, those remaining would have to pay higher rates to maintain services, the cost of renting a house would fall and slum property would fall to zero. The working population would move "into houses of a class quite above those which they can now afford to occupy", which Howard admitted would at least solve the housing problem temporarily. The "wretched slums" would be pulled down and their sites occupied by parks, recreation grounds and allotment gardens.

"For observe what must inevitably happen," he wrote (note that "inevitably"). "A vast field of employment being opened outside London, unless a corresponding field of employment is opened within it, London must die."

In many ways Howard was foreseeing the social cataclysm his ideas eventually wrought on many cities, as people fled to low-density suburbs from the 1920s – a process that turned into a flood in the 1980s onwards – and at the same time their industrial employment began to lie down and die. This process didn't destroy the cities altogether, of course, but the traditional bye-law home communities were deliberately wrecked in the name of 'slum clearance' while vast areas of municipal estates, often built on impeccable garden city principles and ideals, were built to replace them and then declined with the industry. Indeed, it was the lack of Howard's "vast fields of employment" that proved the problem.

But even the need to destroy towns and cities that had been healthy communities for hundreds or even thousands of years failed to shake Howard's almost narcotic rosy vision of a low-density suburban future.

"London must be transformed," he ordered. "Elsewhere the town in invading the country: here the country must invade the town." A new city would, he said, rise on the ashes of the old.

"Easy, comparatively, is it to lay out on virgin soil the plan of a magnificent city . . . Of far greater difficulty is the problem . . . of rebuilding a new city on an old site, and that site occupied by a huge population," warned Howard. If this sounds a little like Pol Pot and the Khmer Rouge, hold on to that thought. Howard may have been an impeccable supporter of human rights, but this is genuinely dangerous stuff, and strands can still be found in the DNA of some influential people in the planning profession.

Howard noted that comprehensive plans for transforming Paris had been developed since 1848, slums had disappeared in Berlin since 1870, 88 acres of Glasgow had been remodelled, 93 acres of squalid slums in Birmingham had become magnificent streets flanked by architectural buildings, and Vienna had completed a stately outer ring and was remodelling her inner city. He neglected to note that none of these was being rebuilt as low-density sprawl, but warned that London would have to be reconstructed on a far more comprehensive scale. Once a group of garden cities was built, "the reconstruction of London must inevitably follow".

Mercifully, as usual, 'the Garden City Geyser' was wrong.

Slum clearance

Building garden cities was, of course, only one leg of Ebenezer Howard's master plan. The other – destruction of our traditional towns and cities as people turned into model citizens and moved to his new settlements – got under way at a serious level with 'slum clearance'. Early in the twentieth century there were, of course, vast areas of slums that needed clearing – basically the cheap and nasty homes thrown up for industrial workers in the first two-thirds of the nineteenth century before the reformers secured decent building standards. But it was all too easy to go from knocking down real slums to knocking down anything that was built before 1914 and had fallen on hard times.

For that was what so many 'slums' actually were – reasonable homes that were economically deprived and overcrowded. From there it was an equally short leap to knocking down bye-law homes, because they weren't part of the garden city vision.

George Orwell saw one in *The Road to Wigan Pier*, which opens with the author sharing a room with three others in Mr & Mrs Brooker's decrepit doss house. "Years earlier the house had been an ordinary dwelling-house, and when the Brookers had taken it and fitted it out as tripe-shop and lodging-house, they had inherited some of the more useless pieces of furniture and had never had the energy to remove them," he noted. "We were therefore sleeping in what was still recognisably a drawing room. Hanging from the ceiling there was a heavy glass chandelier on which the dust was so thick that it was like fur . . ."

The 'slums' they cleared weren't always slums. *Image: Gateshead Council*

In the last quarter of the twentieth century thousands of such houses were 'gentrified' and became useful homes again; in the more expensive areas they can now fetch seven-figure sums. But the urge to destroy the good as well as the bad, because it did not fit the vision, was upon the garden sprawl movement. Poverty, disrepair and overcrowding were always blamed on the housing by those who wanted to destroy it, and pretty soon that became an almost universal view.

The Road to Wigan Pier is a magnificent howl of rage against the squalor, poverty and misery of industrial Britain in the 1930s. Much of it is spent describing the horror of the slums and the need to tackle them. But few readers seem to have noticed that Orwell was almost as critical of the low-density sprawl with which the local authorities were trying to replace these buildings.

> Bishops, politicians, philanthropists and whatnot enjoy talking piously about 'slum clearance', because they can thus divert attention from more serious evils and pretend that if you abolish the slums you abolish poverty. But all this talk has led to surprisingly small results.

Orwell noted that some towns had proceeded with a degree of vigour, some had lagged and Barnsley had spent the money on a new town hall. But where council houses had been built, he was less than impressed with "the row upon row of little red houses, all much liker than two peas". Nevertheless, the intrepid hack journalist in him went to visit a couple of Wigan's new homes, just as he had visited many slum dwellings. While he judged them obviously better than the run-down, overcrowded, verminous slums, he noted that one of the new houses was ill-laid out, draughty, cold, damp and more than a mile to the town, with no bus service.

That could pretty well stand as an obituary for 1930s housing in general. Orwell observed that they were also much more expensive than slum dwellings, much colder and more expensive to heat, and involved costly bus journeys to work and to shop.

> When you rebuild on a large scale, what you do in effect is to scoop out the centre of the town and redistribute it on the outskirts. This is all very well in a way; you have got the people out of fetid alleys into places where they have room to breathe; but from the point of view of the people themselves, what you have done is to pick them up and dump them down five miles from their work.

He noted too that some relocated people missed the "frowzy warmth" of the slum and complained they were freezing on the outer estates. The estates lacked shops and they lacked pubs.

"Certainly most corporation estates are pretty bleak in winter. Some I have been through, perched on treeless, clayey hillsides and swept by icy winds, would be horrible places to live in."

He accepted that the new flats were also unpopular but noted that destroying slums destroys other things as well, and remarked that most rehousing was being done in a pretty inhuman manner. "On balance," he concluded, "the corporation estates are better than the slums, but only by a small margin."

From someone who had seen the full horror of slums, this is quite an indictment. What no one seems to have even been thinking at the time, and Orwell never mentions, is why those slums that needed pulling down weren't replaced with something functional, compact and community-friendly like the bye-law homes of the late-Victorian and Edwardian period. Of course many of these had, by the 1930s, become slums, but like many of the older Victorian and Georgian houses of better quality, they were slums because of disrepair, overcrowding, poverty and lack of modern facilities. A fraction of the cost of acquiring land for outer estates and building semis on them would have seen huge numbers of 'slums' turned into decent, functional, well-equipped and warm homes.

By 1937 almost no one had that vision. If it was built before 1914 and in disrepair, it had to come down. And it didn't even need to be in disrepair, so the good came down with the bad; the pictures Victor Gollancz used to illustrate the first edition of *The Road to Wigan Pier* were a mixture of the real hovels, large Georgian terraces and bye-law homes. The real hovels had gone by the end of the 1950s but slum clearance continues to this day.

Even our travel writers have noticed that 'slum clearance' has been, at best, a mixed blessing. Recounting his voyage by punt down the Trent through Nottingham in *Downstream* (2008),[2] Tom Fort passed The Meadows district of Nottingham, which he noted had become, in the nineteenth century, an area "synonymous with disease, squalor, crime and misery: the worst of slums". Being beside the Trent it was also vulnerable to flooding, and in the great flood of March 1947 five thousand of its buildings were flooded. This gave the council the pretext to sweep it all away and replace it with something it judged better. But sweeping away old buildings is no panacea; as Fort noted, The Meadows had now become "a byword for gangs and guns and drugs rather than crocuses".

And even though everyone agreed there was an acute housing shortage in post-war Britain, it didn't stop the destruction of thousands of perfectly sound homes. 'Slum clearance' had become an obsession between the wars, and there was to be no let-up afterwards – even though the number of homes that could genuinely be called 'slums', i.e. their construction was so inadequate they could never be brought up to acceptable standards, was diminishing fast. But 'slums' could be used to cover anything that wasn't new, that was overcrowded and that required improvement or even maintenance. Once again, overcrowding and decay was blamed on the design of the houses, rather than on the poverty that bred these problems, and the garden sprawl obsession meant few in the 1950s were prepared to stand up to the slum clearers.

From the middle of that decade slum clearance began to push ahead again. In 1954 the standard of fitness for homes was revised and laws relating to clearance orders and compulsory purchase of unfit houses was streamlined. New subsidies were introduced for replacing homes and these came to encourage low-density but high-rise housing in the cities (just what another sinister force threatening our cities – the Modern movement – wanted). Vast areas of traditional townscape were torn down, often against the wishes of their inhabitants, and replaced with junk buildings. Bizarrely, the only thing they left was the street corner pubs.

Comprehensive redevelopment went out of fashion in the 1970s, when people found that traditional, pre-1914 houses, even the little ones, were generally much nicer places to live than much of the tat built since then. But, strangely, as we shall see in Chapter 6, it was to enjoy a revival in the 2000s on the back of Gordon Brown's 'Sustainable Communities Plan', this time called 'housing market renewal'.

Perched on treeless and clayey hillsides.

The Modern movement

We've already seen that few dared question the sprawl lobby's vision of planning during the first half of the twentieth century and beyond. Yet from the 1930s there was a movement that did challenge it, and most effectively, and I'm not talking about those who sought to protect the countryside.

Few in 1942 would have dared come out with statements in a new book like "the crimes of our own century, the mock-Tudor suburbs, the ribbon-development and the imitation classic" or to complain that "around the town spreads unending suburbia, the result of everyone trying to escape the unpleasantness of the modern town, and defeating their purpose by themselves destroying more and more country."

But this wasn't some early Smart Growth pioneer, daring to stand out from the crowd by questioning the low-density dispersal ethos of the sprawl lobby and trying to protect our towns. It was in fact the modernist architect Ralph Tubbs in his book *Living in Cities*,[3] a wartime tract which managed to see the Luftwaffe's onslaught on our cities as an opportunity to knock most of the rest of them down and rebuild according to a vision as destructive as the garden sprawl enthusiasts' own ruinous plans.

They knocked down the houses but left the pubs.

Some day perhaps we will have a truth-and-reconciliation process for architecture's 'Modern movement' to try to heal at least the emotional scars of the
damage it wreaked (possibly far more effectively than the Luftwaffe), of the
lives it blighted and still blights to this day, and of the towns and cities it so
comprehensively wrecked. Remarkably, it still has its admirers.

There's an international DoCoMoMo (DOcumentation and COnservation
of buildings, sites and neighbourhoods of the MOdern MOvement) body,
which, instead of trying to undo the damage the movement did, seeks to preserve
and celebrate it. There are moves afoot to list more of the very worst buildings
created during the movement's high point from the 1950s to the 1970s, even
those created by the 'brutalists' who designed architecture for brutes. It's no
accident that Hitler, Stalin and Mussolini were early admirers; modernism has
always managed to combine the megalomaniac with the banal, creating buildings and structures at once huge and dominating, and cheaply and nastily built.
Clients both private and public could satisfy their desire for ostentation and
effect while paying as little as possible for it – and it's still the same today.

The Second World War and its aftermath marked a struggle for the soul of
the planning movement between the garden city enthusiasts and modernist
architects, many of whom saw themselves as planners too. Ralph Tubbs's most
visible legacy is his hideous buildings such as Hammersmith's Charing Cross
Hospital or Kensington's Baden-Powell House, but while others were busy
fighting the enemies trying to flatten our cities, he and others were hard at
work laying plans – to flatten our cities.

Even in a spirit of reconciliation, I can't bring myself to recount the history
of the Modern movement – if you're at all interested there are thousands of
tomes of hagiography about the likes of Le Corbusier, Ernö Goldfinger, James
Stirling, etc., etc. ad nauseam. But while both garden sprawler and modernist
alike wanted to destroy the towns and cities we had spent 2,000 years or so
shaping to our needs and wants, their plans for the alternative were wholly at
odds, although Patrick Abercrombie at least was prepared to ride both horses.

"Under what flag is this plan to sail?" he wondered in 1945. "For it must
be remembered that two solutions (or many more) might be propounded to
fulfil these external and internal requirements which would be fundamentally
different. Plans prepared by the late Ebenezer Howard and by M. Corbusier
for the same place would be based upon different fundamental conceptions,
though there might be some unity in what they condemn. We are at present in
a highly experimental and undecided stage."[4]

The decades that followed the Second World War saw both the garden
cities movement and the Modern movement pursuing their ends with equal
support from those in power. The result was ruined towns and ruined countryside and a pretty dysfunctional mess.

The two movements were never going to agree. As early as 1951, Ebenezer Howard's disciple and the Town & Country Planning Association (TCPA) luminary F. J. Osborn attacked Le Corbusier's deranged *Unité d'Habitation* in Marseilles (one of the Modern movement's most sacred sites) as a "mad 14-storey glass-house" and complained that UK architects had now invented the "maisonette block, in which two-storey houses are built on top of each other up to eight storeys . . . combining the disadvantages of flats and houses".[5] The following year he visited Marseilles and boasted (to his own less-than-modest satisfaction) that he had "collected all the data necessary to show its [Unité d'Habitation's] economic and social absurdity".

One can only agree with Osborn on this (a rare admission in this book), but things were to get much worse. He noted (as early as 1952) a radio lecture by the head of an English school of architecture praising Le Corbusier, and complained that even architects in the TCPA's students group were as herd-minded as lemmings on modernism. "Now that academic authority is passing into the hands of the Corbusierites, apparent support is given to the opportunist leanings of the LCC [London County Council] and other housing authorities, and the Ministry, and more and more block flats are being built, and density is gradually being increased in normal housing estates and in the new towns."[6] Curiously, Osborn saw this as a conspiracy between "countryside preservationists, the city authorities and the architects", but, while a conspiracy between the latter two was certainly under way, no one in 1952 was paying much heed to those hardy souls trying to protect the countryside from Osborn and his cronies or anyone else, although those who wanted to rip the towns down in the name of modernism certainly pretended their plans would allow containment of cities. As even the tower blocks offered no higher density than the terraces they were demolishing, this argument was unsustainable, but it was enough to convince the likes of Osborn. And, in any case, the garden cities movement had set out with the explicit intention of destroying our traditional cities themselves and replacing them elsewhere. The Modern movement's ambition also included such destruction; it just wanted to rebuild them *in situ*.

As early as 1942, Tubbs's *Living in Cities* had set this out very clearly. He too shared the mutual contempt felt by the garden city boys: "They hope to get the advantages of both town and country, but in vain. The community life of the town, the friendliness of the market and the comfort of surrounding buildings are all missing; time, money and energy are wasted in wearisome travelling; and each new suburban house pushes the country further away." This could almost be the urbanism of a later generation, but actually protecting the comfort of surrounding buildings, community life or friendly markets was not at all the plan. "We must not fail," he bleated. "Often we may have to pull down more. 'Redestruction' may have to precede reconstruction. In that day, our faith in our own civilisation will be tried." Quite.

So what would the cities of the future look like? "Intimate colonnaded shopping boulevards, tall offices admitting sun and air to every room, trees and parks, avenues, squares and terraces replace the old disorder." And where would we live? "The solution is surely terraces around open quadrangles of lawns and trees, punctuated by high blocks of flats. How pleasant to walk from one quadrangle to another, to enjoy the sense of seclusion and the peace of the inner courts, with a skyline ever changing with the silhouettes of towering flats." Oh, what a blissful vision – the inner-city tower block. "For centuries men enjoyed some of these pleasures in the medieval cloisters, in the university 'quads', and in the courts of the Temple or Lincoln's Inn in London." Whether *women* ever enjoyed these pleasures while trying to reach their flat on the eighteenth floor with a child in a buggy and the urine-soaked lift out of order, or dodging the gangs holed up in the deck-access flats across the 'quad' was not something Tubbs and his kind worried about too much as they persuaded local authorities and central government to rip cities apart.

In case anyone doubted the scale of the modernists' ambition, Tubbs included end plates in his book showing drawings of an imaginary city of "yesterday" and how it would be rebuilt as the ideal city of "tomorrow". The old city has a congested core with "no trees or open space", suburban development

The modernists talked of cities with sunlight and fresh air, but in reality they would be motor car cities.

is "neither town nor country", new factories are built on a "bye-pass", there are traffic jams and "needless smoke polluting the air". In the new Tubbsopia, however, the whole place has been completely knocked down bar the medieval cathedral and castle and a small area of high-quality squares and terraces. Nuclear-warfare-style architecture has completely destroyed the rest. The new town has "many-storied offices making possible concentration together with sunshine and fresh air", flats, terraced houses and new residential squares where "children play midst trees and grass – not in the streets", there is a park between industry and residential district with view across river to cathedral and much else beside. Everything is remote from everything else, separated by swathes of grassland and blocks of trees.

And here is perhaps the most sinister aspect of all of this. The "yesterday" city is served by a main-line railway, but there's no sign of it in the "tomorrow" version. In the far distance, well outside the town, is a "co-ordinated railway and bus station", but it looks very much like an afterthought. This was 1942: a time when the vast majority of households had never owned a car and when every last drop of petrol was being fought across the Atlantic through 'wolf packs' of U-boats, yet Tubbs' new city was to be a motor-car city. "Traffic is congested in the towns, not so much because roads are narrow as because of the frequency of crossings," he wrote. "These must be eliminated from primary roads. To achieve this, roads can no longer be entirely on the ground level."

Here we go.

"Primary roads may have to be built at high level, as railways were in the nineteenth century. When this is not possible, 'fly-over' or 'clover leaf' type crossings must ensure an uninterrupted flow of traffic." Multi-storey car parks would be needed, underground if necessary, and "every building must accommodate on its own site parking space for all vehicles visiting it."

The garden cities movement was always a bit wary of admitting its dependence on motor cars, but the modernists were all for it, right from the start. Having smashed down the cities and applied tourniquets of urban motorways, what sort of building should the unfortunate remaining inhabitants expect when the modernist bombers were through and the concrete mixers arrived? It was a misconception, wrote Tubbs, that modern architecture means flat roofs and white concrete walls, just an illusion based on early experimental types. "True modern architecture uses sympathetically all materials, whether steel, concrete, brick, stone or timber."

In fact modernist architects have always been dedicated followers of their peers' fashion. In the 1950s they felt the need to dress up their buildings with a few classical references, in the cladding at least. The 1960s, however, let concrete and glass rip, and, in the case of the brutalists, just concrete. All-over glass then made a come-back and was succeeded by mirror glass in the 1980s.

Return of the white boxes.

There was a brief fad for post-modernism as the 1980s gave way to the 1990s, with a few traditional references and a faintly refreshing ability to get away from the monolithic crassness of the modernists, but it didn't last. By the late 1990s we were back to modernist blocks with a temporary fad for wavy roof lines, before things came full circle with the dawn of the twenty-first century. The ideal building was a white concrete box with a flat roof, just what Tubbs had predicted wouldn't happen. But then he was working with his imagination, not a client on a tight budget.

Our travel writers have seen the results. Visiting Oxford, Bill Bryson wondered what sort of mad seizure was it that gripped the city's planners, architects and college authorities in the 1960s and 1970s.

"Did you know it was once seriously proposed to tear down Jericho, a district of fine artisans' homes, and to run a by-pass right across Christ Church Meadow?"[7] he noted. "These ideas weren't just misguided, they were criminally insane."

His walk around the ancient city was finally arrested by the sight of the Merton College warden's quarters, not by any means the worst building in the city. "Some architect had to design it, had to wander through a city steeped in 800 years of architectural tradition, and with great care conceive of a structure that looked like a toaster with windows. Then a committee of finely educated minds at Merton had to show the most extraordinary indifference to their responsibilities to posterity and say to themselves, 'you know we've been putting up handsome buildings since 1264; let's have an ugly one for a change'."

But all over Britain the walls of hundreds of Jerichos were tumbling down, to the sound of architects' applause. I forget who it was who called the modernists the "monkey with a cardboard box school of architecture", but it hit exactly the right note. You know, you hand the monkey a large, cardboard carton. He plays with it for a while then puts it down on the floor. At that point all the other architects start applauding it, hailing it as a bold, imaginative break from the past, a building with its own strong sense of identity, a sensitive reinterpretation of classical forms and (if this were the post-war world), a bold rejection of bourgeois values. Then the monkey gets showered with awards, gold medals, etc.

But, for a quarter of a century, these people were given free rein to wreck our towns and cities and quite a lot succumbed. Some, like Plymouth, had had their centres completely destroyed by bombing and perhaps were fortunate that they were rebuilt in the 1950s, when architects still retained some sense of form, proportion, decoration and human scale.

Joe Bennett was not impressed at all by Plymouth, however. "It could be Bucharest or Beijing," he complained. "It's the town planner's notion of civic living."[8] He complains that a windswept plaza "where mothers were meant to sit with winsome infants" has become the haunt of winos. But that is, perhaps, the fault of Britain's social and economic breakdown over the half-century after Plymouth was built. In fact its hopeful, hopeless post-Festival of Britain architecture actually does retain some sense of a traditional city centre. But things soon got much worse. By the 1960s it was all systems go to knock down the cities that survived: sometimes in a piecemeal way, juxtaposing hopelessly unsympathetic modernist buildings with traditional city centre architecture, an approach that afflicted cities such as Newcastle; and sometimes by comprehensive redevelopment, which simply carpet-bombed whole areas and replaced it with concrete junk.

And junk it was. It didn't just look like junk, it wasn't just dysfunctional, it didn't just destroy traditional metropolitan life, it didn't just destroy townsfolk's sense of community: it was jerry-built too.

In 2010 the Government's chief construction advisor, Paul Morrell, told a newspaper interviewer[9] that huge expanses of British town and city centres built in the post-war period would have to be torn down if the country were to meet its carbon emission targets. "In the sixties, everything was built cheaper, faster and nastier," he said. "If you are going to try to fix buildings, then really you won't have too many problems with anything built earlier than the fifties or after the eighties. Although you can do some things to buildings from the sixties and seventies, like replacing the roofs, there are probably some places that need to come down entirely."

That should have been obvious in 1968, when a small gas explosion in the 22-storey Ronan Point block of flats in Newham brought a whole corner of the building tumbling down. But the lesson took decades to learn.

So then, the post-war period was spent replacing functional and relatively carbon-efficient and communitarian town and city centres with something that made the people involved in the development very rich, and impoverished those who had to live in the towns permanently.

The triumph of the modernists

The destructive process just described, which should have been controlled by the new planning system after 1947, was actually facilitated by it. The new Conservative government in 1951 set about ripping out the betterment provisions of the 1947 Act, which were supposed to remove speculative profits from the rise in the value of land when planning permission was given (something Labour governments have now tried, and failed, four times to implement), and local authorities were encouraged to make deals with the private sector to redevelop their urban areas. Most of them did and this deal-making soon became a byword for corruption. One or two, such as Newcastle City Council leader T. Dan Smith and the corrupt architect John Poulson, even got caught, but most didn't.

It's difficult to grasp how much of our town and city fabric was torn apart by modernists in the 20 years between 1955 and 1975, or indeed in the decades since, for it still goes on. Certainly there were thousands of tower blocks of flats; Glasgow alone had 300. Then there was all the medium-rise rubbish, the deck-access 'streets in the sky' and all the rest of the hard- or impossible-to-let-today stuff. Office blocks scraped the sky in every city, multi-storey car parks like giant cheese graters grated the eye in every town, shopping centres that looked like ill-designed nuclear power stations replaced traditional shopping centres, high street shops and department stores. Everywhere the motor car was king – everywhere.

Travel writers, understandably, tend to avoid these smashed city centres, but as most town centres had at least a few teeth knocked out by modernists, it's hard to avoid them altogether. Bill Bryson noted he could never live in Inverness thanks to two sensationally ugly modern office buildings, which proved that two inanimate objects could ruin a whole town.[10] "Everything about them – scale, materials, design – was madly inappropriate to the surrounding scene. They weren't just ugly and large but so ill-designed that you could actually walk around them at least twice without ever finding the front entrance." A Newcastle taxi driver told Nik Cohn[11] that Newcastle had become a different city. "They tore down half the town. If I drove you through the old working areas like Byker, round where I was born, you'd hardly find a street standing. All the terraced housing, gone; the little pubs, the corner shops, the local businesses, gone as well. And the industry with them, mind." Stuart Maconie, who tries to be "no knee-jerking enemy of modernism" finds in Tunbridge Wells that "some barbarian of the 1960s dropped a pre-stressed concrete car park right in the middle of town. In my trips across middle England I was to recoil from several of these eyesores."[12]

Frankly, Stuart, you might as well become a knee-jerking enemy of modernism: it saves much pain and anguish in unsuccessful battles to convince yourself that eyesores of no merit have, well, some merit. But 999 times out of 1,000 they don't. In Slough Maconie gave up the effort in the face of the

Bath – a tale of our disorder

Decades later, it's difficult to appreciate just how destructive the post-war ambitions of the Modern movement were. But if anyone is in any doubt, let's recall that even the most historic cities were to be swept away and rebuilt with concrete and glass boxes.

Walter Wilkinson, visiting the city of Bath in 1930, noted that the handsome buildings impose the elegance of the eighteenth century on you. "One can believe in these buildings as the work of thoughtful men," he wrote. "They are charged with human character; they speak of human aspiration and exhibit the achievement of fine minds."

The Luftwaffe launched an attack on Bath in a deliberate attempt to smash an historic city, but the damage was slight compared with Britain's attempt to destroy the Georgian city of Dresden. Into the 1950s Bath was still among the two or three most complete period cities in the world. Everything, from the houses built for the very wealthy, such as the Royal Crescent and the Circus, to the fine terraces of buildings for the ordinarily wealthy and the prosperous artisans, was supported by fine smaller terraces and a sprinkling of older buildings. The city Jane Austen knew was still mostly there a century and a half later.

Even at a period when it was very difficult to get any building listed, Bath had nearly 2,000 and, had they survived, many thousands more would have been listed today. It was a gem, but some deeply stupid people were circling. One of the Modern movement's basic principles was that only the very finest historic buildings should survive. The rest had to go.

In the 15 years between 1960 and 1975, Bath's amazing legacy was attacked with extraordinary ruthlessness by the city council and developers. In 1960 the council published a revised development plan which noted it had already destroyed 480 dwellings as 'unfit' since 1951 and planned to knock down a further 1,370 in the next

Buckingham Gardens car park: "a squalid concrete patch, lowered over by monstrous tower blocks".

And it wasn't just the big cities that had the hell bombed out of them by the modernists. Towns and smaller cities suffered too. Even the historic city of Bath, one of the very finest Georgian cities in Europe and one of the few to have come through the Second World War largely unscathed, copped it big time.

While a few stood out against the destruction, many 'city fathers' adopted the modernist ideas with relish. Some, no doubt, such as T. Dan Smith, were motivated by bribery. It wasn't always money – the London County Council's last planning chairwoman Jane Phillips told me that as soon as she was appointed she was showered with offers of opera tickets, days at the races and helicopter flights around London (no doubt as a prelude to more lucrative bribes), and it took several months of refusing all of it before the developers

---

decade as unfit, plus 1,241 for road building or other development. In 1965, Colin Buchanan (see page 99) was charged with solving Bath's traffic problems; his 'solution' was to drive a new trunk-road through the city centre in a tunnel with extensive areas of demolition for slip roads at either end. The council responded with an even more destructive motorway proposal. As the 1960s unfolded, many other comprehensive development plans followed, aimed at clearing whole areas of Georgian housing. Much of this was actually carried out.

Down came many hundreds of seventeenth- and eighteenth-century buildings; down came listed buildings galore; down came whole areas of the city centre; down came the house where Henry Fielding wrote *Tom Jones*.

Never mind, the council was advised by architects of the Modern movement, including Sir Hugh Casson, a member of the Royal Fine Arts Commission (as so many of them were), at a time when "the Commission was eager to promote modern architecture in place of traditional survival".

But then, as one city planner of the time put it: "If you want Georgian houses, you need Georgian artisans." Or, to put it another way, if you want to carry out vandalism on a truly gargantuan scale, look to the Modern movement.

The destruction of historic Bath was eventually slowed as the 1970s wore on by a determined fightback by citizens. Georgian houses that had been left to decay pending demolition, even the one the fire department set alight to see how fire-resistant it was (and it proved extremely good) were eventually restored. But the city fathers (and presumably mothers) seem to have learned nothing. In 2009 the city's World Heritage Site status was put under threat by an unsympathetic high-rise development alongside the river. As I say, look to the Modern movement.

The triumph of the modernists.

got the message. That's how it was in the sixties; no doubt many municipal politicians, planners and architects succumbed to a greater or lesser extent and many of the rest were just plain mugs.

You can get some idea of the extent of the damage wreaked by looking at a book of pictures of your own town centre in the post-war period and comparing it with what survives. Despite the bomb damage and inter-war development, our Edwardian city centres were still working very well in the 1950s, and those that survive show what great places they could be today. The same could be said of the homes that were swept away and replaced by the accommodation boxes – *Unité d'Habitation* indeed.

It's still going on today, albeit at a slower rate, and we need to find a better way.

Shopping unsustainably

Supermarkets arrived in Britain in the 1950s, along with the era of mass motoring. Since then we've gradually stopped shopping several times a week and shifted to a weekly shop, although given the ever-longer drives to the supermarket, the time spent probably hasn't reduced that much. Try driving to Cribb's Causeway outside Bristol or the Metrocentre in Gateshead on a Saturday lunchtime and see what I mean.

Supermarkets were followed by out-of-town centres and, from the 1980s, patchy efforts have been made to control them. Together, large multiple food stores and out-of-town shopping have killed our town centres and the small shops they contain.

A survey published in 2010[13] found that, in the worst areas of England and Wales, 20 per cent of town-centre shops were empty. In medium-sized towns Margate was worst hit, with 27.2 per cent of its shops empty, but big centres were affected too – with Wolverhampton having 23.9 per cent empty, followed by Bradford, Middlesbrough and Sheffield. Across 700 centres in England and Wales, twice as many shops were vacant at the end of 2009 as one year earlier and, although the problems were worst in the north, the figures had risen sharply even in the south-east, where 9 per cent of shops were vacant. The multiple retailers, meanwhile, were purring and planning large numbers of new stores. Their PR people were getting ready to tell the local papers that their new store 'would create so-many-hundred jobs'. No one ever says it will destroy so-many-hundred jobs. But it will.

And while supermarkets, out-of-town centres and strip malls (think they're uniquely American? Go and look at Croydon's Valley Park, etc., etc.) sucked the vitality out of town centres, another insidious process was at work. The new economics foundation's 2002 report *Ghost Town Britain*[14] demonstrated that we are losing our high streets because they are unable to compete on a level playing field; at that time 50 specialist shops and 20 traditional non-chain pubs were closing each week, and things have since got much worse.

> In the place of real local shops has come a near-identical package of chain stores replicating on the nation's high streets. As a result, the individual character of many of our town centres is evaporating. Retail spaces once filled with independent butchers, newsagents, tobacconists, pubs, bookshops, greengrocers and family-owned general stores are becoming filled with supermarket retailers, fast-food chains and global fashion outlets. Many town centres that have undergone substantial regeneration have even lost the distinctive façades of their high streets, as local building materials have been swapped in favour of identical glass, steel and concrete storefronts that provide the ideal degree of sterility to house a string of big, clone town retailers.

The Campaign to Protect Rural England's subsequent report, *The Lie of the Land*,[15] warned that out-of-town shopping and sprawl was destroying the character of our towns. "All it takes for blandness to triumph is to let events take their course," it said.

nef's 2004 report *Clone Town Britain*[16] struck a real chord by asking why our towns and cities were turning into soulless clones of one another. A survey cited in the report found that an insipid similarity was taking over our towns, with national chains imposing sterile uniformity on both the shopping process and the physical environment.

Urban road building

While garden sprawl enthusiasts were enticing the brightest and best young adults out of our old towns, 'slum clearance' was reducing the towns to rubble and modernists were rebuilding them in totally dysfunctional ways, yet another blitz was launched on our battered towns and cities. The twentieth century became the century in thrall to Willam Morris II; the road builders were coming.

We shall look at the devastation wrought by the roads lobby over the last 100 years or so in the next chapter, but some of its very worst damage was done in the cities. The thought of moving every last single commuter into a big city like London by road should have made even the most obtuse road lobbyist blanch, but it didn't. For the most obtuse there was the example of the United States, where many cities destroyed their centres in an effort to do that. Within 15 years of the end of the Second World War, trams had been eliminated from British cities and the roads lobby was beginning to dream of a world where the car was king and trains had also been eradicated completely.

"Mention of American motorways . . . invites the criticism that 'downtown' congestion has invariably been worsened by motorways in American cities," noted one Brigadier T. I. Lloyd in a 1957 tome *Twilight of the Railways*,[17] which proposed the insane idea of converting all Britain's railways to main roads. Insane it may have been, but the idea was actually pursued for some decades.

Lloyd paused to sneer at the vice-president of the American Transit Association, who pointed out the obvious (at least if you weren't in government or making a mint out of road transport in Britain or America) that "motorways generate extra traffic, requiring yet more motorways, and so on ad infinitum; no city has found a solution 'regardless of how much it has poured into providing conveniences for its motorist'." Brigadier Petrolhead had just, on page 59 of his book, blown the rest of his thesis apart, but he didn't seem to notice and instead drew a lesson from Fort Worth's city architect, Victor Gruen, who was, apparently, "confident of producing the solution with his plan for the central section of Fort Worth, Texas, a city of about 500,000. He proposes motorways leading right into the city but not giving vehicle access (for the automobile commuter) to the downtown streets. The motorways will terminate in car parks or garages."

Instead of foreseeing the inner city destroyed to make way for motorway interchanges and ring roads, as so many were in the 1960s and 1970s, with roads surrounding an inner city rebuilt with tower blocks around a few pedestrian streets that emptied at night, Lloyd was busy plotting a "Fort Worth plan for London". And it so nearly came to pass.

Once petrol rationing ended in the early 1950s, traffic grew rapidly and began to choke our towns. By 1955 we had 3.5 million cars; by 1960 it was 5.5 million and there were forecasts (which proved accurate) of massive future increases.

By 1960 the UK was already building major trunk-roads and motorways between towns to ensure we had a transport system totally unfit for the twenty-first century. But towns remained a massive obstacle to the roads lobby's dreams. Roads Lobby Central, cunningly disguised under the name 'Ministry of Transport', favoured massive urban motorways and in 1961 appointed a study group led by Colin Buchanan, a transport planner who had gained a degree of general acceptability through his scepticism for out-and-out road building. Among the worthies on his group was T. Dan Smith.

The group's report *Traffic in Towns*[18] was published in 1963 and took as its basis that the number of cars on Britain's roads in 2010 would be four times what it was in 1962 (in fact it was five times). The report predicted a number of consequences of this, including a huge expansion of the British motor industry and a huge hit on our balance of payments to pay for fuel; in the event neither of these was very accurate. But the biggest consequence, it said, would be seen in the streets of our cities.

Half a century later, it's difficult to believe that those entrusted with the care of our cities were planning to pull most of them down and replace them with concrete boxes and deck-access buildings surrounded by urban motorways. Patrick Abercrombie began the process in the Second World War with the *County of London Plan*, which proposed creating a series of three ring roads around London. These, it said, "would draw off traffic by the simple and direct expedient of giving it better conditions for its operation". Perhaps, in 1944, it might have been possible not to realise that building roads simply unlocks traffic demand and that the roads 'relieved' by bypasses, ring roads, etc. would soon simply fill up with new traffic unless you physically restrict it. This was not even accepted by central government until the late 1990s, and then simply ignored as the roads lobby regained ascendancy over government policy in the 2000s.

That reality should, however, have been pretty obvious by the 1960s, when planning for London's ring roads and urban motorways in other cities was in full swing, but, of course, Buchanan noted that car owners would soon be a majority in the country, and one that future governments couldn't ignore. They haven't.

Today, *Traffic in Towns* is usually seen as the moment it was realised that unrestricted urban road building would not be possible. It pointed out that British cities lack the room that American cities had for building roads, they are packed with buildings and with history and that (this was 1963) even Americans were beginning to question the desirability of this level of destruction. Despite this, Buchanan reached a strange and curiously equivocal conclusion.

> We believe there is a need in this country for a vigorous programme of urban road building – not rushed into haphazardly, but as the result of careful analysis of probable traffic flows and needs. But we cannot hold out any hope that this by itself will go very far towards solving the problem.

Who was it said that those whom the gods wish to destroy, they first make mad? This was supposed to be, by 1960s standards, a roads sceptic, but he still advocated billions be spent destroying our cities without doing much to solve the problem.

Armed with this philosophy, the Buchanan team looked at various levels of destruction in cities of various sizes. In London they considered four options for a huge chunk of the West End, stretching north roughly from Oxford Street to Euston Road and bounded by Tottenham Court Road and Great Portland Street. The least damaging option would have been piecemeal redevelopment, as was already occurring, and the road system was seen as incapable of coping with the level of traffic generated by a gradual increase in parking spaces. A "minimum redevelopment" option assumed that six-lane freeways had been built around the edges of the area and that pedestrians and shop fronts in Oxford Street had been raised to first-floor level above a widened road (that was 1963's idea of 'minimum redevelopment') but, in the case of Regent Street, its architectural character meant a structure erected along its centre "would require the most careful consideration". For the rest, on-street parking would be banned and there would still need to be comprehensive redevelopment alongside the primary distributor roads.

A "partial redevelopment" scenario would have preserved buildings of historical or architectural interest although the area would have been sur-

Even town centres were sacrificed to the needs of the car.

rounded by a network grid. Howland Street and New Cavendish Street would have become a new dual carriageway (a few yards from Middlesex Hospital) and the area would have been criss-crossed with a new network of internal distributor roads. 'Partial' the redevelopment might have been, but it would have involved knocking down about three-quarters of the area and rebuilding it on a raised deck (I'm not making this up).

Finally there was a "complete redevelopment" option, which meant what it said. The existing road system would be replaced by a system of distributors in hexagonal cells, much of it dual-carriageway and in open cuttings. The team agonised over whether to put pedestrians on the ground and the roads at first floor level ("wonderful urban views can be obtained from high level access roads") or vice versa, and it concluded that traffic was best left at or below ground level and the "pedestrian environment" above to obtain "greater flexibility in the design of buildings". Various futuristic designs were included to show what the brave new world would look like; they look pretty much like the worst 1960s housing estates that have since been pulled down with a massive sigh of relief. The team also produced similarly destructive plans for Newbury, Leeds and Norwich.

Thus heartened by a 'sceptic', the rest of the sixties was spent in an orgy of planning for urban motorways, and some of the plans were implemented. Leeds promoted itself as 'the Motorway City' and huge roads were smashed through Birmingham, Newcastle, Sheffield, Gateshead and many other towns. London was to have a system of ringways, which eventually spawned the Westway elevated motorway and other bits and pieces in inner and outer London, the upgrade of the North Circular and the M25. All this, of course, was supposed to reduce traffic on the rest of the network. Worked well, didn't it?

Eventually, of course, knocking down much of London (and all our other cities) for urban motorways proved politically impossible, but not before huge damage was done. The pace of urban road building slowed after the 1960s but has never ceased. The extension of the M74 into south Glasgow was pursued for decades, and work began building the 8km urban motorway as recently as 2008. Here be dinosaurs.

The inner-city problem

If you attack a city by taking many of its brightest and best young people away to distant suburbs in the country, if you knock much of it down and replace it with dysfunctional grey concrete boxes on dysfunctional grey estates, if you blight much of what's left or destroy it for road schemes and if your mortgage lenders refuse to lend money on properties built before 1914 on the grounds they're probably going to be knocked down for slum clearance or road building shortly, it might occur to someone in authority that you might end up with a bit of a problem. But, for the most part, the problem eluded those who ran the country in the 1960s.

The penny dropped in the 1970s when we were faced with other diverting problems like the 'Barber boom', 'stagflation', the oil crisis, a couple of miners' strikes, the three-day week, a full-blown economic crisis requiring a loan from the IMF, a 'social contract' between trade unions and government that saw several 'winters of discontent' plus several springs, summers and autumns of discontent, etc. All that, flared trousers, the Bay City Rollers and the Austin Allegro.

The new left-wing Labour government of the mid-1970s returned to one of its recurring themes – how to tax the rise in value of land when planning permission was given for its improvement. Two bits of legislation in 1975 and 1976 gave local authorities power to buy land at existing values and the government power to tax land value increases. Both were well intentioned, but at a time of economic crisis they simply added further constraints to city economies, and vacant sites began to appear.

But things began to turn around in 1977 on the back of a White Paper, the decision by building societies to stop 'red lining' (refusing mortgages) in pre-1914 areas and with the Inner Urban Areas Act of 1978. The mortgage lenders' decision brought wealthier people flocking to buy Victorian houses in many (though not all) inner-city suburbs, a process known as 'gentrification', and the Act gave powers for economic assistance in inner areas. For it had been finally accepted that we had an inner-city problem, but the funds to solve it were lacking and it was too little, too late. Even though the Thatcher government kept what funding there was for inner cities going, too many had become ghettoes for the poor and, for a whole host of reasons, people from many ethnic minorities were more or less obliged to live in them, stoking resentment that exploded in riots in the summer of 1981.

Governments of both political stripes have tinkered with the problem in the decades since. Some inner-city areas have become pleasant and prosperous as a result of gentrification or even, sometimes, regeneration. Others remain mired in poverty and neglect. They have been joined by quite a few outer estates – the massive council estates built on the edge of towns and cities before or after the war in pursuit of garden sprawl ideals. With the industrial economy that paid for them shattered and their social fabric torn apart as a result, some towns have become bywords for crime and social breakdown, despite heroic efforts by local authorities at regeneration. These estates were, of course, built on the very best garden sprawl principles. I wonder what their pioneers would make of them.

Chapter 5

Travelling hopelessly – a century of unsustainable transport

All power corrupts and horse power corrupts absolutely.
John Hillaby, *Journey Home*

Hopeless travellers all

Our destructive addiction to road transport has been a long one. The German pastor Karl Moritz decided to walk part of his journey from Richmond to Windsor in 1782 and soon discovered that "A traveller on foot in this country seems to be considered as a sort of wild man or out-of-the way being, who is stared at, pitied, suspected, and shunned by everybody that meets him."[1]

Arriving hot and dusty at an Eton inn, he asked for a room and found himself being looked at as a beggar. Eventually he was shown a room that looked like a prison cell and when he asked for something better, they suggested he try Slough. Poor Slough, ever the butt of everyone's contempt.

Continuing his walk to Oxford, Moritz admitted to a man he intended to walk there, prompting the man to shake his head and hurry indoors. Sitting by the road reading Milton, this gentle scholar found passing coach passengers tapping their heads at him to indicate he was mad.

"When I passed through a village, every old woman testified her pity by an exclamation of 'Good God!'" he recalled.

A mere 224 years later, the writer Joe Bennett also set out westwards from London on foot.[2] He spent an hour trying to hitch-hike near the M25, totally ignored by all the drivers until eventually two shaven-headed men in a van drove past grinning and throwing V-signs at him "with a thrusting, almost sexual, vigour" and one even leaned out of the window to shout something "of an unsupportive nature". In the end he gave up hitching – a sad contrast to 40 years ago when you could hitch anywhere given time; a symptom of our decline from citizens to consumers, I suppose.

Alive and motoring

Alistair Darling's 2008 pre-budget report attracted more interest than usual, for the nation's economy was crumbling before its eyes. The popular press was looking for someone to blame for putting all the nation's economic eggs in the broken basket marked 'financial services', something they had been urging for 30 years. Darling appeased their appetite for tax reduction with a cut in VAT and also announced plans to sort out the mess that would be caused by raising it again later.

Few observers got beyond this issue, but the report's small print assured us that the Climate Change Bill and five-year budgets would make us world leaders in greenhouse-gas emission cuts, although the prospects were actually much worse than this. In the same statement the former transport secretary scrapped an all-party agreement to reform air passenger duty because it would have hurt aviation at a time of economic stress (despite the need to hurt it on grounds of environmental stress). And, while he admitted road transport accounts for around 19 per cent of our emissions (actually it's far more than that), he also announced plans to spend £700 million on increased motorway capacity and up to 200 new carriages on the rail network (a fraction of the number needed and only half of them were delivered before the plan was shelved to save money). In fact, of course, the £700 million was simply an acceleration of part of the Department's overall roads programme, worth around £10 billion at that time.

The Conservatives said the pre-budget report marked the end of New Labour, but one of that movement's architects, Lord Mandelson, was quick to snap back: "New Labour is alive and motoring." But that, of course, was just the problem. As it had been for decades, transport policy was still seen as improving the road and air networks and giving anything that runs on rails life support at best – and closure at worst.

Wheels within wheels

At the centre of our roads addiction has been the transport ministry, ever since its creation in 1919, wherein a web of intrigue at the highest level has relentlessly dedicated itself to destroying transport that moves by rail and expanding transport that moves on roads or runways. 'Poop-poop' should have been the ministry's unofficial motto.

Our transport ministers have mostly been fully signed-up petrolheads or hopeless saps selected for their lack of transport knowledge. Alistair Darling was once described as the worst transport secretary since Nicholas Ridley, although that was going some given that 'Old Nick' held the job at the high point of Margaret Thatcher's quest for 'the great car economy'. Manipulated shamelessly by civil servants who actively support what has been candidly described as 'the roads lobby', one or two ministers have actually surprised everybody by eventually twigging they'd been sold a pup. Their fate has usually been swift and unpleasant.

But had the Edwardian age possessed a non-fossil source of transport fuel, its transportation system would have been quite remarkably sustainable. If people or goods needed to move any distance inland, they used a 20,000-mile road network. A great deal of freight travelled in coastal vessels and a small amount on inland waterways. Within towns, deliveries were taken from railway goods yard to your door in horse-drawn wagons, and most industrial premises had their own siding or wharf. Within towns people moved by suburban railways (already starting to be electrified), by electric trams, horse buses, bicycles or on foot, while London and Glasgow had their first underground railways. Cars were in their infancy; lorries and aircraft were unknown.

But the aftermath of the First World War saw car and lorry manufacturers turn their wartime expansion to peacetime production, and a flood of war-surplus lorries allowed the first haulage companies to form. Prime minister Lloyd George tried to nationalise the railways and put both roads and railways under ministry control, but the roads lobby that had continued growing since its Edwardian childhood successfully fought for control of the roads and left the railways to cope with a botched merger process which eliminated inter-company competition but left the big constraints on rail business untouched.

No sooner was the ministry created than its director general of roads became its highest-paid official, and its main objectives were plainly promotion of road transport and erosion of rail. As early as 1919 the director general was laying plans for 5,000 miles of 'superclass roads', and the first dual carriageway, London's Great West Road, opened in 1925. This was soon being touted as the ideal location for industry – a pattern of road-based employment sprawl that has continued uninterrupted for more than 80 years. By 1929 the ministry was paying local authorities 75 per cent of the cost of building main roads and 60 per cent of the cost of minor ones, while the railways were allowed to soldier on through the 1920s collapse in coal traffic and the 1930s economic depression with obsolete equipment and restrictive Victorian legislation.

Meanwhile the roads lobby was going from strength to strength, with the British Road Federation (BRF) set up in 1932 to represent motoring organisations, oil companies, motor manufacturers, the aggregates and concrete industries and hauliers.

Mr Toad meets Dr Todt

Around the time J. B. Priestley was being driven on his *English Journey*, events in Europe were moving in ways that brought the roads lobby satisfaction. An angry man with a small moustache and big ambitions was building a system of autobahns, ostensibly so that Aryan families could drive their new Volkswagens around, but actually so their sons could drive tanks into neighbouring countries more easily.

The British roads lobby sensed a kindred spirit.[3] An international roads congress in Munich in 1934 helped persuade the British government to pledge £100 million for road building and to take major roads under government control, creating the massive and ever-growing trunk-road network. In 1937 the BRF took a delegation of MPs, councillors, county surveyors and other engineers to Germany to see 'Adolf Hitler's roads'; the ministry declined to attend and the BRF replied it would be sorry the party would not include its 'good friends' at the ministry. Germany's works minister, Dr Fritz Todt, entertained the party royally with a wonderful tour that even included attendance at the meeting of Hitler and Mussolini in Berlin. Back home the delegation came, to recommend Britain adopt the motorway system; Todt later visited London and a German delegation met the transport minister. The following year, the Institution of Highway Engineers recommended that the government build 3,000 miles of motorways, but fortunately the BRF's call to switch money from the defence fund into road building went unheeded, to Dr Todt's disappointment no doubt.

And still it went on, even after the Nazi tanks rolled. In 1943, while Organisation Todt's slave labourers were making munitions to fire at Britain's armed forces, the BRF adopted the County Surveyors Society plan for 1,000 miles of motorway. No sooner had the guns fallen silent than the Society of Motor Manufacturers and Traders sent a delegation to Germany to investigate the autobahns, and was soon urging the ministry to build motorways. The government responded with plans for an 800-mile, ten-year road construction programme, which foundered as it ignored the trivial point that no money was available to build it.

A thousand miles of motorways

The post-war decade of austerity and petrol shortages did nothing to dampen the roads lobby's enthusiasm, and its government was soon committed to 1,000 miles of motorways, with the Preston Bypass opening the programme in 1958.

For 50 years after the Second World War, governments of both political colours remained doggedly faithful to road building, and in 1959 a road builder, Ernest Marples, actually became transport minister – a conflict of interest he managed to circumvent by transferring his Marples Ridgeway shares to his wife. He pursued the relentless programme of road building and rail closures throughout the early 1960s and was later elevated to the House of Lords, accused of tax evasion and died in Monaco where he had fled to evade justice.

The Wilson government promised to change things but didn't, and its best-

A thousand miles of motorways and mess.
Image: Leeds Library and Information Service, from the David Atkinson archive

known transport minister Barbara Castle pursued the Beeching Plan and set up regional construction units to speed up road building. They were most successful – the first 500 miles of motorway took nine years to build; the next 500 just four. Flushed with success, the government immediately proposed another 1,000 miles.

The 1970s saw economic upheaval and the first stirrings of the environmental movement, and the roads programme slowed a little, but 1979 brought a prime minister who supported 'the great car economy' and things were soon running again. Even though the 1980s heralded a severe economic slump and huge reductions in government spending, the appointment of Nicholas Ridley as transport secretary soon had another 51 schemes worth £300 million added to the trunk-roads programme, and things just accelerated through the 1980s and 1990s.

A new deal for transport

A temporary chill hit the roads lobby with New Labour's election in 1997. Before the election the party had noted[4] that the government was spending £3 billion annually on roads, three times what it spent on railways, and that the road network had already grown by 64,000km since the Second World War.

"It is now accepted by almost everyone apart from the DoT that new roads

The more they built, the more we drove.

generate new traffic," it said. "They attract large retail outlets and other services, accessible only by road, and encourage patterns of work travel and commuting which involve long drives. Widening existing roads will have much the
same effect. Labour will scrap plans to widen the M25."[5]

And for a while it looked as if things would change. A 1998 White Paper,
A New Deal for Transport, proposed reducing the need for travel, a new integrated transport commission and more environmental protection. Land use
and transport policy would be integrated and there would be more alternatives
to cars and lorries. A greater proportion of the roads budget would be devoted
to long-neglected maintenance, but the White Paper promised to "promote
carefully targeted capacity improvements to address existing congestion on the
network, where they support our integrated transport policy". Ironically, it
went on to note that "since new roads can lead to more traffic, adding to the
problem not reducing it, all plausible options need to be considered before a
new road is built".

So by 1998 the realisation that road building simply stimulates more traffic
was spreading beyond the environmental movement, and even the previous
Conservative government had set up a Standing Advisory Committee on Trunk
Road Assessment (SACTRA) in 1996 to examine the relationship between
road building and economic growth, the economy's need for transport and the
assessment criteria for trunk-road building. SACTRA pondered these issues for
three years and concluded that transport investment brings little benefit to a

country with a well-developed transport infrastructure. The roads programme slowed, temporarily, but eventually the need to reassure the roads lobby reasserted itself.

As early as 1999, when Chris Mullin became a junior environment and transport minister, the pendulum was swinging back. A conversation with transport minister Gus Macdonald proved revealing.

"'We must avoid being seen as anti-car,' said Gus," wrote Mullin.[6] "Why shouldn't poor people enjoy the same advantages as the car had brought to the middle classes? There was no inconsistency about favouring wider car ownership but less use." Apart from its utter impracticality of course.

"It's becoming clear that we are – rightly – terrified of taking on the car because we fear that, as with taxation, in the privacy of the ballot box the Great British Public will exact revenge on any party that tries to separate them from their beloved vehicles," concluded Mullin.

Perhaps the terror was all too public: the following year tanker drivers blockaded refineries and intimidated the government into fuel tax concessions. For the only time in New Labour's first ten years, the Conservatives went ahead in the opinion polls. As Kipling noted, once you pay the *danegeld*, you never get rid of the Dane.

Already by 2000, the government had begun peddling the line that it wasn't anti-car, merely in favour of making more sensible use of them, and that pretty much survived until New Labour lost office. Still, Mullin concluded, this didn't matter if money continued to go into buses and light rail schemes. Five years later the government axed all light rail schemes.

Just as John Prescott's eclipse and Gordon Brown's ascendancy in the 1999-2003 period ripped the teeth out of the urban renaissance and rural protection policies, so its green transport support eroded. The period 2000-8, when economic problems intervened, saw the government approve around 200 trunk-road schemes, costing billions.

Sixty million people with thirty million cars

With all this encouragement it's not surprising we became a nation wholly dependent on our cars. In 1895 there were about two dozen motor cars on Britain's roads; by the end of the First World War there were 77,000. By 1928, after the first decade of really intensive urban sprawl, that had risen to 981,000, and the inter-war period saw the birth of the dangerous delusion that cars, like low-density suburban homes, were pillars of our individuality and self-sufficiency, rather than the signs of a society in decay.

The 1920s gave us our first motoring travel writer in H. V. Morton, who certainly started off seeing mass motoring as an expression of individuality and did much to promote it, as he believed the motor car would free the traveller from the constraints of the rail network or the limitations of cycling. It would enable fearless travellers to escape the industrial toil that actually paid for his readers to buy their *Daily Express* or *In Search of England*.

"For the first time in history these panting and efficient little machines were beginning to take individuals and families all over England, inaugurating a new age of discovery, called, in the typically deceptive English way, 'motoring'," he enthused.[7] "Probably nothing like it had occurred since the days of the medieval pilgrimage."

But as early as 1930, his contemporary Walter Wilkinson could reflect as he was assailed by motorists in a narrow lane:[8] "There piled up inside me an immense contempt for the poor silly fools who, sealed up in leather and enclosed in glass and metal cases, were rushed away by their silly engines from all that was lovely, exquisite and life-giving in the sunny day".

Morton too eventually began to realise what had been unleashed. "Inevitably the country has changed in appearance," he wrote later. "Monotonous arterial roads take the shortest way from here to there; the petrol stations which punctuate them have developed a peculiar and horrible style of architecture which might have come from some alien planet, and wherever a wide road has been made, there you will find the worst excesses of the jerry-builder and the uncontrolled architect."[9]

A few lonely voices such as Wilkinson railed against the trend, but what he found when he left some peaceful country between Burpham and Wethan and hit a "tar spreading affair" of a road betrays just how far things had already gone by 1933.

> Every thing worth living for disappeared with the first step on that tarry way. Between the car-infested square at Storrington and this main road we had walked the true England, and Sussex undefiled. We had walked with the acres of grass and flowers, with sweet odours and pleasant sounds, by comfortable looking cottages and bright gardens – sounds, scents, sights, and the whole feel of the world harmonious and delighting, and then, suddenly, we were plunged into that main road, and all the damned fuss there is to make the world ugly and uncomfortable.[10]

But even to intelligent commentators such as Morton and, indeed, Priestley, motoring seemed to offer a return to a simpler, more individual way of life than an 'industrial' transport mode such as railways. That, of course, depended on you owning a car and most people didn't in the 1930s; in fact it was the 1980s before a majority of households had access to one.

And by the 1930s the motor industry had become the barometer of the

60 million people with 30 million cars.

nation's economy it was to remain for another 60 years, as vehicle numbers went on rising. After the end of post-war petrol rationing, numbers climbed rapidly and the million vehicle point was reached in 1958. Just 12 years later that was 12 million, 25 million was passed in 1994, 30 million in 2002 and, by 2008, there were 34.2 million licensed vehicles on the UK's roads, more than half as many vehicles as there were people. It had risen by 250,000 in one year, despite the start of the recession, but the Department for Transport comforted itself with the thought that the increase was "less than half the increase seen in the previous year and the lowest year-on-year growth since 1995". Good news, Captain, the ship's only sinking half as fast as she was!

By contrast, the number of goods vehicles peaked at around 400,000 some years ago, but don't be fooled. A series of changes in the law has allowed them to become ever larger, and new road capacity and distribution depots have allowed them to travel ever-greater distances. Once again, Whitehall has been the main promoter: in 1978 the industry found its lobbying to increase the maximum weight of juggernauts from 32 to 38 tonnes was meeting substantial opposition, but a leaked memo from the ministry's freight directorate head Joe Peeler to the deputy permanent secretary welcomed plans for an inquiry into the idea as a way of "getting round political obstacles", and said the extra time and effort required for the inquiry would be a worthwhile investment.

"Recommendations would be made by impartial people of repute who have carefully weighed and sifted the evidence and have come to, one hopes, a sensible conclusion in line with the department's view," he wrote. "As a subsidiary purpose: it should provide a focus for the various road haulage interests to get together, marshal their forces, and act cohesively to produce a really good case . . . An inquiry offers a way of dealing with the political opposition to a more rational position of lorry weights."[11]

The memorandum attracted public notoriety at the time, but the hauliers got their inquiry, its report partly drafted by the ministry, and despite intense public and political opposition they got their heavier lorries too, in 1983.

It's murder on the roads

Our motor vehicles don't just destroy the environment, they destroy lives too. An unfortunate lady called Bridget Driscoll was killed by a speeding motorist near Crystal Palace in 1896 and the following year saw both the first drink-driving conviction and the first child fatality. Ever since it has been a story of slaughter and bloodshed at the level of a major war.

Around a million Britons died in the First World War and about a quarter of a million in the Second. Perhaps it's because most of us are motorists, but no one seems to have noticed that motorists have killed more than twice as many of us as did the combined armed forces of Germany, Japan and Italy in the course of the Second World War. And still it goes on.

If today is an average day, eight or nine police officers will be screwing up their courage to knock on a door to tell a family that one of their loved ones has, quite out of the blue, suffered a horrific, violent death. Some of these will be children. The same will happen tomorrow, and the next day, and the next . . .

Today, 70 adults and children will end up in hospital with serious injuries, many to suffer months of pain or disability, and some will be disabled for the rest of their lives. Today, more than 600 Britons will suffer 'minor injuries' (that means they're serious enough to require medical attention) and they'll also have had the shock and trauma of the crash. Worldwide, more than a million people will die on the roads this year. Don't pass this statistic by – that's a million people murdered by motoring.

We quite rightly remember those who gave their lives fighting to protect our freedom and those who became innocent victims of conflict, but we forget those who die from freedom's misuse. It's not a hot war or a cold war, but it certainly is a major war.

The roads lobby has always worried about road safety, but its principal concern is that public hostility might put a brake on road usage. But we should be hostile; many of us have had ancestors or relatives killed in armed conflicts, but most families have been touched by death on the roads. It's three in my family so far.

We have become an acutely risk-averse society in most human activities, bar one. Crossing the road or travelling in a motor vehicle exposes us to a level of risk we wouldn't dream of accepting in any other activity except perhaps service personnel in armed conflicts or a few very extreme sports. Yes, it is mad.

Taking the train

The new transport ministry created after the First World War had two main concerns – promoting road transport and eroding rail. The 20,000-mile rail network had already seen its uneconomic passenger services significantly pruned in the war, and an enforced merger, collapsing coal traffic and economic problems sent it into serious decline between the wars.

Few of our travel writers in that period took the train, but if they had they would have seen a system struggling with archaic standards and legislation, little investment and antique equipment. While overseas railways were modernising, little happened in the UK.

Further passenger services were axed during the depression and more still in the Second World War, a conflict that imposed vastly increased levels of freight on an already ramshackle system with little or no maintenance. It emerged on its knees and was nationalised in 1948, although road haulage eventually managed to avoid the Attlee government's plans to do the same with it.

But rail nationalisation gave the roads lobby a new opportunity for attack, as it could infiltrate the quangos set up to run the railways and persuade them to start a slow but steady programme of rail closures during the 1950s. The decade did deliver a botched and underfunded modernisation programme, but there was no money for the things that were really needed, such as main-line electrification. Those who believe rail closures began with Dr Beeching and the 1960s are wrong; most of the hopelessly uneconomic lines had already been hacked off by his time and already the roads lobby was looking forward to a time when the rail network could be finished off altogether.

In the last chapter we mentioned Brigadier Lloyd's 1957 *Twilight of the Railways*,[12] which argued that the whole railway system should be closed down and converted into roads. Brigadier Lloyd envisaged that what little public transport was still needed would be supplied by coach operators, and heavy freight such as coal would be "conveyed in purpose-designed freighters bearing little resemblance to conventional lorries". And no doubt even the timid drivers of the day needed to have no fear of such huge monsters: "It is just possible that by the time railway conversion has taken place the entire motor vehicle driving fraternity, professional and amateur, will have become so responsible, and therefore so law-abiding and considerate of one another, that the converted railway system will scarcely need organising in the accepted meaning of the word."

Or perhaps his huge freighters would have left a trail of crushed Austin Cambridges and Morris Minors. Yet this idea sparked a Railway Conversion League, which pursued it for decades.

The failure of the modernisation plan left environmentally dangerous people like transport minister Ernest Marples and British Rail chairman Richard Beeching in charge of the railways. The whole story of the Beeching reports, their plans to progressively destroy almost the entire rail network over a period of decades, the closures that did happen and the few that didn't, the attempt to cure commuter overcrowding with big fare increases, the death of most of BR's freight traffic and Labour's 1964 promise to end the closures and its subsequent enthusiasm for continuing them has been told in detail elsewhere. The programme didn't quite succeed in its entirety but it did vast damage. Today it's hard to believe that Beeching even wanted to close routes like the North London Line, today groaning under the weight of passengers, but he did. And many of the lines he did close would today be equally busy.

Although most of the lines reprieved in the 1960s were in remote rural areas protected on hardship grounds, vast areas of the country were left isolated from rail services. In the first decade of the twenty-first century Ian Marchant recently moved to Devon, and, 40 odd years after Beeching, found things had not improved.

> There was a line from Exeter that ran up to Okehampton, down through Tavistock and on to Plymouth. This was once the London and South Western's main line from Waterloo. It's closed now.[13]

And it wasn't just small and medium-sized towns such as Okehampton or Tavistock that found themselves deprived of sustainable transport; major towns were left isolated. Towns like the Mansfield/Ashfield conurbation, Newcastle-under-Lyme, Gosport, Washington, Bathgate, Hawick, Ebbw Vale and Aberdare were left to depend on bus services.

The 1974 oil crisis should have woken the country up to its fatal dependence on roads, but the railways struggled on through the 1970s and 1980s starved of investment and government support, and even though the 1980s saw renewed managerial vigour, the decade also witnessed further attacks by the ministry. Privatisation was another attempt to finish off the railways before the Channel Tunnel opened and revived rail freight, but once again the sector's vigour, its importance and the rapid growth of traffic over the last 20 years undermined their plans. So, while separating infrastructure from operations and a clumsy system of franchising should have done great harm, a vigorous management and rapidly rising demand have saved the day, so far. But there are still plainly those who would like to finish off the railways.

Taking the tram

Nowhere is this clearer than in the case of light rail. One of Edwardian towns' and cities' biggest assets was their electric tramways. The electric tram arrived in the 1890s in a world when no one possessed cars and only the very wealthy had carriages, and where public transport had hitherto meant limited-stop suburban railways or horse buses. Suddenly freedom of urban movement was achieved for a whole generation, and towns were able to grow in the compact and sustainable way described in Chapter 2.

By 1914, nearly 150 UK towns and cities had their own tramways, as did most cities around the world. Most of the rest of the world didn't stop investing in their tramways in the 1920s and many countries kept them and modernised them to this day, but between the wars, the roads lobby attacked UK tramways with enthusiasm, finishing them off one by one over a 40-year period, concluding in 1962.

The British tram was killed by obsolete and restrictive legislation and our peculiar and usually inaccurate belief that our eccentric way of doing things is better than the rest of the planet's. So by the 1930s British trams looked old-fashioned and worn out, a symbol of a Victorian past a new generation was rejecting. J. B. Priestley's reaction on a visit to Birmingham was typical;[14] he was depressed by the industrial squalor of the Black Country and took it out on the tram as "the least exhilarating mode of progress possible" – just the opposite reaction of the previous generation, which had deserted horse buses and Shanks's pony for the brightly lit trams of the Edwardian world.

"The people show a sound instinct when they desert the tramway for any other and newer kind of conveyance," he moaned. "There is something depressing about the way in which a tram lumbers and groans and grinds along, like a sick elephant."

Perhaps Priestley should have relied on the public transport of a generation or so later. By then even the trolley-buses that often replaced the trams had been replaced by a vehicle with pneumatic tyres and a diesel engine which occasionally went 'poop-poop' and appeared in suburbs and provincial towns at lengthy and irregular intervals.

Every tramway was torn up and replaced with buses.
Image: National Tramway Museum

"Oh we love you Bristol buses, in your British racing green," sang the late Adge Cutler in the 1970s. "Oh we love you Bristol buses, often heard but seldom seen." Damned right. How much of our youth is wasted waiting for buses?

By the 1980s it was pretty obvious to anyone who wasn't a transport civil servant, a roads lobbyist or someone besotted by their car (a small but informed minority, to be honest) that light rail was the big hole in UK urban transport. The lead was taken by the metropolitan passenger transport authorities left over by Margaret Thatcher's destruction of the democratic metropolitan counties, and systems were soon proposed in Greater Manchester, Sheffield and the West Midlands, followed by Croydon, Bristol and south Hampshire. The opening of the first lines in Manchester and Sheffield spurred others to follow, including Leeds, Liverpool, Nottingham, Glasgow, Newcastle-Gateshead, Edinburgh, Cardiff and Middlesbrough. Some were delayed by the 1990s recession but others kept going, and the systems in the West Midlands, Croydon and Nottingham all eventually managed to open. All had slow starts, but soon became popular and successful.

"The Super Tram is a knockout, even though it goes to the wrong place, and in the cafés they dip your bacon sandwich in cooking fat, which still leaves me open-mouthed with admiration," noted Ian Marchant in Sheffield.[15]

The new government in 1997 brought a surge of new interest, and the 1998 transport White Paper promised to start a new light rail system every year. Interest soon boomed again, with a string of extensions proposed in Greater Manchester and work beginning on Nottingham's system, and plans for Portsmouth-Fareham, Liverpool, Edinburgh and Leeds progressed with vigour. Just imagine, more than a decade later, if a new system *had* been started every year: most major conurbations would now have a system and smaller cities would be actively planning them.

But it wasn't to be; of all the retreats from the environment ordered by Gordon Brown, light rail was the most nakedly evident. His chosen weapon of mass-transit destruction was the then transport secretary Alistair Darling, who struck in 2004, telling Parliament that he was canning the Greater Manchester, Leeds and south Hampshire plans, on the bizarre grounds that their cost estimates had risen as construction approached. Every transport project in history has encountered this effect; indeed it's how road schemes have always been justified. Seduce the politicians with a stupidly low 'of-the-order-of' estimate and by the time they discover it they're stuck with it. Although a subsequent study revealed light-rail-scheme costs actually rise less than roads, there was no sign of cuts to the roads budget. But the damage was done and the one surviving scheme, in Liverpool, soon fell foul of ministry pressure and local politicians' squabbling.

There followed a political object lesson. Local politicians in Leeds, Liverpool and Hampshire grumbled and started looking at alternatives, trolleybuses or just bendy buses in Leeds; a guided busway in Hampshire. By contrast, Greater Manchester's politicians melted down with indignation against their Labour colleagues at Westminster and pointed out that tens of millions of pounds had now been wasted. In the end this paid off, and gradually their expansion schemes were reinstated.

The ministry's next wheeze for canning light rail while appearing to do something for the environment was altogether more imaginative. The Congestion Transport Innovation Fund was supposed to allow cities to have expensive projects such as light rail if they accepted congestion charging to pay for it. At first sight, it was a clever idea, but only at first sight: before cities could implement such schemes, they had to secure support in referenda on road pricing.

So, how highly would you rate the possibility of people voting to pay for something they currently enjoy for nothing? Would it be:
(a) almost impossible;
(b) impossible; or
(c) totally impossible?
Those who answered (c) can go to the top of the class.

No doubt this was entirely clear to the cynics who dreamed up the scheme from the Downing Street e-petition against road pricing in 2007, which attracted two million signatures and led to canning of national road pricing proposals. Greater Manchester was the first to ask its citizens whether congestion charging should be used to pay for extensions to Metrolink and, what a surprise, they voted four-to-one against.

London was another obvious place for light rail, given the success of Croydon Tramlink and the Docklands Light Railway (more of a metro really). Ken Livingstone mooted plans during his mayoralty for tramways in west London, from Camden through the centre to Peckham and in East London, while the Croydon system was to be extended to Crystal Palace and elsewhere. But the new mayor Boris Johnson, keen enough to appear green by wobbling around on his bike, soon had them axed.

Only the Edinburgh scheme had been outside Alistair Darling's axe range, which was perhaps just as well, as it served his constituency. Work began in 2009 despite some hysterical local opposition, and one local paper warning that construction in the city centre could threaten local people with 'carbon poisoning', obviously a significant threat for carbon-based organisms.

A handful of light rail schemes have struggled on. How they will fare in this century's economically straitened second decade remains to be seen.

A bus by any other name...

The roads lobby hates trains and it hates trams, but it's altogether more ambivalent about buses. They're road vehicles, they run on fossil fuels and,

best of all, they need road space and can be portrayed as meeting public transport needs while promoting road building. So, while they are a considerably
more fuel-efficient way of moving people than cars and they offer the only
realistic way to provide public transport in remote rural areas and within much
low-density sprawl, they are a distinctly double-edged sword when it comes to
greening our transportation system.

More recently, however, the roads lobby has used buses in a more sinister
way to undermine light rail schemes – by pretending buses can be trams.
'Guided busways' have been tried in several countries and most have rejected
them after discovering they are an expensive way of giving yourself a bus route,
but here they are being enthusiastically promoted as lower-cost alternatives to
light rail. This argument is entirely sound apart from the fact that they are
neither alternatives to light rail nor are they lower-cost.

Attempts have been made to foist guided buses on a sceptical public since
the 1980s, when the hare-brained scheme was hatched to convert the
Marylebone-Aylesbury railway, a scheme both damaging and expensive. The
beauty of rail vehicles is the very low rolling resistance of a steel wheel on a
steel rail; pneumatic-tyred vehicles, by contrast, go around consuming vast
amounts of energy by continuously compressing the air in the tyres and heating
the atmosphere around them. And while an eight-coach passenger train can
carry over a thousand passengers, even an articulated 'bendy bus' can carry
only a small fraction of that. Guided busways also require the pouring of prodigious tonnages of concrete, not because buses need guiding – bus drivers
having, over the course of more than 100 years, mastered the art of steering
– but because it's believed you can con a dumb public into believing they're
getting a high-quality, fixed-link transit system like a light rail scheme. The
public, of course, isn't so dumb.

But Petrolhead Central watched the demise of light rail schemes and pretty
soon had plans for guided buses on the Gosport-Fareham section of the abandoned south Hampshire light railway, on a disused rail alignment between
Luton and Dunstable (to put an end to plans to reopen it for light or heavy rail)
and, maddest of all, between Cambridge and St Ives, where a closed, but still
extant, railway had been the subject of schemes for a light rail system that
could then be extended to Huntingdon.

But Cambridgeshire County Council knew best. It spent two million
pounds persuading a public inquiry that converting the line to a guided busway
would be a good idea, even though buses would be guided only between the
outskirts of the two towns; elsewhere they'd be guided by their drivers working
a steering wheel, just like a real bus. Despite furious local opposition, work
began in 2007 and over 100,000 tonnes of concrete were poured on a scheme
planned to open in 2009.

A local group, the Cambridge and St Ives Railway Organisation (CASTI-RON), had promoted the light railway, which it estimated would have cost around £50 million, but it failed to impress the County Council, which estimated its own scheme would cost £54 million. Later that estimate rose – to £65 million, £78 million, £86 million, £116 million and, by the spring of 2010 with the busway still to open, £161 million (and this in a country that rejected light railways because costs rise during construction). The park-and-ride at St Ives was found to have been built on the wrong gradient, a river viaduct turned out to be less than waterproof, and drainage on a new parallel service road also intended for cyclists proved so inadequate that it resembled a canal when it rained. The rest of the world might have abandoned guided buses, but this was supposed to be the UK exemplar. And perhaps it was.

But there's an even cheaper, nastier way of trying to con the public. Bendy buses with curvy fronts can be made to look very vaguely like a tram and called 'bus rapid transit' – not rapid, not transit, but I suppose they are buses. I'm not making this up; schemes are proposed in Belfast, where light rail plans were dropped; in Bristol, to serve greenfield sprawl development at Ashton Vale; and elsewhere.

Paying a price

Schemes to reduce urban traffic by charging for road space have been discussed by transport planners since the 1980s, and many overseas cities now have such schemes. But the roads lobby has managed to get most UK schemes canned despite the rapidly advancing technology they use. Actually, charging motorists and hauliers for the road space they use rather than levying a flat fee ought to be a 'no brainer' for radical free marketeers, but doesn't seem to be the case; perhaps too many of them are passionate petrolheads.

Ken Livingstone's Central London congestion charging zone was neither particularly technically advanced nor radical in its effects, but it did mark an extraordinary first in British transport planning and succeeded in its aim of reducing congestion and pollution and getting Central London's traffic moving again. Livingstone laid plans to extend the zone to all of London, starting with a zone in north-west London. But this is Britain, and that was almost certainly a factor which cost him re-election in 2008. Boris Johnson knew who had put him in power and scrapped the extension.

Nationally we seem little nearer road-user charging, however fair and equitable it might be and how environmentally necessary, although 2010 saw an unexpected government commitment to lorry road-user charging. For the rest, the century-old pattern of urban sprawl dominated by unsustainable and obsolete road technology remains intact.

Mr Toad would be proud of us. Poop-poop!

PART II

Where we are

Chapter 6

An unsustainable communities plan

People are beginning to believe that government is a mysterious process with which they have no real concern. This is the soil in which autocracies flourish and liberty dies.

J. B. Priestley, *English Journey*

In trust for tomorrow

In 1994, a newly energised Labour Party launched "the most radical and comprehensive environmental policy document ever published by a major political party". *In Trust for Tomorrow*[1] was indeed pretty radical for 1994, and eventually the nation was persuaded to put its trust in New Labour for 13 years. Sadly, however, tomorrow never really came.

The document promised a bag of goodies including an economy transformed, a radical transport policy shifting investment from road to heavy and light rail, a 10-per-cent renewable energy target for 2010, a presumption against opencast mining, no more nuclear power and energy efficiency for all buildings. On planning, there was to be an end to "bias in favour of the developer" and an automatic right for objectors to appeal against planning consents. When New Labour achieved power it plainly wasn't going to be nearly as radical as it had pretended, but it really did start to implement reforms that included Smart Growth elements. Then most of it went in the bin.

The urban renaissance

Even though *In Trust for Tomorrow* was plainly history as soon as the 1997 election was won, some strides were made. An Urban Task Force was set up, which recommended a radical step change in the way we plan towns and cities, and the government published urban, rural and transport White Papers, which marked some of the most radical environmentally friendly policies ever embraced by a British government and challenged the fundamentals of planning and transport policy dominated by the sprawl and roads lobby for nearly a century. It introduced minimum density standards (30 homes to the hectare), 80 years after Tudor Walters laid down maxima. It accepted that building main roads simply generates more traffic. It promoted a genuine urban renaissance. It attempted to restrict destruction of countryside, of agricultural land and of biodiversity by urban development.

The figure who led these bold ambitions was the unlikely one of John Prescott, and despite his famous verbal dyslexia and undignified political exit, he does deserve one gold star in his exercise book for his attempts to bring about beneficial change.

Gordon the Big Engine

New Labour's cautious five-year retreat from urban sprawl, road building, city decay and low-density sprawl ended with a typically British conspiracy – typical because, like all the most successful conspiracies, all those involved knew exactly what they had to do without actually needing to conspire.

Many bodies, human and corporate, were involved but, inevitably, at the centre of all this was the dangerous virus at the centre of the Great Wen – HM Treasury – and the leading pantomime villain was Gordon Brown. Best remembered now for ten years pursuing the keys to Number 10 and three years demonstrating the need to be careful what you wish for, he will perhaps also be remembered for 'squeezing boom and bust out of the system' in his Treasury years before a boom bust the system and he struggled to contain the mess. But his legacy is a wider one, and it isn't one to be proud of.

When the definitive history of New Labour comes to be written, the gradual waning of John Prescott's control of domestic policy and the rapid ascendancy of Gordon Brown around the turn of the century will be seen as key. As early as 1999, Chris Mullin, then a junior environment minister, recorded in his diaries[2] a surprising conversation with permanent secretary Sir Richard Mottram about air traffic control and the Treasury, in which Mottram referred to Gordon Brown as "PM in all but name". Mullin had believed Blair was wholly in charge, but Mottram told him: "Gordon thinks his writ runs everywhere. To some extent we are protected by the deputy prime minister [Prescott], but some secretaries of state and permanent secretaries only find out about Treasury initiatives affecting their departments when they are announced."

Prescott's protection was to prove fragile, and no sooner was the 2001 election won than dismemberment of the Department of the Environment, Transport and the Regions (DETR) began. Its environmental protection functions were given to the agriculture ministry and the rump renamed Department for Transport, Local Government and the Regions. The new secretary of state Stephen Byers tried to keep Prescott's reforms alive despite the latter's waning influence, but powerful enemies were scenting blood, and they were armed with the nastier weapons of our national press.

In October 2001, Byers managed to upset both the City and the roads lobby by putting the hopeless pseudo-private mess that was Railtrack into administration and creating Network Rail under an equally bogus pretence that it was a community-sector company (anything to keep its borrowing off the Public Sector Borrowing Requirement). Anywhere else in Europe, a public company borrowing to improve vital infrastructure wouldn't appear on the PSBR anyway, but this is HM Treasuryland and investing in vital public infrastructure for good commercial reasons is rated on a par with a comet striking the Earth. This is called sound economic management.

Byers' decision not to stuff Railtrack shareholders with huge compensation sparked a vast class action and resulted in the press sinking their fangs into him. They soon found blood with publication of a memo from one of Byers' advisors suggesting it was a good day to get any issue that needed burying out, like councillors' expenses. It was sent at 2.55pm on 11 September 2001.

Spin is all very well – the idea was to make New Labour electable despite the opposition of most of the press – but, as New Labour was starting to discover, it comes back to bite you. Byers was wounded and the papers scented blood. Another leaked email suggested his head of news planned to repeat burying bad news on the day of Princess Margaret's funeral. Criticism from the transport select committee followed and further revelations about Byers' decision to allow the *Daily Express* to change hands. It was an object lesson in where political power lies in the UK; the hyenas had got their victim down and were finishing him off. He resigned in May 2002.

So, environment had been stripped out of the mega-ministry and now transport followed, back to a stand-alone Department for Transport where the roads lobby wanted it. Prescott was left with a rump department to organise local government, planning and regional quangos called the Office of the Deputy Prime Minister (ODPM). By the end of 2002, with Gordon Brown quietly pulling the strings, this whole area of domestic policy had been broken down into manageable lumps and put under the control of ministers loyal to Brown, such as transport secretary Alistair Darling and environment secretary Margaret Beckett, or those fatally wounded, like Prescott.

The 'Sustainable Communities Plan'

Voltaire once said the Holy Roman Empire "was neither holy, nor Roman, nor an empire". Much the same could be said about the Sustainable Communities Plan launched by John Prescott, still deputy prime minister, early in 2003. It wasn't about communities, marking as it did the eclipse of New Labour's genuine desire to restore communities through its urban renaissance and a return to sprawl. It wasn't really a plan, more an abandonment of planning, and it certainly wasn't sustainable, just the opposite. What it actually represented was a surrender document, the final triumph of Gordon Brown's bid to control UK domestic policy as a sort of prime-minister-in-chief and the end of John Prescott's attempts to bring a semblance of sustainability to environment and transport policy.

"We now have an opportunity to do things differently and to break from the past," noted Prescott in his introduction. He wasn't one for subtlety so presumably the irony was unintentional, but after six years in office he might have realised that 'the past' actually included changes he had helped bring about. Ominously, he went on to call for a step change in approach.

The Not-Really-a-Plan Plan[3] set out to tackle "housing supply issues in the South-East, low demand in other parts of the country and the quality of our public spaces". The headline idea was to add three more "growth areas" to the existing (largely brownfield) Thames Gateway – Milton Keynes-South Midlands, London-Stansted-Cambridge-Peterborough and Ashford. Taken together they represented a huge chunk of southern England, stretching from Corby to Faversham. And although the intention was a step change in house-building levels to make housing more affordable, the Plan also worried itself about low demand for housing in the north of England and Midlands and proposed "housing market renewal pathfinders" in some areas, which would knock down tens of thousands of homes to make the remainder *less* affordable. Confusion was obvious throughout.

"Over many years we have been too wasteful of precious greenfield land . . ." it admitted. "The way land is used needs to be adapted to constantly changing demands. Yet our planning system is unresponsive and slow. People have moved out of our cities to seek a better life in suburbs, creating urban sprawl."

Having spotted the problem, it then set about making it much, much worse. Planning was to be made more "efficient" (i.e. ineffective), and ways of bashing local authorities that failed to comply were proposed (and implemented), including new-style local plans and regional spatial strategies. The latter should have been a major weapon in securing sustainable development but were instead used to force sprawl on wiser local authorities. As a result, this vital tool achieved political unpopularity and was abolished by the new government in 2010.

"For more than 30 years this country lost its way," intoned Prescott (who had been responsible for the previous six). And now the glimmers of hope were to be snuffed out.

And let slip the dogs of sprawl

A step change was just what Brown and his acolytes were looking for – why did he ever worry about being prime minister when he already exercised most of the powers without having to take the flak?

Brown's initial weapon of crass destruction was an economist, Kate Barker, whose background as chief European economist at Ford, chief economic advisor to the Confederation of British Industry (CBI), member of the Treasury's panel of independent economic advisors and, since 2001, a member of the Bank of England's all-powerful Monetary Policy Committee, obviously made her the right person to advise the government on, er, housing and planning.

But who cared? Brown was running the show and playing a long game. Barker was commissioned to "conduct a review of issues underlying the lack of supply and responsiveness of housing in the UK" – a textbook bit of pre-judgement that logicians call 'assuming the consequent'. In case she was in any doubt, the Treasury also required her to consider "the role of competition, capacity, technology and finance of the house building industry" and "the interaction of these factors with the planning system and the government's

Everything was sacrificed to the house-building target. *Image: Henry Oliver*

sustainable development objectives". Perhaps it would have been simpler if Brown had just said: "Kate, go out there and give us the ammunition to smash up the planning system," but that might have been a little blunt, even for the man they called 'the great clunking fist'.

The Barker housing review was commissioned at a time that house prices were soaring on the back of the cheap-and-easy credit Brown's economic policies had unleashed and buy-to-let speculators were pushing up prices by buying the homes young first-time-buyers should have had. But Barker's interim report[4] suggested loftier economic concerns, admitting that our house prices were actually less volatile than some of our neighbours' but underlining that we still deserved a good smacking.

"The UK tends to be more sensitive to changes in house prices than in other European countries," it said, i.e, we binge on credit when our house prices go up and grizzle and go bust when they go down. Obviously, none of that was the fault of those peddling cheap credit.

Barker's final report in 2004 provided stronger ammunition to fire at the planning system, claiming 70,000 more homes would have to be built each year in England alone to keep price inflation down to 1.8 per cent, or 120,000 more built to keep it to 1.1 per cent. Five years later we were building 70,000 houses a year fewer and prices were dropping sharply.

Brown obviously thought planners needed undermining further, however, and commissioned Ms Barker to review planning. To no one's surprise, she came back with a report recommending "rationalisation" of planning guidance (i.e. weaker), "faster" planning (i.e. weaker) and a whole raft of other ways of bashing environmental protection. Brown, who always behaved as if the environment had been invented to frustrate the Treasury, seemed to need the comfort blanket of his reviews, however nakedly they might prejudge the issue, and continued trying to batter opponents with them long after he left the Treasury.

Armed with his reviews, Brown set about knocking the planning system into line. He didn't attack the profession per se – never attack a profession unless you have to, they have subtle ways of biting back – but seduced them with the thought that the right of the great unwashed public to interfere in the planning process would be reduced. Some planners have never seemed wholly comfortable with the democratic element introduced in 1947 and obviously believe the whole process is best left to chartered planners, unsullied by unprofessional nonsense.

A quango was set up to take planning decisions on major projects such as motorways, airports and power stations away from elected authorities; councils would be told to consult their residents less and hurry applications through with less effective scrutiny; and planning guidance would be "simplified" into ineffectiveness. Local-authority-led regional planning joint bodies would be abolished and powers would be taken to force higher housing numbers into regional spatial strategies. These would be merged with regional economic strategies and prepared by regional development agency quangos. Bizarrely, this change was introduced by the Local Democracy, Economic Development and Construction Act 2009 – a fine piece of Orwellian newspeak.

The beast of sprawl was thus unchained to make planning more "efficient". Meanwhile the real hollowness of the new approach had been played out behind Whitehall's closed doors.

The Barker Steering Group

To coordinate the new policies, the Barker Steering Group was set up in 2004 and continued to meet until the end of 2005, at which point it renamed itself to avoid having to release any more details under Freedom of Information legislation (whence cometh the following little gems).

It covered the whole range of Barker's recommendations, including the planning gain supplement – Barker's latest suggested way of taxing developers' speculative profits from the uplift in land values when development is approved. She made it clear that this was a central and absolutely vital part of her recommendations, and it did form Labour's fourth attempt to enact the idea since 1947. Vital to the whole process it may have been, but it was subsequently dropped, even though the rest of her package continued to wreak havoc.

The Group's minutes present a fascinating insight into government. It was led by the Treasury and the Office of the Deputy Prime Minister and was attended by other departments including 10 Downing Street, and by Kate Barker herself. And although the public face of Blair resisting Brown continued, it was evident that the prime minister was just appeasing his unruly chancellor by adding Number 10's authority to anything Brown wanted, with his officials constantly backing the Treasury against other departments.

The intervention was supposed, remember, to improve 'affordability' of housing by ensuring more homes for sale were built. At an 'away day' held in 10 Downing Street's Pillared Room on 22 April 2005 the Group heard that "In the short to medium term benefits were around increasing access to home ownership across society as a whole, including the children of existing home owners, and reducing homelessness."[5]

Building homes for sale has, of course, never done anything for homelessness – that requires building socially rented housing, and few of these would be heading for greenfield sites – but the mantra of 'affordability' was chanted throughout the Group's deliberations like the Holy Grail.

The previous March, the Office of the Deputy Prime Minister (ODPM) had warned the Group that "it was likely that high levels of housing would be required to 'shift' affordability and that issues of location and distribution of new housing were important, due to inter-regional migration flows".[6] The members were actually told that the shift in affordability was unlikely to be effected in fewer than ten years and that "there remained a very real possibility that the current research could indicate a weak link between new housing supply and affordability". Yet on this flimsy basis was erected a policy to trash sustainability.

The 'away day' also heard a presentation by Reading University's Professor Geoff Mean, who agreed that the total stock of housing affects prices only in the long term. "The model results were broadly consistent with the scenarios set out in Kate Barker's original report and demonstrated a positive and lasting benefit, provided that higher levels of house building were sustained for at least ten years," he told the meeting.[7] But, curiously, the nation was never actually told the Barker approach would yield no significant house price benefits for a decade or more, even though environmental damage would be huge.

Of course, if the Group had really wanted a rapid improvement in affordability, they'd have just left British banks free to buy junk financial derivatives based on sub-prime mortgages from US banks . . . oh, they did.

Although the Steering Group continued to work on affordability, reality began to intrude by the autumn of 2005 and a dual goal was substituted, dealing with supply and demand through a numerical target "with a longer-term affordability goal, aiming to prevent the house price / earning ratio worsening".[8] "It was recognised that framing the affordability goal in these terms looks unambitious," conceded the Group.

So, here was the government selling a fantasy building target to a sceptical public, but this was New Labour, so presentation mattered. Kate Barker had recommended a national advisory unit on planning and housing and the Steering Group's discussions of the issue soon threw up a problem – it was supposed to be an independent body but how could it be guaranteed that an independent body would make the right recommendations to regional planning bodies and the government?

"The intention was for the NAU [national advisory unit] to be seen as independent, which would imply that its views would be published – though the questions of the scope of these views and the timing of any publication remained," the Group was told. "But there was a need to consider the role of the NAU in a situation where proposed regional targets did not 'stack up' as required, to contribute to the national goal."[9]

Two months later the Group was told[10] that consultations on the unit had proved "not entirely positive" and there was scepticism about its independence – proof perhaps that you can't fool all of the people all of the time. The meeting discussed whether to set it up as a quango or in-house expert panel and the minutes record considerable debate over whether either option would be seen as independent of government.

"The issue of housing growth was considered to be extremely controversial and the 'test' of the NAU's perceived independence might be the extent to which its advice was seen to be critical or widely at variance with government – but the opportunities for this would be limited by the fact that the advice required from the NAU would be 'in support of' the government's affordability goal," the minutes record.[11] Look at those words – "perceived independence" and "the advice required" – and you get the picture.

"Whilst there might be some opportunity for the NAU to express a view different from government's – for example, taking a different view of how housing growth should be balanced across the country – it would not be free, for example, to ignore affordability in favour of a greater emphasis on environmental issues."[12] That, of course, would never do.

In the end the advisory body was set up as the National Housing and Planning Advisory Unit to advise the new Department for Communities and Local Government (DCLG) and did, indeed, pursue a sort of independence through a series of reports. In a 2007 report on housing targets for England,[13] it responded to the government's Green Paper commitment to work up to 240,000 new homes a year with a line that was, indeed, independent. It suggested that additional house building was needed to meet a range of other factors such as the desire for second homes, and came up with an even higher figure of 270,000 new homes. It was independence, but not as we know it.

Dealing with the environment

The Group continued to discuss how to compromise England's environment without anyone objecting, and John Prescott's office presented a draft planning framework to the Downing Street 'away day' to deliver "the Barker recommendations on housing supply and greater responsiveness to the market", but that pesky environment thing remained a problem.

"No. 10 felt that recommendation B (national affordability goal to take account of sustainability) posed credibility problems," says the minutes.[14] "The natural tendency would be for sustainability issues to reduce the level of ambition on housing supply, so better not to include this consideration when setting the NAU recommendations for housing targets."

Heaven forbid the environment should affect macro-economic policy, and a subsequent meeting at the Treasury heard, with relief, that ODPM work on sustainability had produced "some good outcomes, and no show stoppers".[15] This was just as well, as "No. 10 identified the need to draw on research for presentational case".

But a couple of months later a consultant's study of sustainability threw up yet another problem. "The report is also weak on the land take issue – their estimate of available brownfield land is very low," the minutes record.[16] "Richard McCarthy [of ODPM] said that even our estimate, which is much higher than that given by Entec, underestimates what is available."

Given that the whole thing was supposed to provide a rationale for releasing more greenfield land, this was certainly a problem. Tony Blair had told a cabinet committee that he wanted the proposals to have a spatial context, but ODPM was already bribing local authorities to release additional land outside the growth areas with a "growth point" initiative. McCarthy told the meeting the government offices for the regions would need to feed into this process, and this led directly to Whitehall taking control of the strategies' housing targets and, eventually, to their abolition.

But the Group was also working hard to get positive headlines on the sustainability issues, and there were worries that environment ministers were not wholly on board. "There was a need to get DEFRA ministers on side," the Group was told.[17] "Though they were not against the principle of building new homes they were keen to address the environmental impacts, and may look to mitigate the effects."

But the need to spin opposition out of existence remained central to the Group's concerns. As early as December 2004, Number 10 noted that ODPM's housing strategy would "provide an opportunity to highlight the 'green story' to combat the accusation of 'concreting over the countryside'".[18]

"Treasury said that their contacts with industry indicated that it was commonly felt that Government as a whole was actually equivocal about the case for housing growth," say the minutes. "Anecdotally, local publicity (for example, in the East) indicated that Government was losing the communications battle on the case for housing growth . . . The Group agreed that it was important to ensure a positive and consistent Government message about the need for housing growth – communications teams, particularly those in ODPM and No. 10, should continue to focus on this."

Four months later it was reported that a presentational strategy on the case for housing growth would be recommended to ministers. But, by June 2005, Number 10 was still reminding the Group of the need to sell ideas to the public, and showing scepticism that ODPM's planning document would be the first stage in building such consensus.

"Planning document alone could be seen as dismantling Barker package," it told the meeting.[19] "Important to retain message that Barker about infrastructure, planning reform, etc. as well as housing growth."

But the package was already crumbling, as developers had already launched a propaganda war against the planning gain supplement, but work on "communications" continued. September's meeting heard that although work on economic and environmental benefits, affordability, the inevitability of growth and the benefits in tackling it was shaping well, there were still gaps in the economic and environmental cases and a "rebuttal on immigration issues" was needed.[20]

"A spatial element needs to be developed to offset accusations of 'concreting over the countryside'," the meeting heard, as the plans to concrete over the countryside continued, and, sinisterly, the meeting heard of a need to use "conduits other than the traditional media" and work was going on with "regional colleagues and stakeholders" and "paid-for options are also being considered, to bypass the media altogether".

Rebuttal scripts were soon being prepared and ministers brought into line, with David Miliband scheduled to address the "National Housebuilders Federation" (sic), Yvette Cooper talking to *The Guardian* and John Prescott going on the *Trevor MacDonald Programme*.

"The issue seemed to be escalating, with detractors such as CPRE becoming more vocal," the Group was warned.[21] "Responding to this represented a good opportunity to get the message across, and with a good narrative ministers were keen to take on the environmental lobby."

Meanwhile, poor Americans, some with no income, were being persuaded to accept huge mortgages, but these storm clouds were a few years away. But a meeting in October 2005 sounded a prophetic note as it discussed the affordability goal.

"Even a small reduction in house price inflation would have a significant effect in the longer term," it was warned.[22] "It was also recognised that though the affordability goal could only be measured in the long term, a larger-than-expected downturn in the market could quickly make this target look obsolete."

Within three years, the downturn made the whole Barker process look an utter irrelevance, but by then a whole raft of legislation and guidance had been imposed to enforce the process. And in the end, there was nothing really to communicate.

'Eco towns'

One of the strangest offspring of the 'Sustainable Communities Plan' was the so-called 'eco towns' programme. These were supposed to be new towns that would be "exemplar green developments", with a minimum of 5,000 homes. Supposed to "meet the highest standards of sustainability, including low- and zero-carbon technologies and good public transport", according to the DCLG, they were actually a smokescreen for very large-scale greenfield sprawl, a lightning rod for opposition and a useful way for government departments to flog off hard-to-sell, remote, redundant sites such as airfields or ordnance depots at housing development prices.

Plans to build 100,000 of the new homes in the 'growth points' were launched to a sceptical world in 2007. Eco towns' 5-10,000 'low carbon' or even 'zero carbon' homes were supposed to have "strong public transport links to nearby towns and cities" and the first was to be at Oakington Barracks in Cambridgeshire.

"They could use public transport and new green designs to deliver low-cost and low-carbon homes for the future, making good use of brownfield land," said the minister, Yvette Cooper,[23] although she let slip that this wouldn't be sustainably located urban brownfield land – homes could be "built on public sector surplus land such as former MoD or NHS sites" – i.e. a hefty car journey from anywhere useful.

To ensure no one doubted that this was a late revival of a hymn from the Ebenezer Howard Song Book, the Town & Country Planning Association's chair was appointed to report back on further development of eco-town criteria. Soon, Gordon Brown was upping the five eco towns to ten, expressions of interest were sought and expenditure climbed into the millions.

Sceptics were initially floored when more than 50 plans rolled in, but most proved to be simply old, rejected, greenfield sprawl settlement ideas with the dust blown off and a few eco-gimmicks added. Yet no fewer than 15 were shortlisted, although the two impeccable urban brownfield schemes making good use of public transport were rejected, including one at an oil refinery site in Greater Manchester, which could have had a light rail link and been an exemplar of transit-oriented development. But sadly it wouldn't have looked at all like a garden city.

The government's evaluation of the bids noted that none was built on green belt land,[24] hardly surprising as they were all so far from conurbations, and claimed they made good use of brownfield land "including former MoD land, military depots, disused airfields and former mining pits and industrial sites" – anywhere except sustainable locations, in fact. A subsequent analysis by the Campaign to Protect Rural England showed that the vast majority of the eco-town shortlist land was, in fact, greenfield.

If the government had hoped eco towns would generate a favourable view of their sprawl programme, they were to be sorely disappointed. Given the opposition many of the shortlisted schemes provoked, the best it could be seen as was a lightning conductor to direct attention to the rest of the sprawl, which would have accounted for well over 90 per cent of it anyway. Soon protest groups were being set up, celebrities engaged and law suits were flying around. Even a government-appointed panel was scathing about the schemes' poor sustainability, especially their locations and the lack of public transport beyond the usual rotten bus service. Their unpopularity was 'confirmed' when the government announced that its own research showed they enjoyed five-to-one public support.[25]

Slowly, most of the schemes were withdrawn. Their credibility was further damaged by a planning policy statement on eco towns, requiring their new homes to reach only Level 4 on the Code for Sustainable Homes scale – well below the Level 6 all new homes are supposed to meet from 2016. By the time a new shortlist was launched in July 2009 the number of schemes had fallen to four, but another five million pounds was set aside to work them up and six months later a second wave was announced – four sites in West Yorkshire, one in Shoreham Harbour and a possible one in the Dearne Valley – and another five million quid went into the development pot. For the first time a couple of these sites were genuine urban brownfield proposals. And in case insufficient money had been thrown at them, another £62.5 million was put their way early in 2010 to build 600 homes, the first on these sites, to Code Level 4 at least. Finally, on April Fools' Day in 2010, a swathe of rural north Essex along the A120 was threatened with an eco town and another ten million pounds agreed for development.

"Britain is leading the world with these new eco-town standards, which combine affordable housing with new green infrastructure and an exceptional quality of life," said housing minister John Healey.[26] Perhaps 'misleading the world' would have been nearer the mark.

Housing market renewal

We saw in Chapter 4 how decades of 'slum clearance' swept away thousands of good communitarian homes and replaced them with junk housing. Now the 'Sustainable Communities Plan' was to do the same in pursuit of making homes in a raft of northern and Midland towns less affordable.

"Rapidly falling house prices in some parts of the country, particularly deprived parts of northern inner cities and towns that had suffered the effects of industrial decline, resulted in a significant reduction in population," said the DCLG. "This also led to house dereliction, poor services and poor social conditions", and once the houses were empty they became magnets for anti-social behaviour.

Actually, of course, people left the areas because of the industrial decline, not the falling house prices, and many, in any case, lived in socially rented homes. But, the argument went, if you made the housing less affordable, the market would recover and everyone would at least feel better; those who owned homes anyway. Few would still have jobs and those in rented homes would be as miserable as before, but you could build 'family, market homes' on the sites, entrepreneurs would flock to buy them and the local economy would soon match that of Kensington or St Tropez.

On this flimsy foundation, no less than £1.2 billion was spent on the 'housing market renewal pathfinder' areas in England and a further £1 billion budgeted for 2008-11. Much of the money was well enough spent on refurbishment and new homes, but in just three years 16,100 homes were demolished and the pathfinders threatened much bigger destruction to come. And it wasn't the hopelessly located outer estates the sprawl lobby had demanded, where garden city dreams sank beneath global free market reality, that were to go – it was the same bye-law terraces they hated so much.

Many of their residents didn't actually want to move but faced the full rigour of compulsory purchase. And once areas became housing market renewal (HMR) demolition areas, the already low prices just crashed through the floor and thousands of people were forced to accept far less for their homes than they should have got. The housing market may have been renewed but those forced out by court orders found that markets can be renewed downwards as well as upwards. And any real revival of the market was soon wiped out by the credit crunch.

But DCLG still went on claiming the programme had restored confidence, reduced the disparity between markets and made local authorities cooperate. It even had the cheek to claim an important role in the sustainability agenda by having reduced pressure on greenfield sites. It's obvious isn't it? Knock down lots of high-density terraces, replace them with a few low-density homes or patches of windswept grass, and people will stop building on greenfield sites.

In 2008, the Commons Committee of Public Accounts noted "a risk that demolition of sites, rather than newly built houses, will be the programme's legacy" and argued that "the needs of those who wish to remain in an area should not be overlooked in developing more mixed and sustainable communities". Quite.

The stores that ate your town

Throughout the 1980s and 1990s the issue of supermarkets and out-of-town shopping continued to nag at governments of all political persuasions. The 1980s' 'great car economy' had prompted an explosion in out-of-town shopping, and by the 1990s vast, urban-economy-destroying monster proposals were pouring into planners' in-trays, eventually prompting the sequential test and a retail needs test, although it was a weak affair.

But HM Treasury's belief in the unfettered free market was not so easily thwarted. Even though a Competition Commission report in 2000 had warned that supermarkets were threatening product innovation as a result of their supply-chain practices, the mega-stores continued to multiply and prosper while more and more small shops closed every year. Questions began to be asked about what could be done to protect small retailers from the economies of scale enjoyed by the large multiples, especially given the competitive advantage of their out-of-town, car-friendly locations.

Eventually, in 2006, the Office of Fair Trading referred the groceries market to the Competition Commission to see if it was restricting or distorting competition. Optimists hoped the Commission would look at the way super-markets use their muscle to clobber the supply chain, destroy local shopping centres and strong-arm planning authorities into allowing damaging new stores. It was soon evident, however, that the Commission's view of 'consumer interest' was a narrow view of the price of products rather than of issues such as quality, choice and innovation.

"The regulators are not counting the extra value that genuine local shops provide in terms of economic benefit and the social glue that holds communi-ties together," complained the new economics foundation (nef).[27] "This creates an in-built bias in favour of the large supermarkets who distort markets."

Soon the Commission was suggesting adequate consumer choice could be guaranteed by having three grocery outlets larger than 1,400 square metres within a 10-minute drive – that's a two-hour walk, incidentally, for those who don't use cars. (Tesco had, in fact, recommended a 30-minute drive be used – a half-day walk. As nef pointed out, that would mean someone living in Chelmsford would count a store in Romford, Saffron Walden or Leigh-on-Sea as local, or that someone in Balham would consider their local shops to include ones in Cheam, Willesden or Bethnal Green.)

"Unless it makes full use of its powers for the next phase of its inquiry, the big, centralised logistical operations of the supermarkets will continue to drive the homogenisation of business, shop-ping, eating, farming, food, the land-scape, the environment and our daily lives," warned nef. "The endgame could be Britain turning, in effect, into a one-supermarket state."

The flow of small-shop closures became a flood.

As the recession turned the flow of small-shop closures into a flood, Britain moved towards a supermarket state, but the Commission's conclusions ignored all that. Instead of noticing the obvious fact that unfair competition from supermarkets was destroying small shops, the Commission fretted that they were using their strength to prevent other supermarkets opening in towns where they operated. So the main problem it identified was, in effect, that a place whose town centre had been destroyed by a large supermarket lacked a second supermarket to make things worse.

"These proposals stand to accelerate what is in effect a retail *coup d'état*, which has profound implications for our way of life," warned nef.[28]

And, while the Commission recognised the importance of the planning system, it failed to support the threatened retail needs test. "We are offered a bleak prospect of yet more ruthless price wars for food, which undermine farmers' livelihoods, and yet more land-hungry superstores in sprawling, car-dependent suburbs," said CPRE head of rural policy Tom Oliver.[29]

The nef said that if the regulator couldn't prove it could do the job it was set up to do, it should be abolished. It wasn't. In the end it recommended a competition test for planning decisions on large stores, and the government accepted this as an alternative for the retail needs test. Revised planning guidance did at least ask local planning authorities to look at the size of stores and their impact on local economies – which was better than nothing, though not much.

The appliance of science

As sprawl policies took hold during the 2000s, a number of people both inside and outside government began to pin their hopes on work being done by the government's Foresight Programme – the office that's supposed to provide a scientific basis to underpin policy decisions. In 2008 it announced it was to study land use in the UK and, as it was clear that current policies were unsustainable, great things were expected.

Early in 2010 the report, *Land Use Futures*,[30] appeared. The scientists had analysed the finite resources of our land in great detail and observed that it faces increasing challenges as the century wears on. They reminded us that our land provides food, timber and other goods, space for housing, business, transport, energy, recreation and tourism and clean air, water and healthy soils. The report noted new pressures, including rising demographic trends, climate change and rising demand for commercial and residential development, especially in the south and east of England, and called for a more coherent and consistent approach.

Two cheers for that – but (and you sensed there was a 'but' coming, didn't you?) it also told us that, since 1947, "policies to prevent sprawl have been largely successful". Now that may sound funny, but this is a serious problem.

The report stated progress would be made only by identifying how various demands would interact, evaluating the consequences and taking a broad and overarching perspective. OK, so . . . ? A major issue would be whether the land's economic, social and environmental benefits could continue to be delivered *against a backdrop of greater expectations from the market and individuals* (my italics – but of course it can't) and the need to live within environmental limits. It warned that major challenges and rising tensions could arise (bizarrely assuming they hadn't already) unless action were taken.

Then, having identified these challenges, it stopped being all scientific and got all market-friendly instead. It warned that, where land supply was constrained and incomes rising, house prices would rise and pressures on land use in south-east England (with economic growth of 2-2.5 per cent) would intensify. From there it was but a short step to warning that rising incomes would increase market pressure for larger homes and that this pressure in the south-east would necessitate either higher densities or releasing more land for development. This was a government report, so maybe you saw that coming?

By now *Land Use Futures* was busy quoting the Barker reviews (this was supposed to be a science report) and noting "there is a strong economic case that planning controls on land in some areas, especially in the south-east of England, are tighter than can be justified by current valuations of the net costs of development. Releasing land for development in areas of high demand can confer large social welfare gains and would require some relaxation of planning policy." Wonderful thing, science.

"The long-term social, economic and environmental costs and benefits will need to be carefully weighed," it concluded.

So the aspiration many people undoubtedly harbour for a large 'house in the country' had been elevated to the status of scientific determinant. Once, governments aspired to ensure everyone had a decent roof over their heads. But apparently, as politicians of all stripes keep reminding us, 'the age of aspiration is back'.

Well, be careful what you wish for. I suspect most of us would like to live in huge, elegant, detached properties in national parks or areas of outstanding natural beauty. So if aspiration is king, we ought to be building tens of millions of them, with motorway access of course. And if it's not, we need to hear the clunk of report in waste-paper bin, or its electronic equivalent.

Greenfield sprawl and the great crash

The great crash of 2008-9 took house building in England down to 166,000 a year, which at least put an end to the fiction that only raising it to 240,000 a year would bring prices down. And it finally proved beyond doubt that the obsession with home ownership rather than the supply of houses was the real root cause of economic instability. The mad willingness of lenders on both sides of the Atlantic to lend absurd amounts of money during booms to people who couldn't possibly repay it, and their unwillingness to lend anything during busts, proved to be the real root cause. Let's remember that, as late as January 2008, it was still possible to obtain mortgages in the UK for six times one's annual income. The technical economic term for this process is utter lunacy.

But blame was still heaped on planners and conservationists, not the banks, never the banks. Meanwhile Whitehall continued to blather about building 240,000 homes a year in England as late as 2010, by which time the actual figure was not much above 100,000. The 240,000 figure finally disappeared only during the 2010 election campaign, although *Labour's Plan for Housing*,[31] published during the campaign, was still clinging to the idea and attacking the Conservatives' strange knit-your-own planning proposals.

"By scrapping house building targets – likely to lead to fewer homes – they risk the jobs supported by house building and put a brake on Britain's recovery," said the document. "According to city economists, their wider policies to cut investment will drive up unemployment, undermining the ability of people to buy a home and causing a further 20-per-cent drop in house prices."

So, just as in the original Barker review, macroeconomics was firmly back in the driving seat and Gordon Brown's clunking fist was clear in what was supposed to be a vote winner. Seven years after the 'Sustainable Communities Plan' demanded we build many more houses to reduce house prices, the awful spectre of declining house prices was being used as a rationale for, er, building many more houses. If sheer brass neck won elections, Gordon should have romped home.

The new coalition wades in

The new coalition government announced its arrival in 2010 with the intention of becoming the 'greenest government ever', and its new communities secretary Eric Pickles was armed with the knowledge that public anger at urban sprawl had helped defeat Labour. There was actually little agreement between the Conservatives and Labour about spatial planning, and indeed the Liberal Democrats had not shed much ink on it at all. The Conservatives had done so, however, with a pre-election strategy called *Open Source Planning*.

Pickles, a powerful Thatcherite figure, soon used anger at fantasy housing targets, not to impose more sensible ones but simply to scrap decades of regional planning in England altogether, as foreshadowed in *Open Source Planning*. Everything was to be left to local planning authorities; even the extensive national planning guidance was to be scrapped and replaced with a simple statement of national policy. No one had the faintest idea where this would lead; perhaps the 'greenest government ever' simply meant the most naïve. But managing the most overcrowded, polluted and exhausted corner of an overcrowded, polluted and exhausted planet does, sadly, require careful planning. For just around the corner is some very destructive climate change.

Chapter 7

Climate change and other future challenges

More than riches, than great empires, than greasy inventions,
let us have sunlight – simply sunlight.

Walter Wilkinson, *Vagabonds and Puppets*

Let's suppose

Humour me for a minute. Let's suppose, a few years down the line, some clever bunch of scientists proves human-induced (anthropogenic) climate change is a myth. Let's suppose they show there is some natural 'smoking gun' – solar activity, changes in the Earth's orbit, low levels of volcanism or whatever – that can be clearly shown to be responsible for the temperature rises of the last couple of centuries.

What, I wonder, would the reaction be at those bodies set up by the oil and coal industry to deny that anthropogenic climate change exists and to spread confusion and doubt? After the initial giggle of surprise, they would gaze sheepishly at one another and recall all those bogus bits of science they seized upon and embroidered that had now been proven true. On behalf of their paymasters they would rush out press releases saying 'we told you so' to an astonished world, before realising (to their horror) that the coal and oil boys no longer had need of their services. Well, at least one good thing would come out of it.

Folks would be pretty annoyed at the scientists and the politicians that went along with them. But at least they could now crank up their thermostats, depress their accelerators and book themselves long-haul flights with a clear conscience. And where would it all leave Smart Growth?

You might think we could stop worrying about sprawl being car-dependent, or global distribution systems' dependence on fossil fuels. You could actually say stuff your Smart Growth.

But hold on a minute. Long before environmentalists started worrying about climate change, they were worrying about a whole raft of other things. They worried about depletion of natural resources, about destruction of biodiversity, about degradation of our soil and declines in agricultural production and, above all perhaps, about overpopulation. Then along came the 1980s and many stopped worrying about most of those things and started to worry more about climate change.

Now before you throw this book across the room, scaring the cat, let me reassure you that I'm not about to recant the anthropogenic heresy and join one of those wacky 'think tanks' that says climate change has been made up by a bunch of sick, pinko lefties intent on destroying the American way of life. But we do need to realise climate change is far from being the sole reason we need to change.

Limits to growth

The roots of the modern environmental movement go back to the 1970s, when we saw initiatives such as the Club of Rome's *The Limits to Growth*,[1] and *A Blueprint for Survival*.[2] A curious aspect of both is that global warming got little mention. *The Limits to Growth* actually opined that any warming would come as a result of waste heat, not greenhouse gases. "If man's energy needs are someday supplied by nuclear power instead of fossil fuels, this increase in atmospheric CO_2 will eventually cease, one hopes before it has had any measurable ecological or climatological effect," it said.

Ho hum. Perhaps we should remember that if environmentalists of the early 1970s worried about the climate, it was probably about the 'nuclear winter' that would follow an atomic war or the possibility of the ice age resuming. Looking back at the things that did worry people in that era, the main concerns seem to centre on population growth; depletion of resources, especially food, oil and metals; and toxification of the environment by pesticides, etc.

Moving rapidly on, however, it was firmly believed there were limits to growth but that attempts to improve matters would always be undermined until we took urgent action to curb population growth. It was predicted that, unchecked, the world's population would rise from a little over three billion in 1972 to six billion by 2000 – a prediction that proved fairly accurate. In 2008, the UN estimated[3] the world's population was around 6.8 billion and would top seven billion in 2011 and nine billion in 2050.

Some things the green movement of the 1970s did get spectacularly wrong – a great deal of ink was spilled on alarming ourselves that the world would run out of non-ferrous metals, something no one seems at all concerned about today. It underestimated the amount of oil that would be discovered and it foresaw a future where people moved rapidly to a more cooperative and planned 'steady state' existence. Within a decade the world had indeed moved – to decades of less cooperative, less planned, global free-marketism and growth.

But, as we're taking a moment out to look at a parallel universe where climate change is only a minor concern, we might pause to note that many of the awesome (in its traditional sense) predictions of that era are still highly relevant today. The early environmentalists predicted that growth in population, loss of agricultural land to urban sprawl and a decline in vital resources would eventually mean we are unable to feed ourselves. They predicted oil would run short then run out, so we would be unable to move around or sustain agricultural or industrial production. They predicted a world short of water.

Climate change burst into green consciousness in the 1980s and is so immediate a concern that it's tended to push the other challenges to one side. But we should never forget we live in a corner of the planet where gross overpopulation has left us horribly vulnerable to shortages of all these resources. Until now we have been able to use our wealth-generating ability to buy in the things we need from elsewhere. But in a world where the money is following industry eastwards across a planet running ever-shorter of fundamental resources, is everyone confident we will continue to be able to do this in the decades to come?

Peak oil

No one quite agrees when 'peak oil' – the moment when the world's oil supply fails to meet its demand – will happen, or whether it has already happened. But what no one seems to disagree with is the proposition that it isn't very far away. Certainly world oil production stopped going up very much around 2005, and the 2008 price spike was caused by demand exceeding production by just 2 per cent. And in many parts of the world – the United States, Russia, Europe and even the Middle East – production of oil is certainly past its peak. It's claimed that we're currently using about four times as much oil each year as we discover.

In any case, the price will start to climb some time soon, as easy-to-get-at sources are rapidly being depleted and the remaining oil is increasingly in unstable parts of the world or far beneath the ocean. So, one way or another, petrol and diesel (and indeed natural gas) are going to get more and more expensive in the years to come. Just how quickly is a matter of debate, but it is going to happen, whether petrolheads like it or not.

To understand the implications we should look at the US, where property prices have started falling in remote, car-dependent suburbs far faster than in traditional town and city centres, a complete reversal of the trend over the previous 60 years. Of course, commuting distances are much longer in America, but against that is the fact that petrol has been much cheaper there than in the UK. If you live a long way from your work and depend on a car to get there, it's time to start considering the sustainability (in the literal sense) of your lifestyle. Will you still be able to afford it in ten years' time when motoring is much, much more expensive?

Likewise, if your business depends on cheap diesel to distribute goods which spend most of their short lives trundling up and down motorways to meet just-in-time or whatever other demands your customers make, will you still be able to afford that too?

Quite a lot of people believe this won't be a problem – we can use biofuels, we can drive 'low-emission vehicles', we can drive electric vehicles, we can go on more or less as before. For a whole host of reasons, this is not a sensible response. 'Low-emission vehicles' are merely 'slightly-less-high-emission vehicles'. It takes a vast amount of fossil energy to build a steel car of any description and it takes very significant amounts of energy to drive a pneumatic-tyred vehicle around, particularly one that needs to drive when it's cold, drive up hills, etc. Electric vehicles have limited range and long recharge times, and efforts to overcome this are unlikely to result in much improvement.

For some years, environmentalists thought biofuels would provide at least a partial solution. But no sooner did they begin to be produced commercially than a whole list of problems associated with them began to appear. For a start, it takes a vast acreage to generate much worthwhile energy. Then biofuels started to displace food production in parts of the world that desperately need food production. Then producers started converting vast areas of tropical forest and their soils into atmospheric carbon to generate a small reduction in fossil fuel production. Sometimes you could weep.

The end of the era of cheap, convenient road vehicles is still some years away, but it is close enough to require us to start addressing the problem. Currently, we're not.

Peak food

As a species we've never been particularly good at distributing the food we produce. Rich countries are currently eating themselves into obesity and shortening their life spans while poor countries are short of food. But the population of the Earth continues to rise fast and currently we're producing less food than we need. More than 850 million people worldwide suffer hunger.

In 2009, Canada's National Farmers Union warned that rising population, water shortages, climate change and the growing cost of fossil-fuel-based fertiliser mean that things are going to get worse. The oceans were once teeming with fish, but all commercial fish stocks are likely to be exhausted by 2050.

As already mentioned, the UK relies on imports for much of its food, and in 2009 national planning advice ended over 60 years of protection for our most productive farmland. This was so that we could build low-density, car-dependent greenfield housing on it, to keep prices down some time after the next decade.

Yes . . . it tolls for thee.

Peak water

Much of the world is already suffering from insufficient water, and that can only get worse as population rises. Among the countries that are short of water is one called the United Kingdom.

It's been estimated that more than 1.8 billion people around the world will be short of water by 2025. One of the many mad things we're doing to our soil is exhausting the groundwater from our aquifers. When they dry up, local agriculture crashes and people run short of water to drink and short of the water they need for effective sewage management.

Water shortages are likely to hit parts of the east of England, and indeed elaborate measures are needed to keep Essex's planned housing growth supplied with water. Essex, you see, is a very dry place; parts of it are actually drier than parts of Syria. To keep it supplied with water, water is being brought south in a new pipeline from Fenland.

Since the 1930s there has been talk of a British national water grid, but it's never happened because it would cost a bob or two. Given the lack of such a grid, the movement south-eastwards of our economy, employment and population is particularly mad. But economists seem to like it. I wonder if they'll still like it when they can't wash their cars or flush the toilet?

Overpopulation

At the time of writing this book the world's population is around 6.8 billion, but it will have risen significantly by the time you read it. And before 2050 it could have passed nine billion. This will mean world food demand and energy production increasing by around half, and drinking water by about a third. Does anyone seriously believe the planet is capable of sustaining such increases?

More locally, the Government Office for Statistics has predicted that the UK population will top 70 million by 2030, and various people have tried to at least initiate a debate about this (without setting off predictable rants about immigration – responsible for only 44 per cent of the growth – although it's an issue that will have to be addressed). Forum for the Future's 2010 report on the issue, *Growing Pains*,[4] pointed out that, even if conflict could be avoided and a harmonious multicultural society sustained in the face of strong growth, there must eventually come a point at which the growth in population couldn't be sustained any more – it can't go on for ever.

So the report looked at the sustainability impacts and noted many of the issues we've noted here, such as loss of farmland, building on floodplains, food security, water shortages, growth in greenhouse gas emissions, etc. It also looked at the economic aspects of meeting an age imbalance by importing young, economically active people, a self-perpetuating cycle which must be broken one day (perhaps we could tackle ageism in the jobs market?) and the huge extra infrastructure required to support a larger population.

"Whilst a population of 70 million is not inherently unsustainable, managing that level of population sustainably will require an extraordinary combination of planning, investment, and innovation," concludes the report. "And we are likely to have a better quality of life if we set our policies to achieve the lower projections."

And, as Sir David Attenborough noted in April 2009: "I've never seen a problem that wouldn't be easier to solve with fewer people, or harder, ultimately, with more."

Growing Pains suggests planning for population growth, using what we have more efficiently, rethinking what 'growth' means, developing new attitudes to ageing, enhancing family planning, and holding an objective, open and sensible discussion about immigration. To all of which I say 'amen', and would not even venture to suggest that those religions that oppose family planning need to have a good long think about what caring for God's creation entails, because it might get me into all sorts of trouble.

Back in the early 1970s there was a serious national debate about population growth, and slogans such as 'Stop at two' and 'Overpopulation is everybody's baby' were bandied about, but the debate was effectively shut down, partly by the anger of some religious groups and partly because UK population growth was seen as essential to UK economic growth. Even by that time we had spent 100 years boosting our economy through artificially boosting the proportion of young workers by looting the youngest and best from poorer countries, and that has pretty much continued to this day.

Clearly, population growth has to stop eventually, but those who manage our economy have yet to get the message. In June 2010, for instance, the Office for National Statistics published mid-year population estimates which suggested the growth in south-west England – a region to which people had been flocking for retirement or new jobs – had been only 0.4 per cent in the previous year. The South West Regional Development Agency (SWRDA) published a statement[5] bemoaning this as "not good for growth" and ascribed it to the recession prompting a drop in immigration from Europe and to problems people wanting to retire to the region were experiencing in selling their houses.

Now you might imagine that the slowdown in population growth would be cause for celebration in a region that had been a cauldron of fierce debate over its fast-rising population and the consequent urban sprawl afflicting a predominantly rural region. Not a bit of it: SWRDA grudgingly admitted the trend might reduce demand for new housing but suggested this would be outweighed by a drop in building, and its view encapsulated very succinctly the unsustainable nature of economic thinking in recent decades.

"For the SW economy more generally, there will clearly be less growth arising from the inflow of migrant workers and there will be a smaller benefit from the wealth brought by people retiring to the region," it said. Hmm.

Whether the population goes up, stays the same or even drops a little, Britain will remain what it already is, a desperately overcrowded island. Smart Growth planning remains absolutely essential.

Climate change

All right, actually I do believe that anthropogenic climate change is a big problem. How big, I have no idea, and I suspect one of the weaknesses in the current science (ruthlessly exploited by our suicidal contrarian tendency) is that there are big uncertainties. How fast will carbon dioxide increase the temperature? What are the real positive and negative feedbacks? What are the regional effects

Climate change will make things less predictable and more extreme.

likely to be? When will the jet streams break down? When will the thermohaline circulation break down? When will run-away global warming begin?

One of the toughest challenges for climate scientists is predicting how weather patterns will change at any given area of the planet, and for somewhere such as north-west Europe, which has always 'enjoyed' changeable and unpredictable conditions, it's hardest of all. Those contrarians who seize on any area of doubt to pour scorn have exploited this fact to the full. It's reminiscent, perhaps, of those who spent the 1930s arguing that Herr Hitler had no aggressive intentions because . . . well, because the thought of another war like the last was simply unthinkable. Today the thought of giving up mass motoring, flying on holiday or dirt-cheap manufactured goods from the Far

---

The soil-carbon challenge

Europe's soils contain around 75 billion tonnes of organic carbon, and half of it is located in just three countries: Sweden, Finland and the United Kingdom. That's about ten times as much carbon as held by Europe's forest and 50 times Europe's annual greenhouse gas emissions and, were it to become carbon dioxide, would add around 275 billion tonnes of it to our overloaded atmosphere.

UK soils contain around ten billion tonnes of this organic carbon and England's upland soils alone contain more carbon than all the trees in the UK and France put together. But across Europe, including in the UK, soils are losing carbon thanks to drainage and changes in land use.

Much of the UK's soil carbon is in its peat upland areas, and warming and drying is causing them to lose carbon, as does heather burning for sheep or grouse production. Elsewhere, UK soil is losing carbon through conversion to arable soils or by being sealed under hard development such as buildings or roads, which dries the soil, causing it to oxidise.

The soil under grass or forests tends to accumulate carbon, and you can encourage peat to take in carbon by removing drainage from upland areas. Several national parks and other upland management bodies have started to do this – the North Pennines AONB, for instance, has now blocked 270km of drainage channels and restored 1,266 hectares of peat.

Drained lowland peat like Fenland loses carbon to the atmosphere, its depth reducing by 10-20mm each year, and annual UK greenhouse emissions from this source could be two million tonnes a year or more. Yet blocking drainage can result in accumulation of between 0.1mm and 3mm of peat each year.

Converting lowland arable land to grassland would certainly sequester some carbon, but is plainly at odds with the need for food production. All this heightens the importance of halting 'soil sealing' – covering land with buildings – the subject of abortive European attempts to impose a soil directive.

East seems almost as unthinkable. And, as in the 1930s, there are those who stand to gain from manipulating these views.

To be honest, I've no idea what the climate will look like in 30, 40 or 50 years. Looking back over the last 20 or so, I think we can assume it will be more extreme. We are likely to see both hotter, drier summers and cooler, wetter ones. Long periods of drought or deluge (lasting years sometimes) are likely, and winters without frost, with the occasional bitterly cold one thrown in, to keep us on our toes. Sea-level rise will continue and wave climates will change, resulting in the loss of some areas of our overcrowded country to the sea and massive spending on flood and sea defence. The balance of opinion seems to be that the thermohaline circulation breakdown is still several decades away, but when it does happen we will get a climate like Newfoundland's – cool summers and bitterly cold winters. Things will get very different; don't know how, don't know when.

Far mightier minds than mine are wrestling with these problems, but all I would observe is this. I think it was George Eliot who noted that farmers believe things are as bad as they could possibly be and that any change will be for the worse. Could this be because they are utterly dependent on the weather? For that's the truth about climate change – we don't know exactly what the climate will become at any given spot, but it will be different, and whatever the result of that it will adversely affect agriculture, water supply, etc. There's no getting round that. We've enjoyed a pretty stable climate for 6,000 years now and that must be some kind of record. But things are changing and *any* change will be for the worse. It's time to get resilient – and it's time to start learning lessons from other people.

Chapter 8

America – land of dreams

My readers have opportunities of judging for themselves whether the influences and tendencies which I distrust in America, have any existence not in my imagination.

Charles Dickens, *American Notes*

Travel writing

Like Britain, America has had its fair share of travel writers. It's even had its share of British travel writers: Charles Dickens started it off with his *American Notes* (1842), and several others followed, including Walter Wilkinson, who took his puppet show there.[1] The genre can even boast an American travel writer who became a British-living American travel writer and then an American-living, formerly British-living American travel writer in Bill Bryson, who recorded this distinctly mixed Atlantic message in *Notes from a Big Country* (1998).[2] Now, I suppose, he's a British-living, formerly American-living, formerly British-living, American travel writer. I wonder if he gets confused?

We British certainly have a confused attitude to the 'good old US of A'. We slavishly follow its culture and its technology, moaning incessantly as we adopt its television, social networking sites or junk food as essential staples of our way of life. We know we're 'two peoples divided by a common language', but the divide between our two languages, once the subject of so much snooty disdain on this side of the pond, gets ever narrower, envisioning invite after invite to Americanisms. We're even using 'invite' as a noun, which must set on edge the teeth of anyone who ever envisaged the pleasure of receiving an invitation.

But America is still different from the UK in many ways. As Bill Bryson noted in *Notes from a Big Country*: "A remarkable thing about America, if you have been living for a long time in a snug little place like the UK, is how very big and very empty so much of it is. Consider this: Montana, Wyoming and North and South Dakota have an area twice the size of France but a population less than that of south London".

Hmm, I wonder if the good folk of the High Plains region drive around in white vans? Few, I suspect, are Crystal Palace supporters but then, frankly, few

South Londoners are either, except in spirit. But then I grew up on London's 'northern heights' and have the usual mountain dweller's contempt for the cities of the plain, even the parts where my parents were born and where I now live.

But Bryson noted empty space is not something Americans feel smug about; far from it.

> The curious thing is that nearly all Americans, as far as I can tell, don't see it this way. They think the country is way too crowded. Moves are constantly afoot to restrict access to national parks and wilderness areas on the grounds that they are dangerously overrun. Parts of them are unquestionably crowded, but that is only because 98 per cent of visitors arrive by car, and 98 per cent of those venture no more than 400 yards from their metallic wombs.

Bryson is, however, being a little hard on his compatriots (his American compatriots, that is). Because although urban sprawl became an American obsession during the twentieth century in the same way it did in Britain, and although, being American, they did it on a far larger and more successful scale than we did in Britain, we are in no position to criticise. Britain was one of the places that exported the idea that sprawl is a 'good thing' to America and, more importantly, America is at long last doing something about it and coming up with better ways of doing things. In the UK, of course, we still know best.

US sprawl devoured farmland at a phenomenal rate.
Image: US Environmental Protection Agency, Smart Growth Program

For despite the fact that Bryson noted that just 2 per cent of America was developed (in 1998 that was) and had just 86 people to the square mile, compared with 256 in France and over 600 in Britain, like Britain its population isn't evenly spread. In America it's concentrated down the east coast from New England to Florida, spreads into the north-east mid-west (a term which is actually used) and has gone with the wagon trains to the south-west. Vast tracts of America are indeed pretty empty, but quite a lot of it got heavily suburbanised as its vast cities turned into vast suburbs: 'hypersprawl', 'exurbs', 'boomburbs' or just plain sprawl.

So when Bill Bryson calls American pioneer Daniel Boone an idiot for announcing his intention to move because his neighbourhood was becoming too crowded when he saw a wisp of smoke rising from a homesteader's dwelling on a distant mountain, I have to politely disagree. Boone probably knew what would come next: hundreds of square miles of almost identical detached houses with gardens, freeways, shopping malls, strip malls, gas stations, golf courses and diners – all the accoutrements that exurbia brings with it. The far-seeing Mr Boone, you see, knew it would be only a matter of time.

Since Boone's time there's been a steady flow of innovations and inventions across the Atlantic. Over the last 200 years or so we've given them things, they've given us things and we've collectively given stuff to the rest of the world (e.g. 'nylon' – NewYorkLONdon – where it was invented). Science and engineering, communications and politics, economics and the arts, it's been a constant process of exchanging our best ideas. And our worst ideas.

Communication has been one key area. We gave America postage stamps and they hit back with the electric telegraph and the telephone. Radio and television went winging their way west across the Atlantic, followed by the mainframe and personal computers. America responded with the internet and PC operating systems such as DOS, Windows and Apple OS, which made computers useful for more than playing games and pretending school kids could be computer programmers. We replied with the Worldwide Web, so America clobbered us back with *Grand Theft Auto*, which probably served us right.

Nowhere has the interchange been more marked than in television. From the 1950s US TV poured over here with everything from *I Love Lucy* and *The Cisco Kid* to *Superman*. We responded with dramatisations of Dickens and *The Forsyte Saga*, but America proved family sagas could be done bigger and better with *Dynasty* and *Dallas*. *Dr Finlay* passed *Dr Kildare* on a Boeing 707 somewhere in mid-Atlantic while Sir David Frost crossed the ocean to dominate 1970s TV on both sides so often that he joked he sometimes passed himself flying the other way.

Other fields of human activity have also benefited or suffered from this flow. We gave them Keynesianism while they gave us monetarism and the

Chicago School. This was unfair. On the other hand we gave them two world wars and they gave us the weapons and soldiers to help win them. We gave them steam ships and they gave us aircraft – so the carbon guilt's about equal there. They gave us Bill Bryson and we gave them Simon Cowell, so I guess (an Americanism) we owe them big time (another one).

A dangerous export

With a population rising on the back of millions of Europe's huddled masses, America was always going to suffer some sprawl, although many of the nineteenth-and early-twentieth-century emigrants poured into high-density cities. But, even before the First World War, a dangerous idea had crossed the Atlantic from our shores: that sprawl was a *good* thing.

Ebenezer Howard had got his name for his ideal settlement, Garden City, from his stay in America, but the ideas were very much born here and exported over there. Even though the movement was only a few years old, the Garden City Association's former secretary and manager of Letchworth, Thomas Adams, moved to North America before the First World War and spread the idea. Adams was said to be the first person in Britain to make his living entirely from planning; he helped progress the 1909 Town Planning Act and founded the Town Planning Institute, but both left him frustrated at British unwillingness to adopt the sprawl philosophy. So in 1914 he accepted an invitation to become the first town planning advisor to the Dominion of Canada.

Adams had already set out his stall with a speech at a conference in Boston in 1911 where he warned his audience their cities were going to double every 10-20 years.

"Even in Great Britain, every 15 years . . . 500,000 acres of land are covered with houses, factories, workshops and other buildings," he noted. "Now that is a very important fact."

And so it was – he went on to claim that the 1909 Act would secure the planning of 500,000 acres every 15 years, a tacit admission that planned sprawl cities would sprawl at least as fast as unplanned ones. But planning was for "the securing of amenity, convenience and better sanitation" apparently, despite the fact that existing UK legislation was already securing those things.

Canada was trying to cope with nearly a million immigrants who had settled there between 1896 and 1914. Half of these people were living in Canada's towns, there was wild property speculation and little control. It could have been a moment for some sustainable town planning; instead, Canada invited Adams to come and institutionalise sprawl. Within a few years he had junked Canadian towns' grid street pattern that made good use of land and undertook several private design commissions, promoting low-density sprawl at several sites, including Halifax's Richmond district, devastated when a First World War munitions ship blew up.

Garden city ideals quickly spread across North America like the dustbowls of the Depression period as the influence of Adams and other admirers spread. He played a role in founding the American Planning Institute (now the American Institute of Planners) in 1917 and the Town Planning Institute of Canada in 1919. From 1923 to 1930 he was chief planner on the *New York Metropolitan Regional Plan*, in 1932 he became an advisor on home building and home ownership to President Hoover, and in 1935 his *Outline of Town & City Planning* was graced by an introduction by President Roosevelt. So, just as in the UK, the USA and Canada had set up a planning profession capable of protecting the environment but with the recessive sprawl gene firmly within its DNA.

Hypersprawl, exurbs and boomburbs

Adams' arrival was followed by eight decades of sprawl on a scale only Americans could pull off. Much of it was unplanned, facilitated by cheap automobiles and cheap, almost too cheap to price, gasoline. But the planning movement played its part too, providing the intellectual justification for sprawl; zoning laws that rigidly separated housing, shopping and employment; and promoting exemplar low-density suburbs, just as in the UK.

In the 1920s American planners seized on Ebenezer Howard's idea that garden cities should be broken up into 'wards' of 5,000 inhabitants, each with its own local shops, schools and other services, as a way of giving such places an identity, and this featured in Adams' New York plan.

Now it's true that urban areas of such size do have some relevance to planning – it's about the minimum that can support a secondary school, for instance. But city folk tend to take their identity first and foremost from the city, not the suburb, borough, ward or neighbourhood they happen to live in, whose boundaries traditionally tended to be ill-defined (until garden city folks put ring roads around them). An exception, of course, is teenage gangs, but that possibly isn't what Howard had in mind when he turned his baseball cap round and took his posse out to kick ass in the 'hood.

St Ebenezer's ideas, however, soon took root on both sides of the Atlantic, and in America a young planner called Clarence Perry, strongly influenced by garden city planners such as Barry Parker and Raymond Unwin,[3] proposed neighbourhoods with community facilities at the centre and shops around the outside. Perry believed traditional cities had grown through villages merging in an unplanned and unwieldy way, while his neighbourhoods would be separated from each other by main roads to spare them from through traffic. All this actually achieved was to isolate each neighbourhood, place facilities a long way from one another and make the inhabitants fatally car-dependent. But Perry's ideas came back across the Atlantic and strongly influenced Patrick Abercrombie et al.

Perry's ideas were used by Barry Parker at Wythenshawe and in the postwar new towns, most of which developed on the 'neighbourhood' model. In America, the idea was developed by Clarence Stein and Henry Wright at a new development in northern New Jersey called Radburn. This was based on their (accurate) belief that mass motoring would have a profound effect on human society and their (inaccurate) belief that totally segregating routes used by cars and pedestrians was a better approach than the rest of the world's carefully considered philosophy of totally ignoring the problem.

If Radburn sounds a bit like a modern town with pedestrian precincts and traffic calming, don't hold on to that thought. Its pedestrian ways gave access to communal spaces behind the houses while vehicles moved around town on a hierarchy of roads leading to cul-de-sacs behind the houses. It institutionalised the idea that towns should be designed around the motor car, a policy which has wreaked decades of environmental and social destruction. Stein and Wright fixed the idea that low-density suburbia would depend on the motor car – 'Radburn – the town for the motor age' – and while the Radburn idea was little used in America, British planners spent decades squabbling over the neighbourhood philosophy and, worse still, some even adopted the Radburn layout, with disastrous consequences. It litters much post-war new town and council estate planning, and instead of creating the intended close-knit communities it was extraordinarily effective at creating socially deprived ones. The car-free grassland-facing front doors immediately created a sense of isolation while the road round at the back served to isolate homes from the rest of the world. Estate after estate in the UK built on the Radburn principle sank into social problems, and a fortune has been spent over the last 20 years knocking them down and rebuilding them.

"The Radburn layout in particular is a useful reminder that we need to consider the quality of open space and the usefulness of connections," said Oldham Borough Council's *Residential Design Guidelines*.[4] "More of both is not necessarily better."

What would Ebenezer Howard and his followers have made of that?

Heroic sprawl

Much of America's twentieth-century sprawl followed a similar path to Britain's, though on a far vaster scale as they had much more countryside to ruin. America had its own supply of cheap petrol too, allowing people to drive vast 'gas guzzlers' to remote homes, shops and workplaces, and it developed a colossal motor industry and highway network.

"Oh, is the American highway dull," complained Bill Bryson. "As a Briton, you really cannot imagine boredom on this scale (unless you are from Stevenage)."[5]

But if Britain's new towns were dull, consider life in late-twentieth-century US hypersprawl – miles of detached homes, strip malls, shopping complexes, etc. virtually unsupported by public transport, served by highways anything up to 18 lanes wide and where every journey is made in a car. Many traditional urban areas, meanwhile, were sinking into squalor, deprivation and crime. The remains of inter-city rail services were sustained by subsidy and America became the largest greenhouse gas emitter, and largest per-capita greenhouse gas emitter too.

The economic problems of the 1930s placed some restrictions on sprawl, but the post-war world saw it explode on the back of government mortgages for returning GIs; zoning laws that forbade traditional, mixed-use development; and endless, cheap, greenfield land. And it went on, decade after decade: between 1992 and 1997, America built on nearly three million hectares of farmland (about the area of Maryland). By 1994, housing lots exceeding four hectares accounted for more than 55 per cent of the land being developed.

The engine of sprawl on both sides of the Atlantic was the internal combustion engine. In 1922, General Motors set up a unit charged with replacing America's railways and tramways with cars, trucks and buses. It concentrated on the country's 1,200 street and inter-urban railways, which accounted for 90 per cent of all trips made by Americans in the early 1920s. Together with other road industry companies, it created a company to buy tramways, run them down, close them and replace them with buses. It was so successful it fell foul of US law and was hauled up before a federal court in 1949 and fined a massive $5,000. Its roads lobby continued to press politicians (and to buy them sometimes) to build interstate highways and urban freeways.

A 2002 report by Smart Growth America[6] demonstrated how the more US cities sprawled, the higher became the rate of driving and vehicle ownership, while air pollution, road accidents and congestion got worse. The average American was spending the equivalent of 55 eight-hour working days driving each year and, by the end of the twentieth century, sprawl was destroying around a million hectares of open land every year. Inner-city problems in America's rust belt (and elsewhere) made Britain's pale almost into insignificance. Yet sprawl was making many people rich, and millions of America's believed the social isolation it enforced was enriching their lives.

US car dependency has often been 100 per cent, with a complete absence of other means of transport. *Image: US Environmental Protection Agency, Smart Growth Program*

The anti-sprawl movement

As in the UK, some Americans have been trying to protect their land from over-development since the nineteenth century. Scottish-born explorer John Muir (1838-1914), for instance, is revered on both sides of the Atlantic. He helped found the Sierra Club, was active in protecting wilderness areas such as Yosemite, and today is regarded as the father of the national parks movement.

But although sprawl spread across twentieth-century America like a disease and voices were beginning to question it by the 1950s, effective action took longer. Oregon was one state where things began to move in the 1960s, when Governor Mark Hatfield spoke out against the damage speculators were doing to the state's beautiful landscape. When the state's chamber of commerce began touting a 20-mile stretch of Highway 101 as 'Twenty Miracle Miles', Hatfield dubbed it 'Twenty Miserable Miles'. In the 1970s a Bill was brought before the state senate by Governor Tom McCall and two senators, Democrat Ted Hallock and Republican Hector McPherson, and it's an interesting reflection on US politics that opposition to sprawl has always crossed its party political divide, as it does this side of the pond.

The Bill was designed to limit sprawl and protect forests and farmland, and a new state agency was created to take it forward, but although the state's legislation and planning measures have never been 100-per-cent effective, the bene-fits are plain to see. Despite this, Oregon has a well-organised sprawl lobby too, and in the late 2000s tried to bring in legislation to make the state pay compen-sation to landowners refused planning permission for development.

Between 1970 and 2000, twelve states introduced state-wide planning measures aimed at limiting sprawl, with varying degrees of success (although Oregon's remained the most comprehensive), and by that time one-third of all states were pursuing some such reform.

Urbanism . . .

America's cities emerged unscathed from the Second World War, but the dec-ades that followed were to see the same destruction wrought by slum clear-ance, Modern movement architecture and urban road building (or worse) as suffered by UK cities.

'Hack journalists' – Daniel Defoe, George Orwell, etc. – have put in several appearances in this tale, and the tale of US urbanism brings us face-to-face with another. Jane Jacobs was born in 1916 and went through several jobs in jour-nalism before lighting up as associate editor of *Architectural Forum* in 1952. In 1950s New York and other cities she saw the same knock-it-down-and-replace-it-with-a-concrete-box-and-an-urban-freeway policy that was destroy-ing British cities. Around American cities she saw the same suburban sprawl whose origins lay in the garden cities and suburbs movement, horribly mutated. In 1961 she published her ideas in one of the most seminal works of environmentalism and communitarianism ever written, *The Death and Life of Great American Cities.*[7]

Jacobs was one of the first to question the wisdom of the garden sprawl and Modern movement gurus at a time when they enjoyed widespread worship. Ebenezer Howard, she wrote "set spinning powerful and city-destroying ideals", noting his obsession with wholesome housing as a suburban and small town concept, and dubbed him a paternalist rather than a communitarian planner. She accused him of ignoring cities' intricate, many-faceted cultural life and their role in politics and economics.

"Both in his preoccupations and in his omissions, Howard made sense in his own terms but none in terms of city planning," she wrote. "Yet virtually all modern city planning has been adapted from, and embroidered on, this silly substance."[8]

This was powerful, unfashionable stuff but, aware as she was of the sprawl lobby's great influence, she had the courage to characterise Howard's US follow-ers, including Stein, Wright, Bauer and the well-known planner and friend of

F. J. Osborn, Lewis Mumford, by a name Catherine Bauer had used – 'decentrists'.

She was as contemptuous of the Modern movement's great patron saint, Le Corbusier, and especially of his vision of the city reborn as 'The Radiant City' – radiant city! Given its destructive capacity, Radiation City would have been nearer the mark.

Jacobs was, perhaps, the first to make a link between Howard and Le Corbusier, whom she also identifies as a decentrist, for both wanted to trash traditional cities, though in different ways. For while Jacobs noted the antagonism between modernists and decentrists, she was adamant Le Corbusier's Radiant City depended on the Garden City. Garden city planners, she said, wanted "the super block, the project neighbourhood, the unchangeable plan and grass, grass, grass" and had established them as the hallmarks of humane, socially responsible, high-minded planning.

"If the great object of city planning was that Christopher Robin might go hoppety-hoppety on the grass, what was wrong with Le Corbusier?" she wrote. "The decentrists' cries of institutionalization, mechanization, depersonalization seemed to others foolishly sectarian."[9]

With the twentieth century's two great peacetime city destroyers, modernism and sprawl, working in tandem to destroy cities, along came the third Apocalyptic Horseman, urban freeways, to condemn US cities as surely as their British counterparts in the 1960s. And, as Jane Jacobs noted, Le Corbusier would certainly have approved.

The 1960s saw Jacobs fighting all three forces and campaigning against a scheme to knock down Greenwich Village for 'slum clearance', and she fought and won a battle against a plan for a road that would have taken the Village's green space.

New York's master builder of the time, Robert Moses, who had successfully swept away vast areas of the city to let more cars in was reduced to shouting at her: "There is nobody against this – nobody, nobody, nobody, but a bunch of . . . a bunch of mothers!"

. . . and new urbanism

By 1990, a few American architects were challenging the orthodoxy of big boxes, shopping malls, strip malls and urban sprawl. Each had designed neighbourhoods or new settlements that used traditional urban forms and which tried to respect existing urban development, including Andrés Duany's and Elizabeth Plater-Zyberk's Seaside model community in Florida, featuring mixed uses and traditional architectural forms.

Jane Jacobs   (1916-2006)

The radical urbanist Jane Jacobs was born Jane Butzner in Scranton but moved to New York as a teenager during the Great Depression and was soon attracted to the bohemianism of Greenwich Village. After working as a secretary and a stenographer, she eventually broke into journalism the hard way, working as a freelance in her spare time. She married architect Robert Jacobs in 1944 and, pushing a pram around Manhattan, began to accumulate a consumer's view of town planning.

In 1952 she joined the magazine *Architectural Forum* and became increasingly critical of both the sprawl lobby and the modernists' depredations on the vibrancy of city life, a process she later mocked as the "Radiant Garden City Beautiful". Gradually the diverse, lively and vital city she knew was being knocked down for motorways and mega-projects to house the poor, which strongly exacerbated racial segregation. She came to see that cities worked when they were acceptable to citizens.

An essay in *Fortune* magazine won her a Rockefeller Foundation grant, and with this she wrote *The Death and Life of Great American Cities*.

But her attacks hit home and prompted abuse from the sprawl lobby, with Lewis Mumford penning an attack in the *New Yorker* entitled 'Mother Jacobs' Home Remedy for Urban Cancer'. Gender politics has never been the sprawl lobby's strong point, and Jacobs' writing, combining erudite intellectualism with down-home, folksy wisdom, hit home because it touched levels of understanding that the architectural and commercial elite were keen to ignore.

The family moved to Canada in 1968 and Jacobs soon found herself involved in Toronto's community politics. A string of books followed: *The Economy of Cities* (1969), *Cities and the Wealth of Nations: Principles of Economic Life* (1984), *Systems of Survival: A Dialogue on the Moral Foundations of Commerce and Politics* (1994), *The Nature of Economies* (2000) and *Dark Age Ahead* (2004).

Jacobs, now seen as the founding mother of urbanism, knew that even vibrant cities have multiple problems but they also have the potential to solve those problems themselves. Imagining that today's problems can be solved in slow-moving rustic surroundings was a waste of time, she thought. There are too many of us and the opportunities cities offer are too good to waste.

"Big cities and countrysides can get on well together," she wrote. "Big cities need countryside close by. And countryside – from man's point of view – needs big cities, with all their diverse opportunities and productivity, so human beings can be in a position to appreciate the rest of the natural world instead of to curse it."

In 1993, Duany, Plater-Zyberk and other architects formed the Congress for New Urbanism, which has grown steadily since. The Congress states its mission as "the restructuring of public policy and development practices to support the restoration of existing urban centres and towns within coherent metropolitan regions" and "reconfiguration of sprawling suburbs into communities of real neighbourhoods and diverse districts, the conservation of natural environments, and the preservation of our built legacy".

Modernist architects have spent years sniping at this apparently unexceptional statement, and the new urbanists have had to battle to pursue their ideals against forces such as the separate-use zoning and merciless highway development that Jane Jacobs fought against. And it wasn't only sprawl and high-rise town centres that had to be opposed: the new urbanists pursued ideas that would have been commonplace until the twentieth century dictated otherwise, such as footways in town centres and the opportunity for people to meet on the street. They began pursuing higher-density neighbourhoods where pedestrians and cyclists could actually reach shops, schools, health care and even their neighbours without jumping in their cars.

Decades of car dependency are starting to be rolled back.
Image: US Environmental Protection Agency, Smart Growth Program

As Bill Bryson wrote in 1998:

> I had this brought home to me last summer when we were driving across Maine and stopped for coffee in one of those endless zones of shopping malls, motels, petrol stations and fast food places that sprout everywhere in America these days. I needed a particular book and anyway I figured this would give my wife a chance to spend some important quality time with four restive, overheated children. Although the bookshop was no more than 50 or 60 feet away, I discovered there was no way to get there on foot. There was a traffic crossing for cars, but no provision for pedestrians and no way to cross without dodging through three lanes of swiftly turning traffic.[10]

At long last, the tide of opinion is turning against towns with no sidewalks, although plenty still survive. And although few British towns ever went quite this far, there is plenty we can learn.

The new urbanists proposed other shocking things, such as public spaces where people could meet for purposes other than destroying their bodies with dangerous narcotics or industrial quantities of alcohol. They suggested rundown city areas could be regenerated without knocking them down, something we have been forgetting since relearning it in the 1970s. Above all, they suggested something that was heresy to both modernists and the sprawl lobby: that people could live in close proximity without being surrounded by vast areas of grass.

Transit-oriented development

Americans are even more addicted to their cars than we are, but the closing years of the twentieth century saw the birth of another movement, supporting 'transit-oriented development'.

The term goes back to work by the architect Peter Calthorpe, one of the founders of New Urbanism, in California in the late 1980s. He suggested developing dense, mixed-use, pedestrian-friendly and socially and economically diverse neighbourhoods, centred on transit stations. A century ago this would have been pretty commonplace, but America had abandoned it almost entirely.

A body called the Great American Station Foundation was set up in 1995 to revitalise historic railway stations, both to improve public transport and to act as a focus to bring life back to town centres. Such projects soon proved to have enormous potential for both purposes and offered an opportunity to move towns back towards transit rather than the car. In 2002, the organisation was to become the basis for Reconnecting America, with a broader remit.

The basic transit-oriented development idea was to develop compact residential and commercial areas around transit stations or corridors with high-quality service, good pedestrian access, parking controls, traffic management, etc., to maximise the attractiveness of the rail-based option.

Its basic principles are:

- walkable design with pedestrians the highest priority
- railway stations as prominent features of town centres
- regional nodes containing a mixture of uses in close proximity, including office, residential, retail and civic uses
- high-density, high-quality development within a 10-minute walk around a railway station
- transit systems, including trolleys, streetcars, light rail and buses, etc.
- easy use of bicycles, scooters and rollerblades as everyday support transportation systems
- reduced and managed parking inside 10-minute walking circles around town centres and railway stations.

Densification at a transit stop – you can overdo it.
Image: US Environmental Protection Agency, Smart Growth Program

Edwardian towns were compact, functional and mobile.
Image: National Tramway Museum

But the twentieth century sacrificed towns to the motor car and tower block.

Victorian houses were superbly efficient users of land.

While twentieth-century homes just squandered it.

Our town centres and their shops are dying.

Because, just up the road . . .

Ever-bigger motorways won't solve congestion.

America tried and failed. *Image: Nicholle McClelland-Beteille*

America embraced sprawl on the grand scale. *Image: EcoFlight / Bruce Gordon*

But we're still sprawling here too. *Image: Henry Oliver*

Smart Growth is bringing a different kind of development to America.
Image: US Environmental Protection Agency, Smart Growth Program

Decades of car dependency are starting to be rolled back.
Image: US Environmental Protection Agency, Smart Growth Program

Yesterday's garden cities depended on the motor car.

Tomorrow's sustainable towns will be built around different forms of transport.
Image: Jim Harkins

Our town centres must find genuine ways of reviving.

America is finding answers in transit-oriented development.
Image: US Environmental Protection Agency, Smart Growth Program

Americans are deeply devoted to their cars, even more than we are. When Bill Bryson went back to live in a small New England town where he could be within walking distance of the shops in 1998, he soon realised his decision was considered eccentric. Neighbours would draw up alongside him as he walked to offer a lift, and drive off guiltily when it was refused, as if they were leaving the scene of an accident.

"Not long after we moved here we had the people next door round for dinner and – I swear this is true – they drove," he recalled.[11] "I was astounded. (I recall asking them jokingly if they used a light aircraft to get to the super-market, which simply drew blank looks and the mental scratching of my name from all future invitation lists)."

A study by the University of California in the 1990s rated 85 per cent of Americans as "essentially sedentary" and 35 per cent "totally sedentary". "The fact is, Americans not only don't walk anywhere, they won't walk any-where, and woe to anyone who tries to make them," concluded Bryson.

But in case anyone's feeling smug at how superior we are, just look around you – it won't take long to find parents who drive obese kids three or four hundred metres to school every day in a four-wheel-drive gas guzzler. Bizarrely, people feel safer in these lumbering monsters because they have gigantic tyres and the driver sits marginally higher than other drivers. The fact that this makes them less stable, that they're destroying the planet, that people with brains snigger at those who drive them in urban environments doesn't register at all. Hey, they might run into a midsummer blizzard on the school run or a swamp, mountain or desert they hadn't previously spotted on the way to the supermarket. Look around you at the out-of-town shopping, the motorways, the car parks and the rest of it we've excreted on our poor little island in the last 50 years, and let's not get smug at all.

Things have improved in America since the 1990s, and dozens of cities are building transit lines and intensifying the development around them – in con-trast to the UK in the 2000s. New zoning laws and new neighbourhoods around transit stops and corridors began to replace sprawl as America's default mode.

Take Arlington, Virginia, for instance. Its general land use plan now con-centrates dense, mixed-use development at five metro stations known as the Rosslyn-Ballston corridor. Within a few years these 'urban villages' gained 21 million square feet of new office development, 3,000 hotel rooms and 25,000 homes – and saved around 14 square miles of countryside from sprawl. Metro ridership doubled between 1991 and 2002 and nearly 50 per cent of commuter journeys now use it. The corridor became so popular that lack of affordable housing became a problem.

Smart Growth was born from these ideas in the 1990s.

A smart idea

In the autumn of 1991, the Local Government Commission invited architects Peter Calthorpe, Michael Corbett, Andrés Duany, Elizabeth Moule, Elizabeth Plater-Zyberk, Stefanos Polyzoides and Daniel Solomon to develop a new set of principles for land use planning. A group of urban design professionals was then brought together for a meeting at the Ahwahnee Hotel in California's Yosemite National Park. They agreed a set of principles for resource-efficient communities, out of which came both new urbanism and the Smart Growth movement.

The original principles were aimed at elected state and municipal officials, giving them a blueprint for creation of compact, mixed-use, walkable, transit-oriented development. These principles were later joined by Ahwahnee principles for economic development, for water and for climate change.

The Ahwahnee Principles for Resource-Efficient Communities

Community principles
- All planning should be in the form of complete and integrated communities containing housing, shops, workplaces, schools, parks and civic facilities essential to the daily life of the residents.
- Community size should be designed so that housing, jobs, daily needs and other activities are within easy walking distance of each other.
- As many activities as possible should be located within easy walking distance of transit stops.
- A community should contain a diversity of housing types to enable citizens from a wide range of economic levels and age groups to live within its boundaries.
- Businesses within the community should provide a range of job types for the community's residents.
- The location and character of the community should be consistent with a larger transit network.
- The community should have a centre focus that combines commercial, civic, cultural and recreational uses.
- The community should contain an ample supply of specialized open space in the form of squares, greens and parks whose frequent use is encouraged through placement and design.
- Public spaces should be designed to encourage the attention and presence of people at all hours of the day and night.
- Each community or cluster of communities should have a well-defined edge, such as agricultural greenbelts or wildlife corridors, permanently protected from development.
- Streets, pedestrian paths and bike paths should contribute to a system of fully connected and interesting routes to all destinations. Their design should encourage pedestrian and bicycle use by being small and spatially defined by buildings, trees and lighting, and by discouraging high-speed traffic.

The term 'Smart Growth' seems to have been coined in Maryland, where the newly elected governor Parris Glendening took a strong anti-sprawl line from the time of his election in 1995, and within two years the state had adopted a package of around a dozen measures to address sprawl and concentrate development where infrastructure existed, and made a change to tax laws to stop subsidising sprawl. It was called the 'Smart Growth tool bag'.

In 1996 the federal Environmental Protection Agency created the Smart Growth Network, which brought together environmental groups, heritage organisations, professional bodies, developers, the property industry and local and state government. Its mission was stated to be "to encourage development that serves the economy, community and environment". Among its early initiatives, it formulated a set of Smart Growth principles (see box overleaf).

- Wherever possible, the natural terrain, drainage and vegetation of the community should be preserved, with superior examples contained within parks or greenbelts.
- The community design should help conserve resources and minimize waste.
- Communities should provide for the efficient use of water through the use of natural drainage, drought-tolerant landscaping and recycling.
- The street orientation, the placement of buildings and the use of shading should contribute to the energy-efficiency of the community.

Regional principles
- The regional land-use planning structure should be integrated within a larger transportation network built around transit rather than freeways.
- Regions should be bounded by and provide a continuous system of greenbelt/ wildlife corridors to be determined by natural conditions.
- Regional institutions and services (government, stadiums, museums, etc.) should be located in the urban core.
- Materials and methods of construction should be specific to the region, exhibiting a continuity of history and culture and compatibility with the climate to encourage the development of local character and community identity.

Implementation principles
- The general plan should be updated to incorporate the above principles.
- Rather than allowing developer-initiated, piecemeal development, local governments should take charge of the planning process. General plans should designate where new growth, infill or redevelopment will be allowed to occur.
- Prior to any development, a specific plan should be prepared based on these planning principles.
- Plans should be developed through an open process and participants in the process should be provided with visual models of all planning proposals.

Smart Growth and Maryland

The state of Maryland pioneered the use of Smart Growth in the 1990s in response to rapidly rising population and sprawl. Between 1973 and 2002, its population grew by over 30 per cent and its built-up area sprawled by no less than 98 per cent, while a quarter of its farm and forest areas was lost. Its population is still rising – a further million residents are expected by 2030, so urgent measures were needed.

In 1997 the state's Assembly passed the Smart Growth and Neighbourhood Conservation Act to begin the process of curbing the sprawl. Priority funding areas (PFAs), which direct state spending to existing communities and certain other places where growth was expected, were created so that resources could be targeted at sustainable locations rather than subsidising sprawl. Yet 25 per cent of new homes continued to be built outside the PFAs – and swallowed 75 per cent of the land being used for housing.

Baltimore has been a significant beneficiary, with a billion dollars committed to revitalising 28 blocks of Downtown Baltimore's west side to create a vibrant, mixed-use neighbourhood. Lauraville, a quiet older residential neighbourhood of the city, had been cut in half by a six-lane commuter route; this was tamed and substantial investment was made in making the area walkable and enhancing its open spaces.

The town of Cumberland became the state's first Main Street community, where resources were put in to revive a town centre with an eclectic mix of shops, side streets and old buildings. With work to encourage tourism and enhance heritage it became the state's first Certified Heritage Centre.

New legislation since then requires local authorities to include water resources and long-term sustainability in their planning, and a further Act in 2009 strengthened the Smart Growth control.

The new legislation is based on principles which address a wide range of sustainability issues, and local planning commissions must now report on their compliance with Smart Growth indicators every year.

Revitalising Baltimore. *Image: US Environmental Protection Agency, Smart Growth Program*

US Smart Growth Network principles

1. Mix land uses.
2. Take advantage of compact building design.
3. Create housing opportunities and choices for a range of household types, family sizes and incomes.
4. Create walkable neighbourhoods.
5. Foster distinctive, attractive communities with a strong sense of place.
6. Preserve open space, farmland, natural beauty, and critical environmental areas.
7. Reinvest in and strengthen existing communities and achieve more balanced regional development.
8. Provide a variety of transportation choices.
9. Make development decisions predictable, fair, and cost-effective.
10. Encourage citizen and stakeholder participation in development decisions.

From the start, coalition working has been a feature of the Smart Growth movement, with citizens' groups, legislators, professionals, etc. working together.[12] It's an holistic philosophy, based on compact urban development which is walkable, permeable, community-friendly and transit-oriented. It has never confined itself simply to spatial and transport planning, but the early work inevitably concentrated in these areas where the need was most obvious and, early on, it worked through state and city government.

Another trend that came to the fore in the 1990s was the reuse of brownfield land in cities, and a key element of Smart Growth is that it enables you to make best use of existing infrastructure, rather than wasting vast sums of money building new infrastructure on greenfield sites. It's hugely environmentally wasteful to create new sewers, utility networks, roads, schools, hospitals, etc. when such infrastructure lies underused in nearby towns. It wastes land and it burns huge quantities of carbon in creating all the concrete and so on. It wastes vast sums of public money too.

These considerations began to filter into state thinking during the 1990s and soon collided with complaints that American citizens' freedom to build where they like was being infringed. But, as Maryland's state planning director remarked, Smart Growth policies actually put an end to the insidious idea that state governments had an open-ended obligation to fund roads, schools and sewers wherever developers chose to develop, at whatever the cost to the public purse.[13] And states were able to redistribute funds from prosperous sprawl areas to less-well-off but needier older urban areas.

Smart Growth is bringing America a new kind of development.
Image: US Environmental Protection Agency, Smart Growth Program

As America's inner-city problem began to make even Britain's look puny, many of its older cities became known for crime, deprivation and decay; and while the affluent fled to remote suburbs, the poor and disadvantaged remained. But, by the end of the 1990s, several states were aiming to put urban regeneration on a legislative, planning and building code level with new development; some authorities took powers to implement transit-oriented development, mixed-use development, etc.; and Smart Growth coalitions multiplied. Gradually, road building began to cease being the default mode and urban transit suddenly saw an end to its decades of investment starvation. A handful of cities actually began demolishing urban freeways.

Nationally, the movement's momentum began to gather too. The Smart Growth Network had taken it to the heart of government and it survived attempts by economic liberals to destroy it during the George W. Bush administration. The local coalitions and national professional and interest groups needed some national focus, and Smart Growth America was set up as the national coalition in 2000, with more than 100 partner organisations.

In the UK, as we saw in Chapter 6, the old, dismal coalition of roads lobby, sprawl lobby and vested interest continued to undermine attempts to make development more sustainable as the new century went on. But in America the

Smart Growth movement and its constituent parts have continued to gather momentum and support from across the political spectrum. Cities and states began to sign up, and eventually that reached the heart of the federal government in Washington.

Change we could believe in

Perhaps the highest-profile sympathiser was President Barack Obama. During his election campaign in 2008 he was handed a copy of Jane Jacobs' *The Death and Life of Great American Cities* and called it "a great book". Politicians all too often disappoint once elected, and, while Obama may have struggled to legislate on health care or climate change, his administration began another quiet revolution in Washington. Three departments, the Department of Housing and Urban Development (HUD), the Department of Transportation and the Environmental Protection Agency (EPA), which had hitherto largely worked in isolation, were persuaded to work together through a new Partnership for Sustainable Communities to secure sustainable policies with a strong Smart Growth look to them. The 2010 budget backed this with $150 million in support of its six 'liveability principles':

- provide more transportation choices
- promote equitable, affordable housing
- increase economic competitiveness
- support existing communities
- leverage federal investment
- value communities and neighbourhoods.

In support of the Partnership, HUD set up an Office of Sustainable Housing and Communities (OSHC), announced at the New Partners for Smart Growth conference in Seattle in February 2010. The conference was in its ninth year and by that time was attracting over a thousand delegates – something of a contrast with a country that couldn't attract any delegates to a conference on sustainable planning because 'there's nothing the Yanks can teach us'.

Housing and urban development secretary Shaun Donovan told the conference the OSHC would build stronger, more sustainable communities, by connecting housing to jobs, fostering local innovation and building a clean energy economy. Five brownfield areas (brownfield means contaminated land in America, while in the UK it simply means previously developed) close to public transit in areas where affordable housing is needed would become pilots for remediation and redevelopment.

The Partnership is making efforts in another area that sprawl lobbies on both sides of the Atlantic have been determined to ignore too – water. The EPA

Smart Growth has helped Americans rediscover walking.
Image: US Environmental Protection Agency, Smart Growth Program

is working to find out just how much investment is needed to modernise water and sewage infrastructure.

"By targeting these funds toward existing communities that are adopting strategies like transit-oriented, mixed-use development and brownfield redevelopment, states can contribute significantly to community stability while helping preserve treasured rural landscapes," EPA deputy administrator Mathy Stanislaus told the conference.

It's an extraordinary turn-round in 20 years – three ministers (Donovan, Stanislaus and transportation secretary Ray LaHood) crossing America to attend a Smart Growth conference.

OSHC director Shelley Poticha told an interviewer after the conference that one of the big lessons of the last decade is that cities do have the ability to envisage a new future and put it into action in a relatively short period of time.

Look at Salt Lake City, which is planning and building a whole new light rail and commuter and bus system. They are building at a faster pace than anywhere else in the country. One thing they did was to create a shared vision of what they wanted their region to be when it grew up.

They worked very deeply with citizens, the community and business leaders, understanding that the only way they could maintain their shared values with regard to community, family and affordable lifestyles was to think about how they were growing and the kind of infrastructure they were investing in. A lot of the development happening there is infill – recycling old dead shopping malls and strip centres, for example – and it's not just government-led. It's happening through partnerships with the private sector.[14]

Old, dead shopping malls and strip centres – there's a vision of the future. And what America has achieved in just a decade or so shows what can be done. This is change we can believe in because it can happen, but *only* if we believe in it.

California and SB375

"California did not invent sprawl," noted one of the state's conservationists, "but it made sprawl famous." In a state where 50-mile drives to work are commonplace, sprawl has become a way of life for many Californians.

Today the state is part of the movement to make sprawl infamous, and, with Republican Arnold Schwarzenegger as governor, is proving that Smart Growth cuts across America's deep political divide.

Attempts to legislate to ensure that development reduces greenhouse gas emissions go back to 2006, when the state's Assembly enshrined some requirements in state law. The real push came two years later, however, when legislation was introduced into the state's senate that included a range of emission-reduction legislation, including support for transit-oriented development, mixed land use and land-use plans that emphasise compact development and oppose urban sprawl.

The bill, called SB375, soon ran into opposition from the construction industry, which launched a feeble alternative bill of its own, and city mayors, who objected to the state telling them what to do. But although SB375 was damaged, it passed into law. It lost the mandatory targets that would have given its Smart Growth provisions real teeth, but still demands sustainable community strategies, although in its reduced form it doesn't prevent local authorities from approving sprawl developments. But for the first time a state had legislation linking climate change to transportation, housing and land use.

Although critics continued to moan that it was hurting their business, a 2010 report by the Urban Land Institute concluded that SB375 is actually boosting the state economy by reducing the wasteful use of resources that sprawl causes. It pointed out that while brownfield development may cost more than greenfield, long-term savings on municipal costs hugely outweigh this.

Atlanta – capital of sprawl

Atlanta – Atlantic Station. *Image: US Environmental Protection Agency, Smart Growth Program*

Perhaps the city that best deserved the title of 'capital of sprawl' was Atlanta, described in the 1990s as "the fastest growing settlement in human history". It grew from 130 square miles in 1950 to more than 8,000 square miles today. Every day Atlantans collectively drive the distance from the Earth to the sun, and the average employee is driving 66 miles a day – the average! Its cheap, new housing was always built at the edge, so today only 10 per cent of its population lives in the city proper.

And yet . . . this is a story of hope, for the tide has been turned, even in Atlanta. Smart Growth practitioners cite Atlantic Station, a 55-hectare former steel-mill site being redeveloped as retail, offices, hotel, parkland, etc.; or the Atlanta beltline, one of America's more ambitious Smart Growth projects. Along an abandoned rail corridor that circled Atlanta is being built a new transit route, parks and trails – a 'transit greenway' (despite its huge size, Atlanta has less park space than any other American city).

Tysons Corner

Tysons Corner sounds like it belongs in a boxing ring but, situated on the edge of Washington DC, it is classic low-density American sprawl utterly dependent on the car.

Over 50 years it grew from a country crossroads into America's twelfth-largest employment centre and one of its largest retail centres. But its 1,700 acres include 900 acres of car parking, with office parks and chain stores set amidst 167,000 parking spaces – more parking spaces than there are residents and workers combined. Beyond that are long, wide suburban roads without even a sidewalk. But plans have been laid by Virginia's Fairfax County to 'desprawl' Tysons Corner thanks to the planned extension of the DC metro system 23 miles to Dulles Airport. This will pass through Tysons Corner, where four stations are intended to anchor four new urban villages, each with its own character – a shopping district, an arts district, etc. The plan proposes that housing

It will connect neighbourhoods that were once separated by the railroads and will stimulate higher-density development. Another encouraging project is Glenwood Park, a new urban village that, at first sight, could be a pre-war development. A decade ago it was eleven contaminated hectares of derelict industrial land, but eventually it will have 350 homes of a variety of sizes and tenures, shops and offices, and its buildings will incorporate low-impact environmental measures. It's also helping to regenerate surrounding areas that had fallen on hard times. Garages are relegated to the back of homes, a big surprise in a country where houses' front elevation is frequently wholly dominated by a double garage. It's designed around a classic main street and a traditional town square surrounded by three- or four-storey buildings. That sounds very much like traditional town development allied with modern needs and technology.

Glenwood Park's lead developer Charles Brewer says its key thing is its walkability – but that depends on having somewhere to walk to, hence its compactness and having a mix of different elements including parks. To be walkable, says Brewer, the place needs to be interesting and safe – from crime and from "the damned cars". And before we get smug, let's remember all the places in the UK where many people live but which are neither interesting nor walkable nor, indeed, safe from the damned car.

Glenwood Park hasn't been immune from America's recent property crash, of course, but it's surviving and prospering, unlike lots of outer sprawl exurbs.

Atlanta still has far to go, as do many American cities, yet all over America towns are embracing these Smart Growth forms of development. But it was a long road back.

would be packed in with retail and office space, all with the aim of allowing people to commute, shop, meet friends, etc. without getting in their cars – something that would have been considered an un-American activity just a few years ago.

The hope is to draw in an extra 100,000 residents and to create a sort of second metropolis for the region. Sadly, the plans also include tower blocks up to 25 storeys high, which does expose the danger of getting *too* metropolitan in your thinking, but this is no new Manhattan – 10 per cent of the town would still be parks and open spaces. The plan has attracted some criticism from those who feel it may just be too intensified and could create a lot of traffic; some scaling back has occurred and, unfortunately, some more road capacity is included. But it will be fascinating to watch if, and how, Tysons Corner develops, with or without tower blocks.

PART III

Chapter 9

Care and maintenance for a small country – Smart Growth planning

Britain is, for all its topographical diversity and timeless majesty, an exceedingly small-scale place.

Bill Bryson, *Notes from a Small Island*

The road to Wigan

Technically speaking, I suppose, most of us Britons have lived in towns since Victorian times, but today, in practice, most of us live in suburbs. Exactly where urbs end and suburbs begin sounds like a promising PhD thesis, although my Smart-Growth-oriented brain would place the boundary between pre-1914 urban development and low-density twentieth-century sprawl.

Towns are places where people live relatively sustainable lives and suburbs are places where they don't. Towns are where citizens live; suburbs are where consumers live. Towns are places where we can walk to the shops, cycle to school, meet people on the street and chat; suburbs often aren't. Towns are the future; suburbs are going to be one of the future's major challenges.

Towns have surprised and delighted our travel writers, and one particular one seems to attract them in droves. H. V. Morton admitted he was "expecting the worst" as he approached Wigan, imagining dreary streets, stagnant canals and white-faced Wigonians dragging their feet through their horror of a town. But though he knew the jokes about Wigan Pier, he ended up liking the place.

It is surprising to find a place which still bears all the signs of an old-fashioned country town. Its wide main street meanders down a hill in a casual, leisurely way. Along this street are many modern half-timbered buildings. The Corporation of Wigan has made a rule that buildings on the main streets must be rebuilt in the Tudor style, so that in 20 years or so there will not be a more original or better-looking manufacturing town in the north of England.[1]

No doubt it would have been better had the Corporation worried more about preserving what it had than promoting mock-Tudor; what can you say about it except that it was better than most of the junk they've put up since the Second World War and you get used to it, like an old sweater?

But Wigan has been sucking in travel writers for hundreds of years. Celia Fiennes found "Wiggon" a pretty market town built of stone and brick. "Here it is that the fine Channell Coales are in perfection – burns as light as a candle – set the Coales together with some fire and it shall give a snap and burn up light".[2] Daniel Defoe was similarly impressed with the coal.[3] John Wesley found his congregation there "as wild as might be; yet none made the least disturbance" and as he walked down the street they stared, "but none said an uncivil word".[4]

Bill Bryson admired its neat and well looked-after terraces ("every fourth one seemed to be a hairdresser's"),[5] and Wigan has finally managed to breed a travel writer of its own in Stuart Maconie, described by Peter Kay as "the best thing to come out of Wigan since the A58 to Bolton". Maconie notes that modern Wigan is best known for its pies, for Uncle Joe's Mint Balls and as the home of Wallace and Gromit.[6]

But a slump was to follow close behind Morton's visit to Wigan, and inspired its best-known piece of travel writing in George Orwell's *The Road to Wigan Pier*,[7] which catalogues the destruction of people's lives by poverty and still arouses mixed feelings among Wigonians. But, curiously, Walter Wilkinson's Punch & Judy show rolled into Wigan around the same time.[8] He found few people about and he too was horrified by the broken spirit of men, a third of whom were unemployed, squatting on kerbs staring into space. And yet . . . when he brought his puppet show into the town, its qualities still shone through the grinding poverty for, as an elderly local told him, "Well, ah've stood it for 40 years, and ah don't feel mooch like changing nah."

Wilkinson noted that Wigan still had bright and breezy streets, and cafés that looked smart and new wherein sat ladies consuming meat pies for tea, followed by Eccles cakes.

The shops are well stocked, as they well may be, for the town serves a district of a quarter of a million people, and on Saturday night progress through the streets of Wigan amounts to standing patiently until you are

Wigan's bright and breezy streets. *Image: National Tramway Museum*

shoved, I understand. Shopping there is delightful after more pretentious and affected markets. You are served by human beings who are interested in what they are doing, and who take a particular interest in you as a stranger.[9]

In today's average shopping centre, of course, few are shopping for food or household items as these have been leached out by supermarkets only really usable with a car. The range of shops is vastly reduced and is dominated by banks and charity shops. In the evening the centres no longer bustle but accommodate the 'evening economy' – youngsters pouring booze down their necks with almost religious intensity. You know you've reached the 'vodka and vomit' zone in my local shopping centre on a Friday or Saturday night by the line of police vans and an ambulance ready to deal with hostilities or casualties. It's city life, but not citizen life, and the consumer society has become the alcohol-consumer society.

A really sustainable communities plan

We need to find what lessons we can learn from Wigan's long survival through the ups and downs of economics and history. It's easy to see why the housing-led sprawl of the sustainable communities plan (see Chapter 6) is no way to plan sustainable communities, but what would a Smart Growth alternative look like?

The UK is a crowded, cramped and over-exploited little country with 60 million people crammed into a space capable of supporting less than half that, and the English part is more cramped still. Our starting point must surely be recognising that this requires some very careful planning.

But what sort of future population must we plan for? Our country's tottering ecology may well have to sustain even more of these large and destructive primates than it presently does, and all of us will want housing, feeding, watering, employing, educating, defecation facilities (sorry, but that's actually important), recreation, supplying with consumer goods and healing when we're sick.

In 2009, the Office for National Statistics projected the UK population rising from 61.4 million in 2008 to 65.6 million in 2018 and 71.6 million in 2033. This sort of population growth would be unsustainable anywhere, let alone in a desperately overcrowded country, but the popular reaction to the figures demonstrated the immaturity of national debate. There were howls from right-wing parties and newspapers about swamping and retorts from the more liberal press that our economy would collapse at once if our freedom to loot the brightest and best-qualified young people from poor countries were curtailed in any way. Somewhere, the fact that we seem to be generating internal population growth of our own, that recent immigrants have a higher birth rate because they're more likely to be of childbearing age, and that some of them are genuinely fleeing repressive regimes got buried, but it is inescapable that net inward immigration is contributing significantly to our growing population. We have spent more than 100 years subsidising our economy by importing people to do the jobs too unpleasant or lowly paid for us to do, or in areas where wages are insufficient to pay for the basic standard of housing indigenous folk demand. Of course this is also symptomatic of a 100-year drift south-eastwards of Britain's population and governments' increasing inability to deal with this through effective regional policy. Perhaps one day we can learn to celebrate diversity, uncouple the population debate from its racist aspects and treat the issue seriously. Or perhaps rising unemployment will make this country a less attractive place to move to.

Whatever the future population growth, however, we will still be overcrowded and we will need to protect our countryside so it can continue to supply ecosystem services to a rising number of people in a world less able to supply resources from other regions. We've treated rising population as a social challenge and an economic opportunity, but it's also a significant environmental threat. The need for a Smart Growth approach which makes cities more compact grows ever stronger.

The proximity principle

The starting point must be to tackle our addiction to sprawl. Our small and overcrowded country has spent a reckless hundred years squandering land on low-density living. It's time we worked out how to live in closer proximity to each other.

The Campaign to Protect Rural England's 2008 report *The Proximity Principle*[10] by Sustainable Development Commission vice-chair Rebecca Willis called the twentieth century the "century of dispersal" and asked if living ever-further apart was actually what people wanted. She spoke to people in several different housing environments and concluded they worry about a whole range of things when choosing a house, including surroundings, community, service and status. It's dangerous to generalise about whether people prefer garden cities or compact ones, for some like the community and companionship of high-density living while others want peace and privacy. Most proved surprisingly happy with the amount of space they have and were prepared to trade space for proximity to services and meeting their community needs.

Willis found that village centres can provide community interaction in exactly the same way as towns and cities and it's the shared facilities such as pubs, shops, religious buildings and libraries, as well as areas' physical layout, that facilitate human interaction. "People need to see they are part of something bigger," she said.

She warned that the need to find alternatives to car dependency would mean more than just discouraging car use, and concluded compact development would be a crucial tool in mitigating climate change. She said we have long concentrated on novelty and invention since Ebenezer Howard pushed the virtue of new settlements, but new-town reality has seldom matched the ideals that inspired them.

"A focus on proximity would allow us to fulfil environmental and social objectives, as well as meeting housing needs," she concluded. "This could be achieved through planning policy and financing mechanisms that support existing settlements, through a more sophisticated approach to measuring density, through linking transport and planning policy and through encouraging greater community involvement."

How many homes should we build?

This issue is much more complicated than governments of all political persuasions would have you believe. We are endlessly told there is a vast shortage of 'family housing' and that civilisation will end because all under-30s can't own their own homes.

New family homes need not be the priority. *Image: Henry Oliver*

On top of this pile of misleading claims, the Treasury has long pushed the building of raw numbers of houses to keep prices stable, even though house prices have never been stable and never will be. Whitehall has battered opponents with 'household' projections showing strong growth in numbers, necessitating extensive housing construction. A household is, essentially, any adult or group of adults sharing the same kitchen, and apparently the rapid growth in household numbers is all our fault. We're marrying later in life, if at all, and when we do, we get divorced more often. So, to punish us, the countryside must be destroyed. This argument is plainly circular – create more homes for people to live on their own and more of them will live on their own. If you create fewer homes, however, then more people will find ways of living under the same roof, sharing a kitchen and working out how to share a fridge without nicking each other's food.

Much of the rationale for building 240,000 homes a year in England sprang from a government estimate that 223,000 'households' were forming every year. Perhaps, if we lived in a different-dimensional universe where space was flexible, we could simply build these homes and spread ourselves across the landscape with impunity. But remind yourself that the UK is one of the most densely populated parts of Europe and England is one of the most densely populated parts of the world. Sprawl, as a way of planning anything, is totally irresponsible.

Growing old disgracefully . . .

But before we bend under the lash of those household figures, let's take a closer look. A breakdown of the household growth projections for DCLG in 2008 by Anglia Ruskin University[11] showed that no fewer than 155,100 would be single people, 65,200 would be cohabiting couples, 15,300 lone parents and 16,100 multi-person. Married couple households, meanwhile, were declining at 28,400 every year and more than half, 89,800, of the one-person households would be over-55s. Indeed, 48 per cent of the new households would be retired people.

So, despite the fact that the vast majority of the new households would be single people or couples and that the majority would also be over-55s, they were being used as a rationale for building 'family homes' for young, multi-person households on greenfield sites. No doubt it's good politics to play on people's concerns about younger relatives with families struggling to get on the property ladder, but it's poor planning.

Our key challenge is not providing family homes, it's how we're going to accommodate the over-55s, and that becomes more acute the older people become. For that's where the real growth is – around 26 per cent (5.6 million) of English households in 2006 were over-65s, and we can confidently predict that will have grown to 30.4 per cent (7.9 million) by 2026 and that around half of these people will be living alone.

Old people move less often than young ones because they have less need to do so and they sure as hell hate doing it. As a result, these households (over-whelmingly comprising just one or two adults) tend to be rattling around in large houses – 72 per cent of over-65 owner-occupiers and 52 per cent of these over-65 singles live in homes with three or more bedrooms (the figure is lower for those who rent but they are a small and declining minority of elderly people). In fact the proportion of owner-occupiers whose homes have three or more bedrooms goes on rising until we meet the 70-75 age group, and declines slowly after that. A 2009 study by the Universities of York and Cambridge[12] suggested that a change to more suitable accommodation is usually prompted by widowhood, but that this is often only to a two-bedroomed house, with around a quarter of widowed people making such a change. It suggested there could actually be an *increase* of around 630,000 owner-occupier couples over the age of 65 in houses with three or more bedrooms (including 160,000 with four or more) by 2026, plus a further increase in demand for such homes by 145,000 widows and widowers living on their own.

More elderly people are divorcing too – an increase of 650,000-700,000 between 2006 and 2016 is forecast and many of these, on current trends, are likely to want three-bedroomed houses in case their families ever visit (something that apparently is happening less and less). Still, they might come and visit once in a while, mightn't they?

The York-Cambridge study also asked how older people might be encouraged to downsize to something more suitable and release family housing for families. Obstacles included the minimal cost savings yielded by such changes, as smaller homes appeared nearly as expensive to heat and the desire to retain housing equity usually prompts a move to a more upmarket area where council taxes, etc. are higher. In any case, few older people said financial considerations were a factor and most had no plans to move unless their spouse died. Most were content with their existing home and its surroundings and some said they wouldn't move under any circumstances, even ill health, and would adapt their homes as need be and even move downstairs if necessary. Some still lived in homes where they had raised children, some were living close to younger relatives and some were keeping their homes in the belief their relatives would sometimes visit or even come and care for them when the need arose.

"One of our participants had downsized to a smaller flat in a more convenient city centre location than her former home, which had been in a remote rural location," noted the researchers. "She was, however, seeking a larger property because she felt that her status as 'matriarch' of her family had diminished because she could no longer offer her children and grandchildren a place to stay."

Smaller homes were condemned as claustrophobic and pokey, and a move would mean abandoning possessions and hobbies. Homes embodied lifetimes of memories and a place to store mementos, and moving might mean exchanging good neighbours for bad, as well as entailing the whole misery and expense of the moving process. Many older people were adapting their homes rather than moving, and only a small minority, mainly the very elderly who found their house and garden a burden, were looking to move. Even then, the favoured alternative would be another family home such as a bungalow, and few found the specialist retirement housing on offer attractive. Somehow the mistaken idea has taken root that such housing is intended only for the very elderly and infirm, though in fact most providers will not accept such people.

Those who had actually moved had mainly done so as a result of ill health, bereavement or the need to be near young relatives for support, and anecdotal evidence suggests such moves are usually made at the last possible moment, when life had become as challenging as could be.

Here, I suggest, is the real challenge – rather than the lack of land that dominated the planning for housing debate through the 2000s. We are building tens of thousands of greenfield-sprawl houses for families each year and many are being occupied by elderly people without children for whom the housing will soon become unsuitable. It's a problem that America at least is starting to face up to.

Shelley Poticha, director of the US Administration's Office of Sustainable Housing and Communities (at the forefront of federal Smart Growth thinking) said in an interview in early 2010 that the importance of generational diversity in housing will grow as baby boomers and their parents age.

> If you are a family with children, your parents might live several blocks away – close enough for you to reach them, and for the kids to go to grandma's house after school and to be able to get there safely. As people downsize and move into smaller places, having those condos or rental units in locations where they can get around, or being able to take care of prescriptions, go to the library, or volunteer at the local school without having to get in a car [is important].[13]

Here in the UK we spend our time agonising about the economic effects of the 'demographic time bomb' and the housing challenges of young families, but the real challenge is the housing challenge of the 'demographic time bomb' and the economic challenge is to young families. And it's something no politician dare touch, apparently: losing old folk's votes being political suicide.

But on any rational analysis, building unsuitable greenfield-sprawl family homes for elderly people is crazy. The over-55s actually need something very different – they need services such as nearby shops and health care, which towns provide and the countryside and low-density suburbs don't. As people age, maintaining gardens and large homes becomes increasingly impossible, and ill health will stop anyone driving eventually, at which point low-density living becomes a nightmare.

And so many policies conspire to discourage a move to more suitable accommodation. The truly monstrous cost of keeping oneself or relatives in residential care, currently at least £600 a week, from one's own savings or from the value of one's former home causes some of our most vulnerable citizens intense pain in the evening of their lives. Money husbanded over a lifetime of thrift to help their children suddenly starts to be squandered at a previously inconceivable rate, and those who bothered saving watch those savings suddenly leach away. Even the capital released by moving from a big home to a smaller one will quickly vanish to pay for a spouse in care or when you yourself need care – at £30,000 or more a year. The whole issue has become intensely embarrassing to politicians, who know they would never be allowed to reverse the 1990 National Health Service and Community Care Act by their masters at the Treasury. Plainly, looking after our most needy and vulnerable citizens whose decades of toil created the wealth we enjoy would mean a couple of pence on income tax, and that would never do.

To add to this financial disincentive to moving and to reduce politicians' embarrassment about the issue of residential care for the elderly, government policy has increasingly emphasised encouraging people to stay in their own homes as long as possible. No doubt it's superficially comforting to those who fear a move, but it just puts off the inevitable day until they're even more infirm and less able to cope with a move, and it means that even more family homes will remain under-occupied.

. . . or gracefully

In more cynical moments it might be tempting to persuade the press to start a campaign against 'family home blocking' by elderly people, but they seem to have more important concerns, such as building up celebrities and knocking them down or attacking speed cameras, to maximise the number of their readers killed or maimed in road accidents.

But why on Earth are we building family homes outside towns at all, apart from a few socially rented ones? Why aren't the majority of the homes we build aimed at elderly people? The answers, I suspect, are complex and irrational. Most of our need for new family homes is in the social renting sector and that's predominantly an urban need. And the homes we do need are mostly for single people or elderly people, and these won't be out-of-town either. In America they're facing this issue, as described by Shelley Poticha in early 2010.

> Demographic trends in the US clearly show that over the next twenty years, the housing market will focus on smaller households. Singles are going to be the new majority, and they will be looking for something different from the single-family housing we've had for the last 50 years. When we start there and then layer on the issue of climate change, along with the economic need to attract and retain workers, a key ingredient becomes offering choices in different types of homes and places to live, as well as different options for getting around in a community.[14]

We need to find flexible ways of housing the over-55s that meet their needs at their current stage of life and allow them to move without too much fuss to higher levels of provision as their needs change. In England and Wales, buying and selling a home is one of the most traumatic things we ever experience, on a par with divorce, bereavement and redundancy, and the attempt to make it a bit easier through a robust home information pack system was first emasculated by opposition from those professionals who faced exclusion from this trough and finally seen off by the press in pursuit of cheap politicking. So our mad house-buying ritual is now an environmental challenge, as well as a social and economic one, for it encourages us to occupy family homes we don't need.

We need to find ways to encourage older people to free up family homes for families and we need to do much more to create many-layered housing provision for the elderly that allows them to meet their needs and wants, including visits from relatives and access to gardens, and to move to the next stage when need be, without the full horror of the housing market. We must make this provision for them in urban areas, and this is potentially a way of adapting the sprawl on the outer parts of our cities. Maybe older people, who often seem increasingly uneasy being around younger people, would welcome this. Many people are uneasy about the 'Costa Geriatrica' or creating 'grey ghettoes', for we all know that social and health services in such areas struggle with high proportions of elderly people, but perhaps it's time for us all to recognise the fact that concentrating these services in one place means economies of scale and consequent savings.

Town planning in practice

The new coalition government began life in 2010 with a major onslaught on the planning system and, just three months after the election, had the Royal Town Planning Institute[15] and 28 other national bodies warning that its onslaught on regional planning was threatening "economic recovery, meeting housing need and demand, sustainable transport, regeneration, sustainable development and growth, investment in our infrastructure, biodiversity loss, climate change, and reducing inequality" – no small achievement for a government's 'golden 100 days'.

The government had capitalised on the fury whipped up by Gordon Brown's misusing regional strategies in England to impose fantasy housing targets and exacerbate sprawl. This surely needed attention, but provided no justification whatsoever to scrap regional planning altogether – a bit of recessive-gene Thatcherism that should have died with the 1980s, for if ever anywhere needed regional planning it's England, with its insane 90-year drift south-eastwards of economic activity.

For sure, regional planning can be misused, as we've seen with the English regional housing targets and the Northern Ireland Executive's 2010 decision to respond to the 'garden grabbing' furore and the desire of so many of its citizens to litter its countryside with bungalows with new planning guidance actually forbidding densification of urban areas. But it can be a force for so much good – around the same time, in summer 2010, the Welsh Assembly Government introduced strategic planning policies[16] with a strong Smart Growth ethos, concentrating development on brownfield land within existing urban areas and demanding it be located so as to minimise road transport.

How, then, should we go about town planning in practice, to borrow the title of a book[17] by the great high priest of sprawl, Raymond Unwin? In the short term we need to start by looking at ways to eliminate sprawl, then see how to preserve and regenerate our towns and cities, to make them easier to move around in sustainable ways. Then we will need to work out what we do with our addiction to out-of-town shopping, with the dismal legacy of the Modern movement and with the low-density stuff bequeathed to us by the garden sprawl movement.

No pressure then.

How do we fight sprawl?

"Sprawl drains resources from existing communities," says Smart Growth America, and that's just as true over here. The 100-year flight to suburbs and greenfield sprawl of all kinds sucked the vitality out of our towns and cities, leaving them weak and vulnerable to the heavy bombers of slum clearance, road building and modern architecture. Planning and regeneration have tried to alleviate the damage done by dispersal, but the sprawl is still out there, sucking away like a leech.

Stuart Maconie, for instance, found that "Grantham today is more a slip road than a town. For every pedestrian I spot, a score of vans and cars come throbbing through the town at speed. The few of us on foot feel like an afterthought, an irrelevance scuttling along the shop fronts while the lorries roar by".[18]

For 5,000 years we gathered in towns to work, to trade and to live. We met to conduct business, we practised religion, manufactured and traded goods and, above all, we met the rest of the human race there, both the ones we liked and the ones we had to get on with thanks to our proximity. This is known as community. Once we stopped loving towns, we stopped being community beings.

Still in Grantham, Maconie found himself "wandering glumly in the George shopping centre; several of the shops are closed, there are dirty puddles on the floor reflecting the harsh fluorescent lighting and a bad, thin version of Joan Armatrading's *Love and Affection* is piped around the echoing galleries. It's a dreary experience".

It's unfair, of course, to single out Grantham – how many traditional centres have been eroded by destruction of their character buildings, the flight of shops, businesses and homes out of town and crass, ill-designed shopping centres?

So part of our Smart Growth planning policy must be strict controls on greenfield sprawl. This will take very much more than scrapping regional strategies and leaving local planning authorities to flounder around on their own. It will require robust national, regional and local guidance, support for councils and strict countryside protection – something we will look at in the next chapter.

But we must also reconsider building densities for housing. Cities, towns and villages were built at high densities because land was expensive; it's an art we need to rediscover because high-rise has become our limp response to the need for density. Bye-law homes could be built at over 100 to the hectare and you can find them with amenity space at more than 70 to the hectare. One can overdo this, of course; I recently heard of one inner-London flat development at over 1,000 flats to the hectare and that's obviously grotesque. Too many city regeneration schemes have just crammed in far too many offices, shops and flats solely to increase the commercial return. Getting densities right will need care and careful planning.

How should we preserve our towns?

We must also stop pulling down the older parts of our towns without a very good reason. Old buildings are a priceless asset to any community – a truth rediscovered in the 1970s and 1980s and which a dismal coalition of developers, architects, investors and what we could dub 'the style police' has since been debunking. Shoving up short-life garbage-can buildings may wreck our towns, but it's profitable.

So probably we need a presumption against pulling down anything built before 1914 without a good reason and a big question over pulling down shops and public buildings built before 1939. (Perhaps we could have a presumption in favour of pulling down anything built during or near the 1960s? Just a thought.)

Traditional buildings aren't just a community asset and a treat for our eyes, they're also economically valuable. The Prince's Regeneration Trust asked the new economics foundation to examine extending HM Treasury's Listed Places of Worship Grant Scheme to local communities who are restoring historic secular buildings to create employment, safeguard distinctiveness and stimulate regeneration.[19] VAT reimbursement grants would be given for listed buildings owned by charities offering public access and VAT 'refund' grants given for reuse of up to ten locally historic buildings in each of the UK's 88 most deprived areas. The nef concluded that the initial outlay would be between £13 million and £48 million a year, but that within four years the Treasury would actually reap a net and growing benefit. Instead of which we actually tax people for restoring historic buildings and reducing their dependence on the Treasury.

One thing that became clear from discussions during the writing of this book is that we have lost our ability (or at least our courage) to apply the idea of beauty to townscape. Is it because the style police have battered us into silence with cynicism or even 'post-modern irony'? Or have we really lost all

Is it time we stopped knocking down old buildings?

appreciation of urban beauty and become unable to describe it in terms that don't make us cringe with embarrassment?

What should we do with our town centres?

Out-of-town shopping may eventually lie down and die with the era of cheap motoring of course, but it may be too late for our traditional centres by then. We need to find some way of taking action against out-of-town centres now – perhaps through the parking restrictions or taxes on them suggested in the late 1990s or by some form of traffic restraint. The mere suggestion would provoke howls of rage, of course, but for the most part there would be nothing to these apart from pure financial self-interest. In the meantime, no more out-of-town stores should be approved, the size of new in-town stores should be limited and big store numbers rationed.

Then we have to make traditional shopping as attractive as possible. Traditional shop hours haven't always kept up with changes in our working schedules and the demands of a long-hours culture, which is something that will need to be addressed. Another key element will be improving urban public transport – which, as we shall see in Chapter 11, is our key transport challenge. At present, traffic restraint measures including pedestrianisation and reducing parking provision makes town centres more environmentally attractive but deters people from using them, so shopkeepers often oppose pedestrianisation measures as their customers will simply vote with their accelerator feet and go out-of-town. The answer to this is not to build more out-of-town shops or even to open up towns to more traffic, it's to restrict out-of-town centres and to improve sustainable access to town centres.

And high buildings? Well, there will always be some of them in cities and large towns – civic buildings, cinemas, offices, schools, hospitals, etc. But we mustn't let them be the paradigm of prosperity they have become – 'our shopping centre's bigger than yours'. Medium-rise is fine for all but the very largest cities and then only in moderation, and it needs to be permeable by pedestrians, cyclists and trams. Town centres will need to have shop frontages to keep the streets alive. Traffic will be limited but not wholly eliminated. Some of this is done already, of course, but it's usually then undone by some megalomaniac shopping centre.

Reviving our town and city centres must be done with great care to make them places for people. 'Place making' provokes a great deal of interest today, and very good much of it is. And some isn't; bizarrely, you even hear some of the more egotistical modernist architects claiming to do it as they make their places for crazy people. The perverse idea took hold that very tall buildings create 'excitement' (plainly, some people are easily excited). Sometimes they do and often they don't. If we are to allow a few tallish buildings in city centres, they must never again be the city-devouring monsters they've become. You don't actually need high buildings to create urban excitement; London's Covent Garden is exciting and one reason it's exciting is that the Modern movement (which wanted to replace it entirely with tall buildings and a dual carriageway) was prevented from building high buildings or anything else there. The City of London, meanwhile, is absolutely full of high buildings, but it certainly isn't exciting, unless you're making piles of cash of course.

Our new urban renaissance will need people sensitive to the towns they are regenerating, not trying to carve their egos across them or screw the maximum-possible cash out of them. We should forget about 'wow factors', because art galleries don't need to look like battered heaps of baked-bean cans to make them exciting; it should be their contents that do that. Too many 'wow factors' pretty soon turn into 'ow factors' and we don't need 'landmark buildings' to mark our land either, we need well-mannered buildings that impress with their quiet air of belonging without flaunting their egos, or their designers'.

It may upset the style police, but we need towns we can feel comfortable in. Let's banish terms like 'twee', 'bourgeois', 'dinky little', 'retro' and 'reactionary' from architectural criticism, especially when written by twee, bourgeois and reactionary writers in dinky little retro columns. In fact, let's have architecture we like.

How do we make our towns permeable?

Our town streets must be safe and pleasant places to walk or cycle and their centres must have live frontage – shops, restaurants, cafes and, yes, building societies and banks – places that the public enter and leave, in fact, and meet on the street outside. Footways should normally reach right up to them and down to the kerb and, however unpredictable our climate might be, most of this should be in the open air, although there should certainly be more trees. If this were America we should call this Main Street, which has an almost mythical, though much abused and neglected, status. We'll make do with High Street as a generic term, although it's quite likely to be Fore Street or something else altogether, but whatever it's called, it deserves the same degree of respect. These are the beating hearts of our towns and they are being starved of lifeblood by large stores, road builders, sprawlers (a rather broad category) and, saddest of all to admit, ourselves.

We must fight to win back our towns. We must ensure they are 'permeable' so that walkers and cyclists can enjoy reasonably direct routes across them unhindered by motorists or by each other. If anyone produces a town plan with cul-de-sacs or the like, they need to go back to college.

There's been a lot of debate in the last few decades about the European concept of 'shared space' or 'naked streets', which blur the distinction between footway and carriageway to destroy motorists' belief that they own the space and to slow them down. It's a fine idea, but whether it will work in a country where many motorists seem to believe the public highway is, in fact, the public grand prix track, remains to be seen. I suspect one of the problems with the concept is some British cyclists' contempt for pedestrians; shared streets may slow motorists down, but a minority of cyclists may need more persuasion and separation from pedestrians by at least a kerb.

New development must be made permeable.

What do we do with the high rise?

A great deal of the Modern movement's excess in the 1960s and since has been swept away, but much remains. Many of the tower blocks and other garbage-bin buildings from that era remain and need replacing for a whole raft of reasons (including structural weakness and fire safety). Bringing sane urbanism to such areas doesn't necessarily involve densification, although the acres of fly-blown grass around many of these blocks means you certainly don't need to make such places less dense. The object will usually be to start remodelling these areas into something a bit like the townscape knocked down to make way for them (often, curiously, leaving the pubs). We could even adopt the style of residential areas built in the 40 years before the First World War as a sort of 'old urbanism', combined with elements of new urbanism. It wouldn't be perfect because perfect town planning doesn't exist, but its essential elements would be a long-proven model: predominantly low-rise, high-density houses (often in terraces) rather than flats, local schools, shops, health care, pocket parks, allotments and good, frequent, reliable, densely networked, rail-based public transport. Just like our great- and great-great-grandparents enjoyed.

How should we build our towns?

Urbanism, new or old, is never going to be easy (did I ever promise this would be easy?). We have precious few examples of either in this country, and fewer still if you demand transit-oriented development.

The writer Joe Bennett in *Mustn't Grumble*[20] visited Poundbury, the model urbanist community backed by the Prince's Foundation for the Built Environment, and admitted, before he arrived, that he was a bit suspicious of it. So am I, a bit – it was an urban extension on a greenfield site outside Dorchester. But it's got to be better than most of the rubbish development of modern times, and Bennett came to a similar view, noting the inevitably middle-class shops and the Volvos parked halfway up the pavements. Yet, despite these 'ominous signs' he liked the roads curving like old roads, the stone buildings, the little parks and public spaces, the pub in the square and the mix of house sizes and prices, though he was worried it would turn into a middle-class posh suburb; a niceness.

"But I hope I'm wrong," he concluded. "If a way can be found to create a modern village, something that works in the twenty-first century, then I am for it. It has to be better than Slough."

Poor old Slough. Well, perhaps all our urban areas are in need of a bit of 'niceness'; I think it used to be called community.

We really will have to find ways of building houses up to three storeys on small footprints. It's a problem post-war architecture has been trying to crack

Could we rediscover the coherent architectural language even bye-law homes had?

since the 1960s 'town house' without ever really succeeding, although it was never going to work when most of the ground floor was taken up by a garage. It's just a suggestion, but why not look at the late-nineteenth-century terrace for your model and find a way of bringing it up to date? This would require the architecture profession to come up with a consistent architectural language that can easily be replicated by builders in the way quiet classicism was a century or two back. They could replicate it simply, even on the meanest bye-law house, by following a few rules of proportion: this worked fine until along Good Intention Lane came William Morris I who said classicism was a Bad Thing and should be replaced by some kind of vernacular. This might have worked had he specified local vernacular, but his excited followers set off a sort of architectural food fight, grabbing bits of every vernacular tradition they could find and splattering them around the place in grim profusion. So when speculative builders got hold of it, there followed the disaster that was twentieth/ twenty-first-century minor domestic architecture.

What do we do about open space?

One of the less satisfactory features of the fragile urban renaissance policies of the 2000s was not the so-called 'garden grabbing' but the 'playing-field grabbing' and the 'allotment grabbing', although both go back to the free-for-all planning of the 1980s. We need to protect urban open space, and we need to become more imaginative about the ways we provide more of it, and that will be all the more important in the denser urban areas of a sustainable future.

One of the more dismal legacies of the Modern movement is the vast expanse of flat roofs in our cities – but these potentially at least provide places to add greenery. Modernism also created vast areas of windswept grass around the flats and offices it created, and an obvious community use for these would be as allotments – providing gardening opportunities and local food production, and introducing an opportunity for residents to interact socially in some of the most challenging of our residential environments.

And converting small areas of the unproductive-but-high-maintenance mown grassland in our parks to allotment use could provide an opportunity too, although obviously this could happen only in areas where open space provision is good. Of course this would detract from parks' aesthetic appeal and their sense of openness, but set against that would be provision of a productive community resource for parts of large areas that are often at present largely just giant dogs' toilets. I can see the appeal of a chance to let the eye wander through a stretch of uncluttered land after a spell in the city, but I can also see the advantages of allowing people to grow their own vegetables. Not 'garden cities' but 'gardening cities'.

And in the longer term . . .

But perhaps the biggest challenge for the longer term is not how we plan our cities. It's what we do with the sprawl.

A surprising feature of the recent US recession was the sudden crash in house prices in remote, car-dependent suburbs. Although gasoline is far cheaper in America than in Britain, the vast distances Americans commute meant that, suddenly, it wasn't the inner cities that were suffering worst but what were supposed to be affluent outer suburbs. Over here commuting distances are smaller and public transport, though patchy and ramshackle, is generally more generously provided than in America (though they are catching up). So will the same thing happen here? It's got to, eventually. Although outer suburbs often have some sort of poor bus service or, if they're lucky, a suburban railway station, life is pretty difficult for those who depend on them (and believe me – I grew up in a suburb depending on buses). We need to start planning for how we will get people in these areas around when petrol simply becomes too expensive – and too environmentally destructive – to be used freely any more. This will happen, even if we hope it won't.

And a great deal of recent greenfield sprawl has been in areas vulnerable to flooding. The Environment Agency has been yelling itself hoarse for years about this, but councils still sometimes grant permission and sometimes, when they don't, the Planning Inspectorate overrules them.

Rocketing fuel prices, restrictions on motoring and revitalised towns and cities mean much of our sprawl will become a real challenge. When all this comes to pass, where will it leave the garden cities, the garden suburbs, the new town and outer estates, the low-density sprawl that has spread around our towns like morbid obesity? It will leave them as a giant problem.

Some areas we can retrofit, partly densify and link with rail-based transit. Some parts will have to soldier on as best they can, reliant on lousy bus services and far from anywhere people need to be. And some . . . well, some aren't going to make it. Sorry.

So what do we do with the sprawl?

The approach Smart Growth practitioners are taking in America is densifying low-density suburbs around transit stations and stops. Low-density construction is even more prevalent in America than in the UK of course, and traditional town-centre densities on both sides of the pond don't need densification. But we do have vast areas of low-density suburbia that need retrofitting with rail-based transit of one sort or another, and denser service centres created around the new transit stops. The centres can contain shops, schools, health care provision, employment, etc.

This is going to cause intense pain at the Treasury, which currently won't allow light rail schemes even in densely populated cities where ridership would be high. In the rest of the world, however, light rail reaches out into the suburbs, and there are dozens of such schemes being planned in America.

Our remodelled communities will also need to make provision for the elderly – the demographic growth challenge. Low-density sprawl may be these people's preferred choice of home, but old age brings challenges, sometimes soon after retirement, and a low-density sprawl home can rapidly become a prison when health problems and difficulty with driving occur. Yet old people have shown a clear preference to live among other old people – in the bungaloid sprawl near the south coast, for example. This concentration does present challenges for health and social care, but maybe we need to go with the flow here, and find ways of (quietly) intensifying this sprawl and retrofitting it with transit and public services. Maybe we need to start retrofitting parts of our low-density suburbia as urban villages for the elderly, with a range of suitable housing and services. Yes, it's expensive to provide a concentration of elderly people with services, but it also means economies of scale.

To be honest, low-density suburbia really only offers any kind of ideal living at the stage when we have young children and need somewhere for them that's safe from traffic, and in the early years of retirement when we can still manage to garden. For the rest of us it's an attractive dream undermined by our long-hours culture and uncertain economy. If you're in work you don't have time to garden and if you're not you'll probably have to sell the damned place anyway. And if you were in a low-paid job you wouldn't have been able to afford one in the first place.

Look forward half a century or so and I suspect you will find areas of suburban development most distant from town centres, or located in floodplains, or where local employment is lacking, being abandoned. If you don't think that's possible, look at some of the municipal 'outer estates' in some industrial towns. There, the process of abandonment has been masked by attempts at regeneration and the mad policy of preferring to knock down sustainably located inner-city dwellings under 'housing market renewal', but it shows just what could happen. Some of those leafy suburbs that look so attractive in estate agents' adverts now could be the declining slums of tomorrow; hard to countenance if you live in one, but perhaps it's time to look at alternatives. Just imagine that spiral of decline in owner-occupied estates: prices would fall, the poor and socially disadvantaged would move in and an increasing number of homes would remain empty. Then the fabric would deteriorate and social problems such as crime, antisocial behaviour and so on would emerge, hastening the flight of inhabitants. Property prices would drop to the point where nothing would sell and large-scale abandonment would follow. It has happened, and sometimes in spite of public efforts to halt the decline. It's happening in America too. And maybe there would be very good sustainability reasons not to halt the decline...

Countryside is often destroyed, industry blows away like thistledown, but housing tends to stay even when the industry that paid for it has blown away. Don't imagine it won't happen even in areas that appear prosperous today. We really do need to come up with solutions to the sprawl lobby's malignant legacy.

Future compact

Inevitably, even saying these things will spark furious opposition. Our future towns and cities need to be more compact than those we live in today, but around this point the sprawl lobby will start bleating about 'town cramming' as if we haven't comfortably been cramming ourselves in towns for the last 5,000 years or so. So we must tread carefully.

Much of our traditional urban fabric won't need densifying, of course, just protecting and enhancing, so perhaps it's time to designate most or all of our remaining pre-1914 residential and retail development as conservation areas, giving a presumption against demolition and a power to prevent it. Then we need to find ways of enhancing it. Much of our pre-1939 retail development may need similar protection. But housing development since 1918 is a different matter, as much of it was a product of the sprawl lobby or the modernists.

But we do need to densify with care. There has been a fair bit of densification in city centres on the back of recent regeneration, and much of it has gone too far. Hardly anywhere outside city centres needs buildings over four or five storeys. We don't need tower blocks of flats, and while mixed use is an admirable thing, you get the clear impression that hundreds of flats are added to already over-dense town centre regeneration schemes just to make them pay. Think the traditional city centre of 100 years ago and you're on the right lines. It's the low-density areas that need densification.

Sadly, densification of low-density suburbs is likely to be a battlefield; it needn't be, but people are extraordinarily defensive of their homes, even of relatively poor-quality ones. While thousands of people were happy enough to be saved from the Modern movement's tower blocks, suggest to anyone with a remote suburban plot that it's unsustainable and out come angry red-faced folk waving tabloid newspapers. It's understandable, but it's frustrating too.

In 2006, for instance, a local paper got hold of an unpublished draft report by the Milton Keynes Partnership looking at ways of dealing with some of the really badly built 1960s Milton Keynes Development Corporation homes.

We need towns that work like traditional ones did.

Milton Keynes was always a sustainability disaster, built at ruinously low densities and utterly dependent on the motor car, so its bus services were always both poor and heavily subsidised. Built around a one-kilometre grid of roads and with a centre dominated by vast, empty rain-swept plazas, everything is as far away from everything else as possible and attempting to walk anywhere is probably grounds for sectioning. Many of the early homes had significant structural problems too and were expensive to heat.

The report proposed demolishing some homes on six estates and replacing them with higher-density buildings so an extra 14,000 could be added to the city's housing stock, thus slightly reducing its dependence on its default mode, greenfield sprawl. Some main roads were to be downgraded to residential and some mixed-use development was planned. Higher-density development and consequent public transport improvements would lift the older estates out of their deprivation and improve sustainability.

Smart Growth urban planning policies

- Living and working in closer proximity.
- Ending greenfield sprawl.
- Development making best use of existing urban infrastructure, facilities and services.
- Building in context, respecting and enhancing traditional buildings, townscape and heritage.
- Transit-oriented development.
- A public-transport accessibility standard in planning.
- Ending out-of-town shopping.
- Protecting and enhancing small shops and traditional shopping centres.
- An urban renaissance based on communitarian place making and urbanism.
- Permeable development.
- Low- or medium-rise development except in the centre of large cities.
- Urban tree-planting, roof planting, open space protection and enhancement.
- Building to Lifetime Homes standards (which ensure homes are accessible for people with mobility difficulties).
- Building to meet the needs of elderly people.
- Promoting an attractive appearance to building and townscape via the planning system.
- Promoting reclamation and restoration of brownfield land.

And in the longer term:
- Taking opportunities to densify low-density areas near rail-based transit.

It was a bit cagey about exactly what was to come down but, with some judicious leaking and stirring by the sprawl lobby, residents were soon up in arms. After a less-than-enlightening debate, the proposals, which could have accommodated a fifth of the growth demanded at Milton Keynes, were dropped and greenfield sprawl was left to go it alone.

So Mondeo man will not drive off quietly, I fear. For decades we've been perfectly happy to sling long-established communities out of their homes in the name of slum clearance or housing-market renewal, but sustainability does not enjoy such support. It may be that we shall have to wait until low-density sprawl does enter its long-term, fatal decline before action is taken. There is a better way – across the Atlantic they're densifying neighbourhoods and pursuing urbanism and transit-oriented development. A 2007 study by Reconnecting America[21] showed that families in car-dependent neighbourhoods spent an average of 25 per cent of their income on transportation, while those who lived near transit stops spent just 9 per cent. So we must get the message across that building housing near transit points is a key element of affordability as well as of sustainability. This change is going to take decades, and we may well have to fight for it.

Social networking sites

I wonder what we'll make of the early twenty-first century craze for social networking sites when we look back in 20 years or so. Will they have flourished and developed into something even bigger, or will they have withered and died into something middle-aged people remember with nostalgia from their youth? I don't actually have the faintest idea.

But I would just remind everyone besotted with virtual social networking that we have real social networking sites that have been functioning very effectively for thousands of years. They're called village, town or city centres.

Environmentalists have long been suspicious of humanity's endless movement to the towns, a suspicion that goes back at least to Ebenezer Howard and his chums. But we have to realise that urban life is the only sustainable option for a desperately overcrowded corner of a desperately overcrowded planet. Too often environmentalism is about fear of the future, for very good reasons. But here is an opportunity to make the best of things – and to make things better.

So when people attack Slough for looking downmarket, for not having Windsor's historic buildings, for having housing sprawl, just remember that we can't all have rich inhabitants or 1,000 years of history or avoid inheriting the mess the garden sprawl and Modern movements created.

But we can fix these things – and we can look after our countryside too.

Rating neighbourhoods

A key element in Smart Growth is close attention to how sustainably development is located. Is it within walking distance of shops, schools, public transport, etc.? Does it make best use of existing infrastructure? Does it reduce or increase our need to drive to work?

In 2010 the US Green Building Council launched the seventh of its 'LEED' (Leadership in Energy and Environmental Design) rating systems. The earlier LEED systems covered the sustainable construction of buildings, but LEED Neighbourhood Development was developed with the Congress for the New Urbanism and Natural Resources Defense Council as a way of integrating the principles of Smart Growth with new urbanism and green building. The three-stage certification system verifies whether a development's location and design meet accepted high levels of environmentally responsible, sustainable development.

The ratings are designed to encourage development within or near existing communities and public infrastructure. They emphasise connectivity via public transit, cycling or walking.

UK planning guidance has historically contained a lot of advice about location but has lacked a single, coherent focus on sustainability of location in relation to transport and facilities. In an effort to fill this vacuum, the Campaign for Better Transport published its *Masterplanning Checklist for Sustainable Transport in New Developments* in 2008.[22] "We must develop a totally different paradigm for twenty-first-century housing, although it might also be viewed as a return to an earlier paradigm represented by the densely built and highly sustainable urban form of housing in every century up until the last one," it says.

Rating neighbourhoods examines areas' location and public transport provision to show how sustainably their inhabitants can travel.
Image: US Environmental Protection Agency, Smart Growth Program

Chapter 10

Care and maintenance of the countryside

My journey showed that although Britain is a grossly over-crowded collection of islands, it is still possible to visit remote places and to find solitude and beauty.

Robin Page, *Journeys into Britain*

Loving our countryside

We love our countryside – most of us do anyway – and it's a well-worn platitude that we're loving it to death. But rural beauty is a powerful thing, and many of our travel writers have reflected this. Cobbett was particularly enthusiastic.

"In looking from a hill, over this valley, early in the morning, in November, it presented one of the most beautiful sights that my eyes ever beheld," he enthused about the Hampshire Downs, although he was ever ready to dub downland beautiful. "This is a beautiful country," noted George Borrow about Wales, and even J. B. Priestley, not a man easily moved by ethereal things, admitted he was smitten. In the Cotswolds he declared: "The beauty of the Cotswolds belongs to England, and England should see that she keeps it." He suggested they be turned into a national park.

> It may be necessary to banish from these hills the grimmer realities of our economic life, to make it artificially secure in its fairy tale of grey old stones and misty valleys, but even then . . . the move will be worth making. There will remain a countryside that will be able to give both body and spirit a holiday . . .[1]

We tend to assume that H. V. Morton was similarly smitten, and to some extent he was, but as he clattered through the countryside in the bull-nose car built by William Morris II you can tell it was the prospect of the next slice of history in a town that really excited him. He eulogised Roseland, "a Garden of Eden that cannot be described in pen or paint"[2] and grew all poetic about the Lake District, "Over the dark hills and the pale waters is an unearthly radiance which is not that of either sun or moon, but something, it seems, like the cold light which washes the mountains of dead moons. Above the hills burns the first small star . . ." But it was no good; Carlisle's history was calling and off went the little Morris car.

Besottedness with the countryside is not universal, however. Robbie Coltrane professed himself a city boy, a bit prejudiced about what lies beyond city boundaries.

"My greatest fear is that I am going to meet a lot of people with long-chop sideboards, some of whom will try to wrestle me to the ground, and that I'll discover villages where everyone has the same face and a virgin is a girl who runs faster than her brother".[3] Hmm, perhaps Mr Coltrane spent too long playing a forensic psychiatrist in *Cracker*.

But the countryside has been a central concern for our travel writers all down the centuries, although often their principal concerns were the wretched weather, the awfulness of road travel and the disgusting state of the inns, so some things plainly never change. In the eighteenth century, many became obsessed by agricultural improvement; Cobbett, in the space of an average page, became enraged by so many rural problems you wonder he didn't simply explode with anger.

Writers in the early twentieth century sought to soothe their readers with the glories of the countryside, and while the recent explosion in UK travelogues will have covered just about every aspect of our island life somewhere, only a minority have actually identified urbanisation and road building as real threats to the countryside.

Yet throughout the twentieth century, rural planning policy was at least as confused as urban. For we demand so much of our shrinking and overcrowded countryside. We celebrate its beauty and we seek to enjoy that by living in it, driving through it, walking through it, sweating across it on a mountain bike, flying across it in a light aircraft or microlight or gouging big holes in it with a 4x4, something Mr Toad would have adored. We expect it to provide a substantial amount of our food, timber and building materials. We expect it to nurture wildlife, we observe nature and celebrate biodiversity, or we exploit it with rod, hound or gun. And we depend on it for our water, our flood control and some of our oxygen. It provides us with that uniquely prosaically named function – ecosystem services.

Mark Twain famously advised us to buy land because they aren't making it any more, but we sure are using it up at a rate of knots. It isn't only a matter of urban sprawl; we're building roads, airports, harbours, nuclear power stations, open-cast coal mines, quarries, leisure resorts, golf courses and much else, and some forms of agriculture are still degrading the land.

'The land' – what a range of emotions those words can arouse. 'Our land' – *terra nostra* – powerful, dangerous words in any language. 'The soil' is more comforting altogether, but no less under threat.

No wonder we love our countryside, but that doesn't always translate into protection.

The soil beneath our feet

The countryside debate involves a massive range of issues – agriculture, beauty, Common Agricultural Policy, dairy farming, ecosystem services, factory farming, golf courses, horticulture, isolation, jam production, kennels, land reform, mechanisation, national parks, oat prices, pollination, right to roam, subsidy, transport, ugliness, villages, water supply, extreme sports, yields, zoology – or maybe access, biodiversity, carbon sequestration . . . Well, you get the picture, it's a complex issue.

But let's start at the bottom, with the soil. I return to William Cobbett, who would break off rants about the enclosure acts, rotten boroughs, farm prices or whatever to observe the soil his horse was treading in detail.

> The soil over which I have come today, is generally a stony sand upon a bed of gravel. With the exception of the land round Crookham and the other villages, nothing can well be poorer or more villainously ugly. It is all first cousin to Hounslow Heath, of which it is, in fact, a continuation to the westward. There is a clay at the bottom of the gravel; so that you have here nasty stagnant pools without fertility of the soil.[4]

But we have stopped taking our soil seriously. We depend on it for everything we eat and drink and we treat it like dirt. Many environmentalists take far less notice of it than of the other media: air and water. The European Union has long had powerful legislation to protect air and water but it didn't even entertain plans for a soil framework directive until 2006 and even this fairly modest proposal fell foul of bickering among member states, notably of course the UK. The UK's main objection was regulation of land contamination, and we needn't concern ourselves in this book with the ins and outs, despite the importance of this issue for regeneration of industrial areas. But there was another, unspoken, element to the objection: Europe wanted to control soil sealing – preventing soil carrying out its natural functions of drainage, carbon sequestration, flood prevention, groundwater recharge, biodiversity support, etc. by covering it with hard development such as buildings or roads.

Soil is wonderful stuff. The average back garden is said to contain more species of bacteria than the entire Atlantic Ocean. Soil keeps prodigious amounts of carbon out of the atmosphere, and moorland, woodland and even grassland actually take up carbon (arable land, sadly, emits it). Whitehall fought the directive energetically on the specious grounds that it isn't a trans-boundary issue; in fact, it didn't want Europe protecting its soils from green-field sprawl.

Yet if Smart Growth policies were applied to the UK for just one reason it should be to prevent soil sealing. In an uncertain world with an ailing climate, it makes no sense to destroy our food and water provider, our flood controller, our sole effective carbon sequestrator and the thing on which our entire bio-diversity depends. Unless you plan to make lots of money destroying the environment, of course.

Battle fields

In the last chapter we looked at regenerating our towns and densifying our suburbs, but we also need to address how best to protect undeveloped land.

Those who promote or profit from destroying land would have you believe we haven't lost much countryside in the last 100 years. For although a vast area of land was lost to speculative housing development between the wars, it is difficult to quantify exactly how much. It only began to be quantified accurately when the government, in 1930, set up a Land Utilization Survey to examine every acre of land. In charge of this latter-day *Domesday Book* was someone largely forgotten today who deserves to be a hero of the environmental movement: the great geographer Sir Laurence Dudley Stamp. At a time of huge economic stress and long before the land satellite was even dreamed of, Stamp set out to use the Mark One Eyeball. While European dictators were recruiting their young folk to conquer the world, Stamp recruited a young army to survey our land – schoolchildren.

Armed with 1:10,000 maps covering two miles by three, his young army was sent out to survey their areas and record on their maps what every field was being used for, in a few simple categories. Local directors of education provided the administration and around a quarter of a million schoolchildren took part.

"Many teachers organised it most skilfully; they introduced an element of competition among the children, seeing who could be the most accurate observers, recording the facts properly, seeing who could produce the best maps, the most neatly executed and the most fully documented," recalled Stamp.[5]

Would today's children perform as well? I suspect the answer is yes, although some might wonder how to connect their map to a laptop and would be working despite an inevitable background chorus of anxious parents. The 1930s parents, Stamp recalled, took a lively interest and found time to help. Would we do that in our long-hours culture?

But through this it became possible to see for the first time just how fast we were destroying our land. With a depressed land market, no development control and road transport opening vast areas to development, it was found that around 25,000 hectares of England and Wales – an area the size of the Isle of Wight – was being lost to suburban development in the late 1930s *every year*.[6]

Such exposure of the damage they were doing was not at all popular with the sprawl lobby. Stamp had noted that the survey drew an arbitrary line between houses with small gardens or back yards unlikely to be used for vegetable production and those large enough to produce fruit, flowers or vegetables, and rated them unproductive or productive accordingly. "It was found that the limit was something in the order of 12 houses per acre," noted Stamp.[7]

Just how productive even large 1930s gardens with their shrubberies, rose gardens and tennis courts were is open to question, of course, but this density was just the maximum residential density demanded by the sprawl lobby. Yet despite this concession to their dreams of a vegetable-growing legumocracy (see below), Stamp soon became one of their hate figures. For he refused to share their strange belief that building houses on farmland was the best way to increase its productivity.

In 1956 F. J. Osborn and Lewis Mumford's transatlantic mutual admiration society underwent a small tiff when Osborn chided Mumford for not querying some of Dudley Stamp's "ramshackle figures of urban encroachment on farmland which, after a long controversy, I have discredited".[8] No figures Sir Laurence Dudley Stamp ever produced were ramshackle, but Osborn soon had a kicking party organised to discredit them. He encouraged academics at Wye Agricultural College to produce a pamphlet supporting Osborn's strange view that produce from gardens of low-density housing was greater in agricultural value than the produce from the whole area of farmland destroyed to build the houses.

"Their conclusion is that the best way to increase food production in England is to build houses at 10 or 12 an acre and that some is lost if you go up to 14 or 16 an acre," claimed Osborn. "I had proved this by simpler arguments, but few took any notice. *Floreat Scientia*!"[9]

Obvious, isn't it? Cover a piece of farmland with buildings, driveways, garages, sheds, roads, footways, etc. and you get more from a few garden vegetable plots than from the whole area. But, a decade after the UK had almost been starved into submission because it couldn't produce all its own food, Dudley Stamp was shaken into responding. He suggested a twofold response, firstly by avoiding building on the best-quality farmland.

"The second would be to regard very open densities, such as 10 persons to the acre, as being an extravagance which we really cannot afford in this country, and to look therefore for higher densities," he wrote. "Both these trends have caused a tremendous amount of opposition among certain groups."[10] Stamp patiently pointed out that "a new settlement of the garden city type" left 15-25 per cent of the land not covered in roads, pathways, houses, garages and paths, so only one-fifth of its former area could be cultivated. Even though statistics were limited, he pointed out that amateur gardeners could not obtain as much produce as a professional market gardener on five times as much land. "This would seem to be quite obvious," he concluded.

Except when it contradicted the gospel of the Blessed Ebenezer of course. But Stamp was fighting back by now.

"It is, however, pointed out that not only do fresh vegetables from one's own garden have special virtues which it is difficult to estimate, but also in terms of cash they represent a very considerable saving to the housewife as well as a considerable contribution in aggregate to the national larder," he wrote.[11] "Calculations based on retail prices of vegetables naturally give some very high figures of the value of produce per acre. There are those who have then compared these figures with the average output of ordinary farmland. Quite clearly this is not comparing like with like." *Floreat Scientia*? A triumph for the science of geography perhaps.

Long after the 1950s gentlemen scientists had departed Wye College's cloisters, however, it achieved notoriety in the early twenty-first century when its bosses at Imperial College cooked up a secret scheme for a stunning new science campus in the Kent countryside to be financed by thousands of greenfield sprawl homes. Eventually the resulting furore proved too much for the local politicians, even though they had previously tried to secure it behind closed doors.

Food for thought

You would think a country wholly unable to feed itself in an uncertain world would have learned from the U-boat campaigns, which came far nearer to defeating our nation in both world wars than armies or air forces ever did. But the last 50 years have seen the slow erosion of protection for farmland, which was a lesson learned in those conflicts.

In 2010, the Department for Environment, Food and Rural Affairs produced its *Food 2030 Strategy*, reminding us that "we need to ensure that we can feed ourselves in the years to come by growing enough food sustainably".[12] Oddly, it contained not a single word about protecting UK farmland from development. It put an end to 60 years of using the planning system to protect farmland, and ministers could hardly claim they were unaware of the issue; at the same time they were over in Brussels arguing we didn't need a soil directive to limit soil sealing. The *Strategy*, however, had more important concerns, like "helping to foster an internationally competitive industry without reliance on subsidy and protection". It was hazy about how much of our food we do produce at home but did admit that much of the world's farmland faces degradation and gave Johnny Foreigner some pretty stern advice about how to protect *his* land.

So apparently we can rest easy in our beds, secure in the knowledge that a world where the population is shooting up and food production is levelling off will always be willing to supply us with the food we need, and we'll be equally sure our bankers won't place the wonga we need to pay for it on a three-legged mule in a selling plate at Devon & Exeter such as financial derivatives. We are sure, aren't we?

In 2009, however, the Sustainable Development Commission (SDC) had published *Food Security and Sustainability*,[13] a report which painted a less optimistic picture. UK food production has been in genteel decline since the early 1990s and our population has been rising. Things are better than in 1939, when we produced about a third of our food, but the strong protection given to the best farmland has been eroded and today we actually produce little more than 60 per cent of our food and less than 80 per cent of the foodstuffs that can be grown in the UK. We're more or less self-sufficient in meat, dairy and cereals but grow only around 50 per cent of our vegetables and 10 per cent of our fruit. And high production has a price of its own, with the Commission noting the large acreage of polytunnels in the England–Wales border country. "Its localness has come at some cost," it noted.

Optimistically, the Commission also observed that the forthcoming Foresight report would be an opportunity for a "long-needed policy correction".

"The loss of food-growing land – to building, roads, 'development' – cannot be ignored," it urged. "Soil is the most precious resource and everywhere needs to be kept in good condition to feed people while promoting ecosystems support." It recommended DEFRA give greater urgency to its soil strategy and food production.

Well, as we saw in Chapter 6, the Foresight report *Land Use Futures* suggested it should be ignored in parts of the country because people wanted to live in bigger homes and not have to get stuck in traffic jams when they drive to work.

The SDC report was actually followed by DEFRA's soil strategy,[14] which even dared articulate the 's-word' – sealing – despite the government's opposition to the soil directive. It noted that the planning system was "increasingly recognising the importance of mitigating the impacts of soil sealing, particularly in relation to urban drainage and maintaining green infrastructure" and stressed the importance of the brownfield housing target and that "appropriate consideration" be given to protecting good agricultural soils from development. It promised to work with the Department for Communities and Local Government (DCLG) to protect "important soils" (and the unimportant ones are where, exactly?) and considered the need for a policy update. DCLG responded with planning guidance ignoring, for the first time since the Second World War, the importance of protecting soils.

DEFRA's soil strategy assured us that a long-term review of all types of land management was under way to optimise land use and management. But it let the cat out of the bag by admitting this was mostly the forthcoming Foresight report, whose response to the threat of low-density and greenfield development was to justify it because the market wanted it.

Any Smart Growth policy for the UK must include strong protection for all soils, a presumption against soil sealing and mitigation of losses to soil sealing by unsealing equivalent areas where it does occur. Our soils are far too important to our very survival to be squandered on housing sprawl and road building, even to appease the great god Market.

What would Cobbett have made of our casual disregard of our soil? Standing outside an inn in Dover he was (most unusually for him) in two minds about whether to visit France or to return to the 'Wen', so he decided to toss the bridle upon his horse's neck and let him decide the matter.

"I am sure he is more fit to decide on such a point than our ministers are to decide on any point connected with the happiness, greatness and honour of this kingdom," he decided.[15] You can see what he meant.

Defending our land

Defending our land had real significance in 1940 when H. V. Morton took charge of a Home Guard unit and kept watch for invaders from a church tower.

It is a still night. And now the clouds part and the moon, shining through, casts green shadows so that I can see the little hamlet lying below among haystacks and fields, the lime-washed cottages with front gardens bright with Canterbury bells, geraniums and poppies; and I think that a more peaceful bit of old England could not be found than this village of ours. Yet in every cottage sleeps an armed man . . ."[16]

Paper was in short supply in wartime Britain, but the government was well aware that books about the glories of the British countryside would strengthen the morale of a soldier in a sandy trench at Tobruk or a sailor in a wet, swinging hammock in a storm-tossed Atlantic escort vessel.

Today our land faces a different sort of invasion, for we are the invaders and there are those who would convince us environmental salvation lies in rejecting the traditions of rural conservation. We live in a country where even senior environmentalists can talk about 'NIMBY NGOs', but let's remember it was the wonder of nature, the glories of wildlife and the beauty of the countryside that inspired many people to become environmentalists in the first place.

How, then, should we protect our precious greenfield land resource? I can see no alternative to using the planning system, which can be an incredibly effective force for environmental protection when used properly. That doesn't mean we won't need some new planning guidance of course, as we will need to strengthen the protection greenfield land receives (and some brownfield land at remote sites unsuitable for development). We need to put in place a hard-to-overcome-except-where-there-are-remarkably-good-reasons-for-doing-so presumption against developing them. And where greenfield land is sealed for development, we need to ensure an equivalent area is unsealed. This may seem extreme, but extreme environmental stress requires extreme environmental protection. It's not a luxury actually, it's a necessity, especially in a country where there are always politicians ready to find excuses for more sprawl. Homes! Employment! The economy! The free market! A century of planning tradition! I've just had a fat bribe from a developer!

Yes, we need some pretty robust planning rules.

How should we designate our landscapes?

I sat down and tried to list all our current landscape, amenity, cultural, historical, archaeological, scientific and biodiversity land designations and gave up at 25. The trouble is, they don't protect most of the country. Often they overlap and many protect only small areas. Around 20 per cent of England and smaller proportions of the rest of the UK is covered by one or another. And, green belts apart, virtually none does anything to restrict sprawl and even less to promote a Smart Growth approach. Perhaps it's time for a look at them.

In 2009, a report to Natural England's Board[17] discussed the quango's future strategy on designations and wondered if a blank-sheet approach was needed. "If we were starting from scratch, in the same position as the 1945-50 Parliament, how would we set about the creation of a series of designations and for what purposes?" the board was asked.

But answer came there none. The board "welcomed the opportunity to have an informed and transparent debate about the future of protected areas" and made other comments, but its courage went no further because "we should be mindful of the sensitive nature of this debate and in particular the views of key stakeholders and the public". Right . . . and so?

"The Board agreed that while a full review is needed, the time is not right given current political and economic uncertainties and the need to bring partners fully into our thinking".[18] Well, one shouldn't ignore the political pressure placed on quangos even when governments aren't trying to 'bash' them. Still, we can go further, can't we?

There is a peculiar belief among the public that all undeveloped countryside is 'green belt', but this is far from the case. England has 14 green belt areas surrounding many, though not all, of its major conurbations and collectively covering just 13 per cent of England. Some large conurbations such as Leicester and Hull have no green belt at all, and every year around 2 per cent of England's new homes are built in green belts. Scotland has eight green belt areas plus three in the pipeline, while Wales has just the one around Cardiff.

Green belts are a distinctly double-edged weapon; they undoubtedly set limits on conurbations' expansion but sometimes at the price of encouraging development to leapfrog them to the country beyond. As early as 1970 the *Strategic Plan for the South East* noted that a "ring city" was forming around the capital, helped along of course by the growth areas such as south Essex, Milton Keynes and Area 8, between Reading, Bracknell and Aldershot. The countryside around the conurbation was protected, but at the expense of the countryside beyond it and forced commuters to travel further. Green belts around cities have, however, provided wonderful places to build orbital motorways. Other designations present even less restraint to sprawl, and big housing developments have even been proposed for Areas of Outstanding Natural Beauty such as the North Wessex Downs, Chilterns and Kent Downs.

So could the existing system be used to provide a higher level of protection?

One possibility would be to exploit the public's rather naïve belief that all countryside is green belt by simply enshrining that in planning law and making all greenfield and fully restored brownfield land 'green belt'. It would certainly have the regulatory value of simplicity and would not override the more restrictive designations such as national parks. On the other hand, it might be harder to persuade planning authorities to take it any more seriously than they

Green belts – just the place for orbital motorways.

do the ill-defined (and even iller-defended) 'greenfield site'. But if all greenfield land were designated green belt, then all green belt policies would simply be extended and it would be up to central and local government to say where it should *not* apply – the reverse of the present situation. That could, however, prompt long-term erosion of the green belt concept, so perhaps we need to be more ambitious.

Another possibility might be to create a formal 'greenfield' designation for all greenfield land and a requirement for it to be identified in local plans. It could then be divided into different levels of protection, such as listed buildings, but there would be a danger that the lowest categories of greenfield land might enjoy no more protection than they do already. And while it could provide a high degree of protection against sprawl, how much would it do to promote 'transit-oriented development' and siting new developments where they had access to good-quality rail-based public transport?

A more complex system, which would keep planners gainfully employed for a long time, would involve zoning all land according to a whole range of spatial, environmental, transport and social criteria:

- greenfield/brownfield status
- proximity to city/town/village centre
- proximity to rail-based public transport

- proximity to bus services
- proximity to employment
- proximity to education
- proximity to shops
- proximity to health care
- proximity to community facilities
- walkability/cycle access
- flood vulnerability or potential for alleviation
- agricultural/horticultural importance
- nature conservation/biodiversity value
- landscape quality
- townscape quality
- historic quality
- potential for carbon sequestration
- potential/presence of woodland.

This long, but far from exhaustive, list is obviously far too complicated to impose by a protected area system; it would need the rejig of the planning system we've discussed already. Nevertheless, development of the protected area system might still provide some powerful weapons to fight sprawl.

How will we survive in the country?

It's inescapable that country life is going to be a challenge in a low-carbon world. Even in an era of cheap petrol, rural areas are losing services such as shops, pubs, schools, health facilities, post offices, etc. And this of course makes people even more dependent on their cars. Even if punitive carbon restriction measures aren't imposed on the sacred motorist any time soon, fuel is going to get more and more expensive year after year.

Greenfield sprawl is sometimes justified by saying it will allow threatened services to survive, but this is generally tosh, as at least one travel writer has noted. Paul Gogarty's canal voyage along *The Water Road*[19] took him to the village of King's Sutton, south of Banbury. There he learned the 1966 population had been 600; by 2002 it had risen to 2,000, but where it had previously had six grocers and three butchers, it was now down to one general store. Blame the motor car and the out-of-town supermarket; blame a long-hours culture that squeezes shopping to a once-a-week megashop; blame our desire for ever more consumer goods at ever-lower prices. Yes, blame the lot.

And while we can, in the longer term, reopen some rural rail services, remote areas are going to remain heavily dependent on road transport, so what will they do when fossil fuel power is just too expensive? Well, perhaps here the electric vehicle will come into its own. Its range is short, but generally it will do a trip to the local town once a day and, whatever the carbon and national grid implications of such a vast increase in demand for electricity, here surely is one thing we will have to protect to some extent. For the rest, bus services will have to be improved and no doubt innovation will build on initiatives such as community bus services and demand-responsive transport.

Despite that, we shall have to revive local services. Here surely is an opportunity for little 'big societies' to organise multiple service centres in villages, with some public help. A few villages are already experimenting with community-controlled facilities running community centres, shops, pubs, post offices, doctors' surgeries, etc. Smart Growth is, after all, about reviving communities.

How do we protect our beautiful countryside?

Somewhere, within my not-particularly-long life, we've lost something important. I'm not sure when we lost it, but when I heard a Very Important Planner dismiss concerns about greenfield development as merely the loss of "just some worthless farmland", I realised that the loss is a critically dangerous one.

Farmland is never worthless – its value to agriculture may vary, but its importance runs much deeper. Our farmland is central to our identity even if we never set foot in the countryside. We all sprang from soil somewhere or

Just some worthless farmland.

other on this planet; it is part of who we are and means much more than the food, water or ecosystem services it provides. Much more.

While avoiding the trap of saying our countryside is part of our Englishness, our Scottishness, our Welshness or even our Northern Irishness, it is still part of our national identity. It is the garden within which our towns sit, whatever our ethnic origins. Virtually all of us, whatever our origins, have had an intimate relationship with the countryside somewhere within very recent generations. Farming is something all our forebears practised for thousands of years, and they hunted and gathered from the land for millions before that. I don't buy the argument there's no need to worry about the British countryside if your ethnic origins lie elsewhere. If you live here, it's your countryside and with you lies the vast opportunity it offers and the deep responsibility on all of us to protect it. I know rural communities (anywhere on the planet) can seem hostile to incomers, but just as anyone whose ethnic origins lie within these shores can travel anywhere in the world and appreciate the country there, so anyone can enjoy it here.

And yes, it's true that virtually all of the countryside in these islands is the product of human intervention since 3,000BC (by successive waves of immigrants, incidentally), but for most of those millennia it was a balance between human activity and nature. We exploited our land and we defended our land, and then came industry and most of us flocked to the cities while some remained to steward the land. And then came Ebenezer Howard and his chums to build suburbs upon the Earth and William Morris II and his kind to give the suburbs wheels. And we began to love the countryside to death.

"The astonishing fact about the British countryside", wrote Wynford Vaughan-Thomas in 1979,[20] "is that so much of it is still there." There is, of course, a fair bit less today than in 1979 and Vaughan-Thomas could see why, for he suggested that a bird's-eye view would show "the motorway runs relentlessly through the green countryside . . . The bull-dozers are laying out approach roads for the new factory on a 'green' site. Another small part of Britain is disappearing under its carpet of asphalt and concrete."

And just look at the difference three decades can make. We've stopped building factories on the English countryside and now we build them on the Chinese countryside, so trashing our land is now confined to the building of houses, supermarkets, distribution warehouses and motorways.

Destroying our rural areas risks losing our food security, our water supply, our flood defence, our wildlife and our place for recreation. But it also means losing something very much more fundamental, something not even the most radical environmental economist could ever put a price on. We risk losing the exquisite beauty of our countryside.

I can get pretty cross about destruction of farmland and food production. I can get irked about plans to build more homes in south and east England than the region could ever provide with water. I can get really annoyed about destruction of wildlife or biodiversity. But it's when I see the landscapes I love – and not just the amazing bits – wantonly destroyed to make someone a pile of cash in pursuit of some unsustainable theory about household formation or whatever, that the tinder bursts into flame. Righteous anger is, in the true sense of the word, a terrible thing – it should strike terror. They are stealing our heart, our soul, our fundamental sense of being, call it what you like, but destroying the beauty of our land cuts to the heart of what we are.

No one should ever try to put a financial value on this. You can put a price on a great painting, but that's not its value. And a great painting, even in a private collection, is something with value to me. I don't own any of the British countryside either but, just as I feel a sense of loss if I hear that a great work of art or historic building has been destroyed, I can get really furious when another slice of countryside disappears under Mondeo hutches.

So when somebody calls you a NIMBY for defending the countryside, thank them. The way people have been accused of hypocrisy via this label for defending their local environment shows the depths some people will go to make money out of wrecking it. Wear it as a badge of pride. "Not in my backyard and not in anybody else's. Take your junk development and go. This is our land."

Beauty raped is beauty destroyed. It is vital, central to our well-being. We need, we all of us need, to say this has to stop.

Smart Growth in the country

It might be objected at this point that Smart Growth is essentially an urban development policy, and certainly its roots lie in urban spatial, transport and community planning, although opposition to sprawl has featured from the start. But now US Smart Growth practitioners are asking how such policies can be applied to help growth in rural areas while protecting natural and working lands and preserving the character of existing communities.

In 2010 the International City/County Management Association, an American local government body, published *Putting Smart Growth to Work in Rural Communities*,[21] a report for the US Environmental Protection Agency. Three objectives underpinned the report:

- support the rural landscape by creating an economic climate that enhances the viability of working lands and conserves natural lands
- help existing places to thrive by taking care of assets and investments such as downtowns, main streets, existing infrastructure, and places that the community values

- create great new places by building vibrant, enduring neighbourhoods and communities that people, especially young people, don't want to leave.

Rural America's economic and environmental challenges are not exactly the same as ours, but it's plain there are at least echoes and useful lessons for our towns and villages. William Cobbett was one of the first to demand we give at least as much attention to the countryside as the town, though that derived from his contempt for urban areas. But surely the two are different sides of the same coin and we cannot fix one without fixing the other.

Smart Growth rural planning policies

- Avoidance of 'soil sealing'.
- Protection of undeveloped land except in exceptional circumstances.
- Use of the planning system to protect our land through measures such as new protected area designations, expansion of green belt designation, etc.
- Support for services in villages through flexible, multi-use buildings.
- Protection of soils and promotion of peat formation and carbon sequestration in upland areas.
- Support for tree planting, reafforestation, rewilding, wetland and other 'natural uses', especially where it helps to mitigate climate change.
- Strict protection for farmland in planning guidance.
- Support for local food production.
- Acceptance that beauty is a factor in all countryside protection.
- Landscape-scale conservation and ecological networks.
- Encouragement of quiet recreation.

And in the longer term:
- Restoration of some remote and unsustainable low-density sprawl settlements and out-of-town shopping centres for greenfield uses.
- A system for funding 'unsealing' brownfield land at remote sites to be paid for by a tax on any greenfield land development.

Chapter 11

Smart Growth transport

I sometimes think it would be a good thing if every motor-car could be put out of action for six months to give us time to think where all this is leading us.

H. V. Morton, *I Saw Two Englands*

The great transformation

Shortly before the Second World War, H. V. Morton travelled to Kent,[1] and even this passionate motoring pioneer had to admit that no road infested with robbers, footpads and highwaymen 200 years before would have been half as dangerous as the road to the coast. A quarter of a century earlier, he noted, everyone would have gone by train, but by the late 1930s buses and cars had transformed the face of the countryside and the grim automotive slaughter had begun. "Few of us realise how complete was the transformation," he noted.

So let's remember things can change quite quickly; within a couple of years of Morton's run to the coast, very strict petrol rationing was in force and private cars were pretty much off the road. Today we face equally huge challenges and, as in 1938, most of us seem to be pretending they don't exist. And even if climate change weren't a problem, we could run our towns and cities as communities that work and protect our countryside from further destruction. But part of this process will involve transport changes that some may find painful. We need to start planning a very different transport future and we need to start in the towns.

The symbiotic twins go for a drive

Politicians love to talk about inter-urban transport, whether it's 1,000 more miles of motorway or high-speed rail links. It's the sort of policy they think will impress electors and will carve their names across our landscape. But the transport that needs fixing first is within cities, for it's in the cities that fossil fuel is squandered the most inefficiently, the most pollutingly and the most pointlessly.

In Chapter 9 we came across the key urbanist concept of the permeable town – an antidote to the endless unbroken streets and cul-de-sacs of garden sprawl towns. Our traditional cities developed at high densities but with routes for pedestrians and cyclists to penetrate them without going all round the world. So we must make our towns and cities permeable again, allowing walkers and cyclists to move freely and directly, even if the two do need to be kept apart by at least a kerb. They also need to be compact, for transport reasons.

J. B. Priestley found Hull "a sound and sensible city",[2] even its docks contrasting starkly with the usual murk found in the gloomy docks of cities like London or Liverpool: "Its docks have daylight in them," he exclaimed.

But, talking to a Hull shipping agent, he discovered one deficiency in what he otherwise rated a well-run city. The agent noted that in Hull, as in some other cities, new workmen's quarters had been created outside the town, and said the dock workers should have been rehoused in their old districts, close to where they worked. Most dockers, he explained, have no regular work. They had to 'stand a ship', i.e. go down to the docks in the early morning to see if they were needed and then again in the afternoon. If the morning yielded no work, they had to wait around until the afternoon. Once, they could return to their firesides in the interim but, thanks to the relocation of their new homes outside the city by well-meaning people, that would mean a lengthy and expensive bus or tram ride, so instead they hung around, spending their desperately meagre cash on food and drink.

"Thus they are worse off than they were before, simply because they have been removed so far from their work," noted Priestley. "Their womenfolk especially grumble about it."

Like so many others, the Hull dockers were victims of the sprawl movement (and curiously Hull, despite long-term population decline, is still ripping down compact inner areas and replacing them with greenfield sprawl). Indeed, many of the places the British now inhabit are low-density sprawl, utterly dependent on low-quality bus services or cars. The car is king because there's really no alternative.

Joe Bennett's strange ramble in the steps of H. V. Morton[3] found him in a Chester pub where he met a woman called Annie from Telford, who related her unfavourable account of the new town.

"You've got to drive everywhere," she told him. "Not like here. Everything's all bunched up together up here. It's nice. Besides, I wouldn't go out in Telford, not after dark. I just go home, lock the door and don't hear a thing."

The transport problem in a nutshell – and even if that slanders Telford's crime record, it's the fear that suburban isolation generates that's the problem – locking our doors and not hearing a thing.

The link between the sprawl lobby and roads lobby is inescapable. Early in 2009, ministers announced a £170 million package of funding for transport infrastructure paid for in a novel way.[4] Money for the 29 projects was to come from a new pot called the community infrastructure fund, a joint Department for Communities and Local Government and Department for Transport fund to pay for transport schemes that support housing growth. Urban regeneration certainly needs transport funding at this sort of level to fund light rail schemes, metros, railway stations, interchanges, etc. But that would be to misunderstand the nature of what has been seen as 'housing growth', which normally means greenfield schemes, and the transport needed to support them is mostly roads, despite the claim by the then transport minister Paul Clark, who welcomed the "quality and range" of the schemes to be funded.

"Around 60 per cent of the schemes that we are supporting include sustainable transport initiatives – reflecting a real commitment to supporting housing growth through sustainable means," he said.

Note the weasel words – "include sustainable alternatives". The minister had just conceded that 40 per cent of the schemes he'd just approved were wholly unsustainable and all the rest included unsustainable elements, for 40 per cent of the schemes were pure road building and the rest had some elements, often very minor, of public transport funding.

Let's look at this 'sustainable development' – £21 million for 'Postwick Hub', a highway interchange to form the first stage of the Norwich Northern Relief Road planned to open up a vast area of greenfield land for sprawl; £11.2 million for a junction on the A12 at Haven Gateway to serve a 'growth point' (more sprawl); £9.9 million to dual the A414 to relieve some of the congestion exacerbated by the London-Harlow-Stansted sprawl corridor, sorry 'growth area'; £16.5 million for Victoria Way in the Ashford growth area; £6.5 million for a grade-separated junction on the A38 at Branston to support a growth point at Burton-on-Trent; and so it went on. And the 60 per cent with sustainable alternatives? One or two, such as a new interchange at Reading station, were genuinely worthwhile, but there were some curious candidates for 'sustainability' too. There was £20 million for the South East Hampshire Bus Rapid Transit – the replacement of the abandoned but genuinely sustainable south Hampshire light rail scheme with an expensive and pointless guided busway along part of its route.

'Bus rapid transit' – bendy buses with curvy fronts to fool people – featured strongly. There was £5.3 million for a Northampton-Wellingborough bus rapid transit, to bring a bus service to some of the sprawl planned for Northamptonshire. This was originally meant to have a (pointless) guidance system on dedicated bus lanes but the cost soon turned it into an extra lane on the A45, which wouldn't even be confined to buses. Like the Sustainable Communities Plan (see Chapter 6), it was another Holy Roman Empire moment – not rapid, not transit and this time not even just buses either. There was £3.2 million for the West of Worcester Bus Rapid Transit corridor, basically just a bus route with nicer bus stops. There was £5.6 million for a Milton Keynes Busway, which was, well, a busway to link new sprawl east of the town. £9.78 million would buy the nice-sounding Plymouth East End Community Transport Improvements, which helped buses, pedestrians and cyclists and that well-known community transport initiative, highway improvements. And what were these for?

"This is welcome investment much needed to pave the way for that part of Plymouth's growth on the eastern side of the city," announced Plymouth Sutton MP Linda Gilroy. Growth, that is, not sprawl, never sprawl, although it's ominously called the 'Eastern Corridor', which sounds eerily like one of those concepts Hitler used to justify aggression.

So, basically, here was a broke country proposing to spend a sixth of a billion pounds to demonstrate the symbiotic links between sprawl and road building.

"We know that good transport links are vital to successful communities and these projects will unlock the potential for new housing where it is needed," said the then housing minister Margaret Beckett.

"Poop-poop!" said Mr Toad.

Still travelling hopelessly

A report for the European Environment Agency in 2009[5] revealed that no less than 87.5 per cent of UK passenger transport is by car and, across the 29 other European countries studied, only Norway (87.9 per cent) and Lithuania (90.6 per cent) travelled so unsustainably. Most did much better. Rail was only attracting 6.1 per cent of UK passenger transport while in France the figure is 9.4 per cent, even in that less densely populated, predominantly rural country. The same goes for freight, where 88.1 per cent of UK movement is by lorry, exceeded only by Italy, Luxembourg, Denmark, Greece, Portugal, Spain, Ireland and Iceland, none of which ever had the dense industrial railway or waterway systems we used to enjoy. Rail attracts 11.8 per cent of UK freight; in Germany the figure is 21.4 per cent and in Austria 33.8 per cent.

While other sectors of the economy, such as power generation, are working out how to make substantial reductions in their carbon emissions to meet targets, transport remains obstinately unreformed. Which, of course, offers huge opportunities for reform – and Smart Growth offers particular benefits here.

Driving across the pond

Where the UK managed 100 years of sprawl, America managed 100 years of hypersprawl, but in both cases the engine was the internal combustion engine. But while Smart Growth policies are reversing the trend over there, we're still

Transit-oriented development and greenhouse emissions

Transit-oriented development brings mobility to cities, but it's becoming clear that it is also really good at reducing carbon emissions.

A report[6] for America's Center for Transit Oriented Development examined the potential greenhouse gas reductions that transit-oriented development can achieve in the transport sector. The researchers found that the transport greenhouse gas emissions of households living near transit stops in a central city were 43-per-cent lower than those of households in an average location in that city. In the most location-efficient transit zones, this was as high as 78 per cent.

Transit Oriented Development and the Potential for VMT-Related Greenhouse Gas Emissions Reductions was funded through an agreement with the US Federal Transit Administration. Transport accounts for around 28 per cent of US greenhouse gas emissions, and household car usage accounts for 61 per cent of that.

The study calculated how the form in which we build our cities affects household vehicle travel and looked at how three different development scenarios would affect Chicago – business as usual, accommodating growth in both city and suburbs, and concentrating growth in transit zones proportional to the growth that's already there. Greenhouse gas emissions were reduced by 36 per cent if development proceeded in a compact and efficient manner.

"Individuals and families that live near transit centres own fewer automobiles, drive fewer miles, and leave a much smaller carbon footprint than those who don't," said Scott Bernstein, president of the Center for Neighbourhood Technology, which led the research.

Transit-oriented development.
Image: US Environmental Protection Agency, Smart Growth Program

bleating about 'low-emission cars' and the social implications of putting any restrictions on flying.

Take Baltimore, for instance, the city fictionalised in *The Wire* and held up by the then shadow minister Chris Grayling in 2009 as typifying life in 'broken' Britain. The once-prosperous industrial city lost a third of its inhabitants between 1950 and 2000 while its outer suburbs gained a million new residents thanks to construction of a massive highway network allowing commuters to live in the 'exurbs' and drive to the centre. A familiar and self-reinforcing inner-city pattern emerged of excluded underclass, declining public services, crime, abandoned buildings, etc.

But in Baltimore today, as in dozens of US cities, rising gasoline prices mean many people can no longer afford the long drive to work, and the house price crash that set off the 2008 recession has hit those distant suburbs hardest. Not long ago they were the best things on realtors' books; today they're some of the hardest to sell, and not only have some new developments been left half finished, in some parts of America they've even been demolished. Welcome to the post-oil future.

Suddenly sprawl has become a dirty word and the land of the free market is investing billions of dollars in rail-based urban and inter-urban transit, while departments of Smart Growth proliferate in town and city halls and state capitals. Towns are being densified around transit stops and high-density living is becoming fashionable again. People are surprised to discover they can move between home, work and shops without a car.

Baltimore itself already has examples of successful transit-oriented development, such as Clipper Mill, Mount Vernon Square and other neighbourhoods that developed around historic tramlines. Denver, meanwhile, once one of America's most sprawl-and-motorway-addicted cities, has imposed a sales tax to pay for a rail-based transit plan. In 2006 it opened 19 miles of light railway through its metropolitan area and quickly saw the centre repopulating. This prompted approval of the $6.2 billion FasTracks project for six light and heavy rail lines in the Denver-Aurora and Boulder areas of Colorado. Urban expansion is now taking place around the stations, and this pattern is being repeated in many places across America, assisted by Barack Obama's stimulus package, and similar trends can be found in parts of Canada and Australia too.

How can we reduce transport's carbon emissions?

It is a truth universally recognised, and universally forgotten as soon as we get in our cars, that we urgently need to drive less. Because our transport system is carbon-rotten.

Keith Buchan's *A Low Carbon Transport Policy for the UK*[7] estimated that UK transport greenhouse emissions are much higher than the figures usually quoted by ministers, etc. Transport is usually said to account for about 23.5 per cent of UK emissions but this conveniently omits the emissions from refining the fuel, manufacturing the vehicles, etc. Add them in and the figure rises to 28.3 per cent, and that excludes international goods and passenger movement. When you add *them* in it shoots transport's share of UK emissions up to 33 per cent, with road transport accounting for 70 per cent of the total and

Road transport accounts for at least a quarter of UK carbon emissions.

aviation 21 per cent. When you break down the transport, you find cars account for more than half these emissions, heavy goods vehicles for just under a quarter and light vans for about an eighth.

But while other emitters face trading schemes and other restrictions, and this may even one day hit aviation and shipping despite their wriggling out of the Kyoto Protocol, any restriction on road transport emissions faces a wall of public opposition carefully fostered by much of the press. The government's 2007 report *Towards a Sustainable Transport System*[8] may have stipulated that emissions should be reduced to avoid dangerous climate change, but things are still heading towards, er, dangerous climate change. Overall UK emissions fell 6 per cent between 1990 and 2005 but transport emissions rose 10.6 per cent (or 24.6 per cent if you include international aviation and shipping), and there's still no clear national policy to reverse this.

Politicians of all parties remain utterly petrified of the issue, and the only real restraint seems to be lack of cash for road building. In 2009 the government dropped two billion pounds' worth of plans for widening the M1, M25 and M62 and came up with an alternative scheme of 'hard shoulder running' (presumably so that breaking down on motorways became still more hazardous), but a study[9] by Professor Phil Goodwin of the Department of Transport's own figures found these expensive alternatives would mean speeds on these routes would still fall as a result of congestion, but by only 3.5 per cent by 2025, compared with a slightly larger fall if the money were not spent. As Goodwin points out, road schemes are appraised in isolation.

In all forecasts and appraisals, all traffic which is using the 'long-distance' roads is included indiscriminately, even if it is just making short hops on the motorway as part of a mainly urban journey. Yet at the same time, all policies in the urban areas which have an effect on the volume of that traffic are ignored.

In other words, we are concentrating on the easy bits and ignoring the much harder urban congestion problems. We should be looking at motorists' whole journeys, not just the motorway hop. In cities, Goodwin recommended:
- road or congestion charging
- 'smarter choices' that help people to discover alternatives to the car
- improved public transport and cycle and pedestrian facilities
- reallocation of road space to the most productive, or most needy, users
- real-time information systems
- better land-use planning
- increased use of IT for teleworking, online shopping or transport management.

For years engineers have just about kept the cities moving with complex traffic management measures, and the only real restraints have been applied by congestion and parking controls, both of which leave much to be desired. Complex and effective techniques exist, but the UK has been ignoring them.

Transport remains the big untackled area in UK climate policy, yet Buchan's report points out that transport usage is strongly related to income, while hitting something like electricity supply affects disproportionately those on low incomes. What matters, he argues, is not how big the percentage reduction we achieve by 2020 or 2050, but how *soon* we make the cuts. A tonne of carbon emitted in 2011 will have caused 39 years of ill-effects by 2050, while a tonne emitted in 2049 will have caused just one year's.

But politicians across the spectrum remain paralysed. In 2009, Tony Blair visited Beijing on behalf of The Climate Group, an organisation of large companies in the UK, USA and Australia, to help launch a report telling China, which had spent much of the previous 15 years quietly and effectively lobbying to be permitted to ignore action on climate change, how well it was doing. Speaking in a country where tens of thousands die on the roads each year and where road traffic is expected to triple in the next decade to the point where China produces 20 per cent of the world's traffic fumes, Blair maintained that nothing must be done to curb traffic.

"I think it is completely unrealistic to say to people you can't have a car, you can't use a motorbike," he said. "It is just not going to happen."

This was pretty much the message of the government's national strategy for climate and energy in 2009, which said that if meeting an 80-per-cent carbon reduction target meant hitting people's desire to drive or fly, then even bigger cuts would have to be made in other sectors.

There are quick hits to be made if politicians had an ounce of courage, but many would involve simple behavioural changes that would still set the barmier bits of the press whining and grizzling. Yet a 'smarter choices' philosophy is designed to offer individuals and companies active management opportunities to use vehicles less with minimal pain. Buchan's policy package addresses wider concerns than Goodwin's, but there are elements in common:

• a public transport accessibility standard for land-use planning
• a national public transport city travelcard
• smarter choice schemes for workplaces
• higher development densities
• rail electrification and capacity improvements
• air travel taxation
• consistent planning for transit schemes
• changes to fuel duty and vehicle efficiency
• charging lorries for the damage they do (which is wide-ranging and extensive)
• safeguarding for rail/road interchange sites
• rail freight investment.

A common element is land-use planning and here, in embryo, is the beginnings of a Smart Growth transport policy. Buchan's work, unusually in the UK, endorses a Smart Growth approach, while Goodwin calls for planning to ensure that origins and destinations are as close as possible.

"While journey lengths have grown hugely, the number of journeys has been relatively static, as has the total amount of time spent travelling," says *A Low Carbon Transport Policy for the UK*. Low-density development, car-dependent shops, employment and leisure facilities and a hugely improved road system have made car travel an indispensable thing to most people, and the growth in house prices has diminished the percentage of their income they spend on motoring. The result has been us motoring more and more each year – an annual average 4,700 miles in 1975, 5,300 miles in 1985 and 6,700 miles in 1995, for instance. Goods travelled ever further too. Underlying all these effects, says Buchan, is the low cost of road travel.

What would a Smart Growth transport policy for the UK look like?

Let's take a deep breath and upset the tabloids straight away by admitting that a Smart Growth transport policy could adversely affect the motorist, the air passenger, the haulier, the out-of-town shopper and even the importer of cheap goods. Of course it could also greatly enrich our environment, our economy,

We need more light rail . . . *Image: Jim Harkins*

our society and our individual lives, but, hey, why worry about such trifles? Would it mean more speed cameras?

The first thing we need to fix is the cities.

Politicians, of course, love to tout grandiose schemes for ultra-high-speed railway lines at election time, safe in the knowledge the bills won't arrive in their term of office and they can always appease the press with plans for new motorways. But the most urgent need is not inter-urban transport, it's city transport, and we need to provide cities with rail-based transit.

Some have it already, of course. Most cities have some suburban heavy rail presence and a small handful of lines have seen some significant investment in the last half-century. Some have metros, such as the London Underground, Docklands Light Railway, Tyne & Wear Metro or Glasgow Underground. And Greater Manchester, Sheffield, the West Midlands, Croydon, Blackpool, Nottingham and Edinburgh have at least the beginnings of a light rail network.

But we need very much more. The 19 billion quid postulated as the price of taking the ultra-high-speed HS2 route from somewhere in north London to Birmingham would pay to provide at least the beginnings of a system in all the UK's conurbations with more than 250,000 people. Some preliminary work by the Smart Growth UK Steering Group revealed that in most of these conurbations there had been at least some development work on light rail schemes

... and metro systems.

between 1985 and 2010, and in some cases this was fairly well advanced, to the point of advance works in a handful of cases.

So let's propose a multi-phase policy for urban rail development. In the first ten years the aim would be to introduce a light rail or metro system to those conurbations that lack one and, for those that already have one, use development work already carried out to begin extending their systems. In those where no such work had been done, plans would have to be drawn up, with the intention of at least beginning work by the end of the decade. Nor would opportunities to improve the suburban rail network in the cities be neglected; they would have to form part of the plan too.

In the second decade work would continue, with the aim of creating increasingly comprehensive systems in cities with substantial systems and growing those that were just starting out. The process of bringing light rail to cities with fewer than 250,000 people would also begin. The third decade would see major conurbations eventually enjoying dense and comprehensive systems, and increasing provision in smaller cities and even large towns.

Meanwhile, the bus network would be improved to provide services anywhere that rail-based transport was unavailable, and a better system developed to regulate it while still enjoying the benefits of competition.

Complementing the rail network in the towns would be a range of 'smarter choices' measures including traffic control and restraint. This would be applied progressively across the three decades and tailored to whatever best suited the town in question. More road space would be allocated to pedestrians and cyclists and protecting them from other users.

Sorting out our unsustainable inter-urban transport would have to follow too. To some extent the rising cost of fuel will make car journeys increasingly unattractive, but we will need substantial investment in both local and inter-urban rail, including electrification, to demonstrate the viability of alternatives. Another target must be rail capacity problems in our major cities, where substantial investment to sort out bottlenecks is often likely to lead to greater benefits than ultra-high-speed inter-urban routes. Such routes should still be on the horizon, but only as a lower priority, perhaps to keep politicians in their comfort zone at election time. In the longer term, extra capacity for high-speed rail or even rail freight routes could even be provided by shutting one carriageway on motorways.

Aviation is sure to become an early casualty of rising fuel prices anyway, given the total lack of non-fossil-fuel alternatives. A Smart Growth policy would scrap all airport expansion straight away and, as flying declines, might see part or all of some airports released for development for which their rail access may make them particularly suitable.

How will we travel around the sprawl?

The biggest challenge will be moving around within our massive dismal legacy of sprawl. In Chapter 10 we looked at densification around transit stops, something that's already happening in America. But many UK cities lack transit altogether and represent the most pressing need, so providing transit-oriented development to our many, many low-density suburbs may have to wait a little, but not too long. Most have at least a railway station, and a start could be made by improving these services, but under-investment and lack of capacity will hinder this. The longer-term answer will have to be the development of transit, transit-oriented development around transit stops, densification and new services. For the time being, I suspect, cities that currently lack transit will mostly have to soldier on with bus services and declining standards as road commuting becomes more expensive and the areas' attraction wanes. A few may be so inaccessible they will enter a terminal decline.

How will we get between towns?

If aviation is set for decline and long-distance driving is set to follow, then responsible governments should be looking at alternatives. So as a very first step we need to safeguard the alignment (the disused trackbeds) of our former railway lines. Often in the decades since closure they have been damaged by buildings or roads, but substantial lengths of alignment still survive and are an asset too precious to waste. Safeguarding most of them would involve the same requirements as safeguarding road schemes, something that's been done on a vast and expensive scale over the past half century, so please let's not hear we can't afford it. So, if your house stands on a former rail alignment that looks as if it might go somewhere useful, perhaps it's time to think about a move.

So what should we safeguard? Network Rail has done some work on new lines needed to meet anticipated growth in passenger and freight demand over the next decade, and in 2009 the Association of Train Operating Companies (ATOC) published a report[10] noting that the rail network is now carrying 30 per cent more passengers than 45 years ago on a considerably smaller network, and wondering what to do about it. It said 27 new lines and 68 stations had opened since 1995 but that more are plainly needed.

ATOC suggested that 14 places in England have a positive business case for a new line, to serve communities of 15,000 or more which currently lack a service, and also identified a number of potential new stations. Beyond these it identified a further six lines where the ratio of benefits to costs was one or less, but where the line could be justified on the basis of economic regeneration or employment benefits (an approach already used in Wales and Scotland). Most of these schemes had short lead times and, taken together, could bring direct or indirect rail access to around one million people.

And that's just the schemes that meet current business cases. We need to be more ambitious over the long term. The Campaign for Better Transport has recommended no fewer than 138 lines in England and Wales that should be protected from development as they have reopening potential, and that list is not exhaustive; as the advertising slogan had it, the only limit is our imagination.

We need to safeguard these routes from development, from road building and, amazingly and sadly, from the recreational cycling lobby. Long ago, protecting abandoned rail alignments by converting them to footpaths and cycle tracks was seen as a way of preserving them until an era of wiser transport policies prevailed. Well, that era is coming down the track, but what will it encounter on at least some of the railway formations so protected? Sad to say, it will meet militant recreational cyclists fighting to prevent them being reopened as railways.

If you think this sounds barmy, it's already happened. Mostly, so far, it's just been heritage railways, like the Eden Valley Railway in Cumbria, which found a disused railway it wanted to reopen abruptly sold for conversion to part of a long-distance cycle route. But it's no longer just happening to heritage railways: in 2009 the Department for Transport sparked rage when it announced that £3.8 million was to be spent upgrading a footpath and cycleway on part of the former Matlock–Buxton main line closed in the 1970s. The outrage, which took the Department by surprise, was sparked because not only was a heritage railway trying to reopen the Matlock–Buxton section, but mainline rail operators were also keen to reopen it as part of a useful new trunk route from the East Midlands to Greater Manchester. But while the Department could find nearly four million quid to help cyclists enjoy a car ride with a bike ride in the country, it couldn't find even four quid to support sustainable transport.

It would be nice to think of cross-country cycle routes doing much for sustainable transport, but I suspect that in most cases they're used for recreational trips from A to B and back to A again. There's nothing at all wrong with that, of course, but all too often it also involves getting there in a large motor vehicle like a 4x4. And there's certainly something wrong with frustrating the mass sustainable transport offered by rail reopenings.

How will we get around the countryside?
Rural transportation is going to be a real problem in the UK, where most country areas have been left without rail passenger services. Large-scale rail reopening would benefit many areas, but not all, and while rail services offer relatively fast ways of moving around the country, they seldom facilitate the complex local journeys people make. Bus services will have to substantially improve, of course, but country dwellers' heavy reliance on cars is certainly a challenge.

Back in Chapter 1, I asked whether you could sustain your present lifestyle without a car, and that is surely an even more pertinent question in the countryside. When vehicle fuel becomes too expensive, or is restricted or curtailed because of carbon controls, that will hit most strongly in the countryside.

The current response to that question (were it ever asked) would be using electric cars, and a great deal of effort is being made to convince us they are more environmentally benign than petrol or diesel cars so politicians can look green without upsetting those who believe everything they read in the papers. A scheme called Plugged In Places was launched in 2009 for pilot area electric vehicle infrastructure, including 2,500 charge points in Greater London, north-east England and Milton Keynes. This was supposed to be part of a £450 million programme to support "a flourishing early market for ultra-low-carbon vehicles".

"Decarbonising transport isn't an aspiration – it's a reality," said the then transport secretary Andrew Adonis.[11]

The only flaw in this is that there's no such thing as an ultra-low-carbon vehicle – it takes vast amounts of carbon to turn a tonne of steel into anything and the alternative vehicle fuels, hydrogen or electricity, require vast amounts of carbon to produce. But the message was plainly 'keep driving and don't worry'.

But even though our country dwellers 30 or 40 years hence may have to rely in part on electric cars, their journeys are likely to be significantly limited. Refuelling a petrol or diesel car takes about five minutes and gives you 300-400 miles of motoring; recharging an electric vehicle takes several hours and takes you a few tens of miles; 100 top whack. Then there's several hours of recharging ahead.

It's been suggested that electric cars could carry massive battery packs that would extend their range, but it also extends their weight and hence reduces their energy efficiency. Maybe there will be a breakthrough in battery technology, but it hasn't happened in more than a century of looking. Maybe. Perhaps electric cars could carry massive, interchangeable battery packs which could be manhandled out and replaced every 80-100 miles, but the logistics of this for 30 million cars beggar belief. Each service station would need dozens of assistants and a vast recharging area, and currently the national grid lacks the capacity to do this unless some very tight restrictions were placed on recharging hours. Perhaps it could be done with vast investment, but it's neither cheap nor user-friendly.

Nor would it be particularly green, as a substantial amount of our electricity today comes from coal or natural gas. In future these will have to be replaced by low-carbon alternatives, but these will certainly be more expensive and probably more scarce. So electric cars (and vans) will probably only suit drivers who travel fewer than 100 miles a day.

Given their limited range they are least useful in the country, but I suspect their use will increase as other car usage declines. They will at least allow even people in remote areas to make at least one return trip daily to their local town, even if it proves costly. So getting around the country in the longer term will be a challenge, but not a wholly insurmountable one if we accept that things will be different.

How will we move goods about?

Here's another major challenge, but addressing it will probably be moving us well outside the Smart Growth area. We will plainly need to move goods around by lorry, plane or motor ship a great deal less. We've already seen that dumb growth planning has enabled the distribution industry to create an unsustainable network based on motorways and massive distribution depots, which will have to be put into reverse over the next half-century. It happened, we afforded it, so it can unhappen and we can afford that too. We need to start planning ways of moving a considerably higher proportion of our goods by rail or water.

What we can't afford is not to do it.

How will we travel abroad?

Politicians may talk glibly about 'ultra-low-carbon vehicles' but no one has mentioned even vaguely low-carbon aircraft. It takes a vast amount of energy to suspend 300 tonnes of metal plus passengers plus luggage plus fuel seven or eight miles above the ground for hours at a time. It takes roughly the same amount of fuel to move one airline seat plus passenger from London to Miami and back as the average family car uses in a year, so flying one wide-bodied jet across the Atlantic and back just once uses as much fossil fuel as several hundred cars do in a year. There is no glimmer of an alternative to fossil fuels for air travel, as it would mean using hundreds of hectares of precious arable land for biofuel every time a long-haul plane took off.

Here again we are probably a bit outside the Smart Growth area, but this is important. There really is no alternative to fossil fuels for flying. I'm sorry, I know we've all enjoyed jetting off on holiday but it's soon going to be much more expensive and is already an intolerable burden on our environment. A vast amount of land has been squandered in building airports, and domestic aviation has done huge economic damage to the railways.

Sorry about this, but we have to look at ways of living that reduce flying. First to go should probably be flying on holiday. It needn't mean the end of trips to the Mediterranean, and high speed rail links are already being built across Europe. We may need a second Channel Tunnel, but why not?

Time to get smart

Of all the areas where UK thinking needs a healthy dose of sustainability, transport is probably top of the list. Fortunately it's also the area where a Smart Growth approach can yield real benefits, starting with our cities. Smart Growth is, of course, an holistic philosophy: you don't just improve the transport, you also improve the planning, the communities, the housing, the towns and the countryside. And when you've done that you can toddle off and contemplate ways of radically improving your own life – *but not before.*

The latter is not part of the Smart Growth philosophy, of course, but don't let that stand in your way.

Smart Growth transport planning policies

- An end to major road building.
- An end to airport construction and expansion.
- Creation of rail-based transit in all major conurbations as a priority.
- Creation of rail-based transit in all conurbations.
- Road or congestion charging.
- 'Smarter choice' schemes.
- Enhancement of cycling and walking facilities.
- Protection of most disused railway trackbeds as a priority.
- Railway station and line reopening.
- Rail electrification.
- Air travel taxation.
- Regular and reliable bus services where these are the most sustainable option.
- Promotion and creation of rail–road freight interchanges
- Rail freight investment.
- Charging lorries for the damage they do.

And in the longer term:
- Creation of dense rail-based transit networks in all conurbations.
- Consideration of reduced capacity on some major inter-urban roads.
- Support for electric vehicles in rural areas.
- Capacity reduction and closure of airports.
- High-speed inter-urban railways.

Chapter 12

From consumers to citizens

There used to be a kind of unspoken nobility about living in Britain.
Bill Bryson, *Notes from a Small Island*

Moral cowards or just social cowards?

We have spent the last 100 years or so running away from one another. In a small and overcrowded country whose population is shooting upwards this is plainly barmy, but it's what we've been doing. Maybe we just dislike each other more with every year that passes – where once a party wall sufficed, we've successively separated our homes with privet hedges, feather-edged fences and six-foot larch-lap panels in a bid to keep our neighbours at bay. When we venture out, we armour-plate ourselves with a tonne or so of steel, from which we can roar abuse at other drivers without fear of getting thumped the way you would if you tried it on the street. When we go shopping we step from our hermetically sealed vehicles straight into a supermarket or covered shopping centre, protected from attack by security men and CCTV cameras. We have become pathetic, craven, social cowards, scared of our own shadows.

A 2010 YouGov survey[1] clearly showed the decline in neighbourliness. Nearly 49 per cent of UK adults admitted they now know more about the daily activities of their favourite celebrity than of their neighbour, and the problem is most acute among the young, where 62 per cent of 18-24-year-olds and 72 per cent of students admitted this was the case (even 39 per cent of retired folk said so too). Visiting neighbours' homes is also a dying custom, apparently, with 39 per cent of us admitting we never do so, including 50 per cent of 18-24-year-olds and 60 per cent of 25-34-year-olds. Only 18 per cent of the 18-34 group wished people visited them more at home, and only 49 per cent of 18-24-year-olds believed the people in their area were friendly. Yet despite the usual prejudice about 'unfriendly Londoners', the proportion who said their neighbours have never popped round for a chat was exactly the same (43 per cent) in London as in the north of England or Scotland. How things have changed!

Walter Wilkinson, pushing his puppet show through Somerset, noted that George Borrow's wanderings in the nineteenth century met many people on

The retreat from one another.

roads "thick with pedestrian wanderers",[2] but already by 1927, he found that if he saw anything on the roads it would be a car, "an impersonal affair with its occupants hidden away". But in that era he still met people out and about in the towns and villages. He even managed to attract crowds of children to his puppet show, yet no-one accused him of being a strange man or had him arrested.

"Some inquisitive boys followed from the school and we all lunched together, which was good company for me," he recorded in a Somerset village.[3] "They investigated my affairs with the usual frankness and intensity, and I tried to probe their little lives." Imagine writing that today.

And Wilkinson could see what made towns work: "This country town has a kindly soul, a wide hospitable street . . . and a leisurely, pleasant manner. There is a comfortable old red-brick feeling in the place; it is a human town with human names over the shop windows, instead of those distorted business names, those insane slogans . . . Here the constable, who was chatting to the loungers at every street corner, nodded . . ."[4]

That was Dunstable, believe it or not, later cut in half by traffic on the A5 and today being engulfed by sprawl. Nowadays we want to venture on to the streets as little as possible, sensibly scared of the traffic and stupidly afraid of our fellow citizens. By day our town centre streets see fewer and fewer people, on mid-week nights they are deserted and on weekend evenings they either remain deserted or are noisily occupied by boozed-up youngsters and tough police officers more likely to be bundling loungers into vans than chatting to them. This may be an 'evening economy' but it's not a functioning community and certainly not one to try to negotiate on foot.

How many of our towns have been smashed to accommodate the motor car?

As Iain Sinclair noted: "Dartford is a town that can't be negotiated on foot . . . Finding Dartford station means battling across fenced roads, dropping into pedestrian underpasses, detouring the long way around civic centres, coping with the river."[5] Then it got worse; he reached Stone Crossing: "Warehouses, roundabouts, fountains. Roads peter out into swamp . . . no pubs, no shops, no humans."

And definitely no community, just the Bluewater shopping city.

Anomie

Politicians have talked about Britain's 'broken society', although frankly, the ones who talk about broken societies are those least likely to come into contact with it. Actually, most of Britain's society isn't broken but it is weak and it's been getting weaker for decades, and politicians who have put the economy before the environment or society must carry much of the blame. Many of our recent travel writers seem fascinated with our society's increasingly dysfunctional nature and the utter dislocation of many people, particularly younger people, from social norms. And it isn't just books like Nik Cohn's *Yes We Have No*, in which he went looking for "the republic" of those wholly at odds with society.

Paul Gogarty's circumnavigation of England in *The Water Road*[6] brought him into close and uncomfortable proximity with areas where the economy has been shattered. In Birmingham, drunks cast his moored boat adrift as he slept. In the Potteries a girl aged thirteen or fourteen greeted him familiarly and, when he responded in kind, asked: "Do you want some?" Unsure whether she meant sex or drugs, he picked his way through some teenage drunks and eventually was able to ask about the girl, to be told that about 50 girls were working the local streets and many were thirteen or fourteen, more likely to be offering sex than drugs.

"Dear Stoke-on-Trent," John Hillaby had written 30-odd years earlier.[7] "By far the dirtiest place I walked through and by far the friendliest." But of course that was before we closed the ceramics industry and moved it to countries with little environmental or social protection.

In Wigan, Gogarty was pelted with stones and in Manchester he was warned to avoid the Ashton Canal, where boaters were shot at, had concrete dropped from bridges or had gangs run through their narrow-boats stealing everything they could find. In Blackburn the kids were stoning the ducks and a few miles further on they'd already shot some, while outside Leeds he encountered a gang who burned cars and buildings and threatened boaters.

But at least Gogarty had the wit to realise that vandalism and antisocial behaviour aren't just modern phenomena, and recalled Robert Louis Stevenson recounting a canal voyage where "crop-headed children" spat on his boat from bridges and threw stones at it. "Unfortunately the knowledge I'm not the first victim of little shits doesn't really help," sighed Gogarty.

But he is not one of your usual hangers and floggers. He wondered whether teaching the wildfowl assassins to steer and maintain a boat, or giving them some challenge, might actually teach them some respect, and people he met in the Potteries quickly got him to the bottom of things. They told him that, 40 years before, most people had families and jobs. Today's teenage single mums are the children of teenage single mums and have no one to show them how to bring children up. No one had a job, no one could cook, sew or look after themselves and family life had completely imploded. That was 2002, around the time the UK was comforting itself it was 'the world's fourth largest economy'. Today it is no longer the fourth largest but is still pretty 'large' thanks to vast quantities of electronic money sloshing through the City of London, to the benefit of a tiny segment of our society. Meanwhile, vast swathes of the country are dependent on rotten service jobs or no jobs at all. Give people secure and rewarding jobs and many, if not most, of our social problems will disappear.

Once upon a time, this country made its living by growing things and then made its living by growing and making things. But for the last 30 years we've made much of our living pumping oil and gas out of the North Sea and, increasingly over the last 300 years, we've made our money by investing. That's why so many people no longer have proper jobs.

Opportunities to turn corners

Half a century or so ago, Jane Jacobs set out four conditions for generating "exuberant diversity" in city streets:

- The district, and indeed as many of its internal parts as possible, must serve more than one primary function; preferably more than two. These must ensure the presence of people who go outdoors on different schedules and are in the place for different purposes, but who are able to use many facilities in common.
- Most blocks must be short; that is, streets and opportunities to turn corners must be frequent.
- The district must mingle buildings that vary in age and condition,

including a good proportion of older ones, so that they vary in the economic yield they produce. This mingling must be fairly close-grained.

- There must be a sufficiently dense concentration of people, for whatever purposes they may be there. This includes dense concentration in the case of people who are there because of residence.[8]

These principles still work for me, give or take a bit. Sometime around 1975 we began to take these lessons on board, then spent the next quarter-century forgetting them. But, assuming Jacobs was right, now would be a good time for a rethink about many of the comprehensive redevelopment schemes being touted in so many cities as the road to regeneration. Just increasing the office floorspace doesn't increase the number of jobs for office workers, increasing the retail floorspace doesn't increase the money we spend in shops, increasing low-density 'family homes' around our cities doesn't bring entrepreneurs to depressed areas desperate to invest, bunging up tin sheds near motorways doesn't add anything to our gross national product (it just makes people truck things further), and building vast quantities of tatty flats in city centres doesn't mean anyone wants to live in them. But that, in a nutshell, is pretty much recent regeneration policy; oh yes, that and 'landmark buildings' and 'wow factors'.

This is a book about why the UK needs Smart Growth, and, while it's too early to write its history in America after a mere 20 years, it's clear that the three basic legs of the approach are spatial planning, transport planning and community. We've seen that we need to follow the same principles as those in the US on spatial and transport planning, even if the exact policies might be different, but what do we need to do with our communities? What is a community anyway?

The dictionary isn't much help because 'community' is a word with a whole variety of meanings, anything from just the people who live in one area to a self-selecting group of people who visit the same websites. Plainly we want something more than this – we need a definition that's at once less broad and not too specific. For community – in the positive sense of people who share some sense of common identity, purpose and, above all perhaps, responsibility for the place they live in – is an idea we need to rediscover. A real community, be it a city, town or village, is not just made up of individual men, women and children, nor just consumers, it is made up of citizens. And that, ill-defined as it is, is something we have to work at. We need a physical environment that allows us to work at it – or maybe even necessitates our working at it – and we need to rediscover the values that make communities function.

We aren't going to get there by blathering about 'our broken society' either. People who talk about this sort of thing normally only mean people poorer than themselves, but if any bit of British society is 'broken' it's the plutocrats who brought about the 2008 financial crash.

B-road Britain

We live in a society that is relentlessly ageist and wholly uncomfortable with itself. In *B-Road Britain*,[9] Robbie Coltrane watched a traditional shoemaker at work and reflected that such accumulations of human knowledge bind generations and communities together. "I sometimes wonder if it explains why there seems to be more respect and better communication in less developed countries that there is in Britain," he wrote. "If you are going to spend your life doing what your father did and something goes wrong, you contact your father for advice. But if you leave home and go into a job that didn't exist when the previous generation was growing up, such as computing, then you won't have much to talk about with your dad when you come home in your fancy Armani suit." He concluded that traditions play a big part in holding generations together, without necessarily becoming reactionary or backward.

But an awful lot of our mass culture, our everyday discourse even, has come to rely on ageist humour, decrying tradition and ridiculing our sense of community. It's 'post-modern irony' apparently, and it breeds a cynicism which seems to prevent us talking about things like beauty in the environment.

Community is certainly not in good health, and that certainly includes the deprived areas such as those our travel writers have recorded. When nine-year-old Shannon Matthews disappeared from her home in Dewsbury for 24 days in 2008, many were ready to point the finger at the run-down Dewsbury Moor estate and shake their heads with a sort of "what do you expect?" expression when the full truth about her disappearance and dysfunctional family was revealed. "Dewsbury . . . ah yes, wasn't that where that 7/7 bomber came from?"

Poor Dewsbury: once it was a centre of the woollen industry, although it specialised in 'shoddy' – a poor cloth made from recycled material, and somehow the label survived when globalisation made Yorkshire's woollen industry an early victim. By the 1970s pretty much all that was left was a bed manufacturer.

The Dewsbury Moor estate was a classic bit of 1930s municipal sprawl-lobby housing. It probably seemed like a good idea to move mill workers out of their traditional terraces in Dewsbury up to new brick-built council cottages with gardens built on impeccable garden-city principles. But they were built up on the bleak moorland and good intentions did nothing to improve the climate of this exposed spot. Its low-income residents had to rely on the usual poor bus services to get into town or jobs in Cleckheaton or Heckmondwike, and when the employment laid down and died, the estate inevitably spiralled into deprivation and social problems.

And yet . . . no sooner had Shannon Matthews disappeared than hundreds of local people, from the town and the estate, turned out to spend their evenings and weekends searching for her. The local community centre was turned into an operations room to support the efforts of the searchers and coordinate information. Most homes in the district sported posters of the missing girl and a media campaign was organised. Leaflet drops were organised across West Yorkshire, local taxi firms took volunteers around for free and 25,000 leaflets were handed out by volunteers at a Leeds United match. Local children planted flowers for their missing schoolmate and there was local anger that a working-class girl like Shannon hadn't provoked the same level of attention as middle-class Madeleine McCann.

Well, events proved the cynics justified about the case, but there's a more important lesson here. I wonder if local people would have shown so much community spirit in an affluent, greenfield sprawl suburb somewhere, or a gated development for wealthy folks?

But the impression of an area doesn't just deter investors, it saps local people's spirit too. When the new economics foundation (nef) went to Dewsbury to ask local people their ambitions, the main one was "not to be embarrassed any more" – it really had got that bad. But once they were invited to imagine something more ambitious they began to do so, and nef found they were interested in the long-term future and realised there were no quick fixes. When it asked them what they wanted Dewsbury to be like in 2025-30, they revelled in an opportunity to discuss things with their fellow citizens. But people have been crushed by decades of "you can't buck the markets" – an almost fascistic combination of moral, economic and political pressure.

Our retreat into dumb growth is a symptom of that. It's no accident that the late nineteenth and early twentieth century saw not only the growth of sustainable, communitarian living patterns but also the flowering of extraordinary social progress – emancipation of women; social provision for the elderly, the disabled and the poor; universal education; public health and sanitation. Bye-law homes and urban electric tramways were as much an expression of this as water and sewerage or votes for women.

And that has continued to frighten some people, notably those who like to see economic power concentrated in a few hands. This goes well beyond party politics; for most of the twentieth century all of the political parties accepted these things as progress, but in recent decades the mainstream parties have in fact, if not in theory, run away from them.

My belief is that we have spent 100 years ripping apart the urban areas that allowed us, or required us, to act in communitarian ways, and replacing them with low-density semi-detached or detached houses or high-rise blocks, which deter us from doing so. This began a process of community destruction far more insidious than the culprits normally identified as being at the root of this decline: television, the internet, etc. When Dame Henrietta Barnett ordered the cottages at Hampstead Garden Suburb to be separated by privet hedges, she

Space invaders – how to destroy a community.

set in train not the orderly movement of disadvantaged communities from overcrowded inner cities to new utopias, just a mighty onslaught on her own ideal of community. Ebenezer Howard may have dreamed of commonwealths of idealists drinking cocoa and tending their collective allotments, but the world he created was a world best suited to misanthropists and we have, accordingly, come to hate our neighbours. Truly, the road to hell is not only paved with good intentions, it is lined with cars, carports, drives, hedges, fences, block paving and semi-detached people.

How do we foster communities?

So what is a community in the sense I mean? Finally, here, I have to admit I don't know. It's not something you can define, still less something you can create deliberately. You know it when you see it and you can see when it isn't there. Community, in all the richness of 5,000 years of human interaction, is not so much the elephant in the room as the air in the room; take it away and you're in big trouble.

You can sense it in a traditional high street when you have a short, humorous conversation with a shopkeeper, waiter or market trader. You can see it when the bus driver steps down to help an elderly passenger across the road. You can see it when people greet people they know on the street or near the shops. You can see it when people walk their kids to school. You can see it when people flock to a public meeting to complain about some monstrosity before the planning system. You can sense it in their anger when the monstrosity is bulldozed through the planning system because politicians who imagine they are 'business-friendly' have neutered it. You can sense it when people get together to campaign for better train services or lower fares. You can sense it in a million ways.

And you can sense a community dying too. It dies when a road cuts it in half. It dies when the pub shuts, when the post office shuts, when the local shops shut. It dies when the industry that has sustained it for generations goes. It dies when the countryside surrounding it is splattered with semi-detached boxes. It dies when you knock down the old buildings. It dies when you knock down the terraced houses.

Nik Cohn noticed this when he went to visit his daughter in an area of Salford featured in TV documentaries about inner-city blight, where half the homes were for sale and many others taken over by dope dealers.

> Thirty years ago, any one of the terraced streets might have been the model for the early Coronation Street. Now the houses are mostly abandoned, their windows bricked up, their front doors shielded by steel-plated armour. Where residents hang on, the roofs are festooned with barbed wire and prison bars protect the living rooms.[10]

You know communities when you see them. *Image: National Tramway Museum*

A decade and more after Cohn's visit, the priceless remaining stock of bye-law homes in Lancashire and Greater Manchester was still being flattened in the name of 'housing market renewal' – the mad government attempt to increase the value of homes by earmarking many for demolition, compulsorily purchasing them at far below their market rate and leaving them to fall into this spiral of destruction. Governments have pursued madness of this kind for three-quarters of a century now, egged on by the successors of the garden cities movement.

The movement's other legacy of course is sprawl, and here community is mighty hard to discern. You can't see it in the drive to work. You can't see it in the drive to the supermarket. You can't see it in the drive to school. You can hear the last near-death echo of it in a conversation with the supermarket checkout person and you can actually see the moment of its final death when 'self-checkout tills' are installed. You can hear its last echo when we venture on to the car park where our front garden once was to wash the car and happen to encounter a neighbour. But you can't see it when you drive to the car wash and you can't see it in our back gardens because there's a two-metre larch fence blocking the view. You can't see it in our boarded-up high streets, you can't see it when the local paper lies down and dies and you can't see it when people applaud the drivel in their daily newspaper about the evils of speed cameras, of domestic waste recycling, of scientists daring to suggest their lifestyles are unsustainable. And you certainly don't see it when we retreat inside our homes – our castles – and only venture out in our steel safety cage.

What do we do about this? You can't really create communities. You can create the conditions in which communities may thrive and if you do, they probably will. But communities are like children – you do your best for them but if they grow up to thrive, they will probably do so in ways you don't expect. That usually comes as a shock to parents who foresee their offspring doing what they did, only better, but children usually have other plans. That's the way with communities.

"Cities happen to be problems in organised complexity," said Jane Jacobs,[11] and you know what she meant. They'll always be problems and making them work properly is part of the fun. We'll start on that road when we stop believing the 100-year fallacies of the garden cities movement and remind ourselves that its founding fathers (and many since) actually wanted to destroy our cities.

Smart Growth communities

But even if you can't create instant community, you can at least create the conditions in which communities can thrive.

The US Smart Growth movement's origins lay in opposition to sprawl and car dependency and support for compact, permeable and transit-oriented

And you know when the community has gone.

development, but, from the start, the reinvigoration of communities was a central theme, and the movement has since widened its horizons to cover a whole range of sustainable development issues, as described by Smart Growth America (SGA) on its website:

> Sprawl drains resources away from existing communities. Sprawl's transformation of the American landscape has led to declining cities and inner suburbs, while imposing daunting new infrastructure and public service costs on suburban communities. Many inner suburban communities are suffering from the same neglect and disinvestment as their urban neighbours. Even suburban jurisdictions on the metropolitan fringe are not immune from sprawl's pernicious effects on their economy. Because rapid residential growth often fails to pay for itself, many local officials feel forced to accept any commercial development in whatever form it comes – typically, cookie-cutter shopping centres and big-box stores. These patterns lead to the same problems – increasing traffic, marginal services, lack of open space and rising taxes – that many residents tried to leave behind.[12]

If I knew what a 'cookie-cutter shopping centre' was, I would probably say you could apply that observation pretty much exactly in the UK. Sprawl has spent 100 years dragging wealth out of sustainable communities and it's a tribute to their robustness that they survive at all. The SGA goes on:

We lose more than beautiful buildings from sprawl. We also lose the community character that makes each place unique. This character, made up of the architecture, people, and landscape of a particular place, offers regions some of the best opportunities for economic development. Many of the most impressive examples of revitalization around the country, whether urban downtowns or rural main streets, have had the preservation of historic architecture and character at their core.

That was a lesson we learned the hard way in the 1970s – and seem to have forgotten a generation later. 'Main Street' is still an important strand in American thinking in a way the High Street has never quite achieved over here. In the US 2008 presidential election much was made of the contrast between Wall Street and Main Street, but in truth multiple retailers, shopping malls and strip malls have done at least as much damage to Main Street as to High Street. The SGA again:

> Few places are as hallowed in the American psyche as the classic Main Street. With its human-scale architecture of retail shops, offices and apartments above, and wide sidewalks, these places represent some of what is best about American town building. With many suburban-style, generic malls falling out of favour with consumers and developers alike (which incidentally provide additional Smart Growth development opportunities), the people are returning to Main Street for shopping, strolling or just to find a peaceful place to people-watch.

America, like the UK, has actually got a very long way to go in this direction. But at least the penny has started to drop. Here we're still finding excuses to build edge-of-town supermarkets, vast indoor shopping centres and retail parks for bulky goods and, indeed, other goods. This has to stop and we have to find a way of hurting big retailing in the way it's hurt small retailing. Big retailers took over the world through a process they had the cheek to call the 'free market', through which they used their commercial muscle to destroy small shops, so I daresay it will just be free marketism when they get to taste some of their own medicine.

Then we've got to protect what's left of our old towns. SGA points out:

> While cities pay consultants thousands of dollars to come up with the Next Big Thing (usually with a huge government subsidy attached), some creative communities have realized that their best assets are what drew them to the place originally. Historic architecture, diverse neigh-bourhoods and scenic vistas are just a few of the assets that can be built upon for successful and long-term economic revitalization.

High Street UK

At some stage we're going to have to tackle the vast out-of-town shopping dinosaurs, the dysfunctional hypermarkets and the malformed malls. And we're also going to have to find ways of revitalising our high streets, sunk into economic decline and 'clone town' uniformity.

A good place to start is the new economics foundation (nef)'s High Street UK programme, which helps communities design and implement town centre plans, strategies and actions to enhance their existing assets. High Street UK programmes are driven by local people and supported nationally by nef, which will work with local businesses, residents' organisations, public bodies, the voluntary sector and youth and faith groups on local coordination, design, promotion and economic development over a two-year period.

The aim is to support a resilient local independent sector that retains more local money in the local economy – national chains take the profits away, which is one way money drains out of an area. A coordination group communicates the vision, philosophy and activities through partnerships and a communications programme, a design group works to improve the town centre's appearance and protect its historic assets, a promotion group markets the town and an economic development group works to strengthen the economic base.

Two very different towns, Brentford and Malvern, have been implementing programmes. High Street Malvern has promoted a shared-space system, expanded recreational and leisure activities such as arts and craft fairs and walking events, published a visitors' guide, improved public amenities and campaigned to preserve historic buildings. It's early days, but it's a positive answer to the power of giant, clone retailers and a necessary step if we are to rebuild living communities.

Many of our high streets are desperately in need of help.

There are so many examples of how preserving old urban development has yielded vast economic, social and environmental benefits in the UK that it continues to amaze me so much destruction continues. London's Covent Garden, Regent Street or Piccadilly, Newcastle's Grey Street or the centres of the hundreds of towns and villages that resisted the 1960s/1970s Modern movement's call to destroy and went for conservation instead – all continue to stand the commercial and community tests of time. Yet still we bung up new shopping centres which, in 25 years, will be hard-to-let eyesores just as their predecessors were, polluting their neighbourhoods and dragging them down like foundering supertankers.

What shall we do with the economy?

You weren't expecting a treatise on economics and you're not going to get one. It's pretty obvious to anyone by now that the twin pillars of the late twentieth / early twenty-first century UK economy – financial services and North Sea oil and gas – aren't going to provide much of our corn in the future. The trouble is, we haven't much idea what to replace them with. During the 2010 general election campaign it was also pretty obvious that none of our mainstream politicians had much idea, apart from some flimsy rhetoric about reviving our manufacturing industry. But to achieve that would require a fundamental over-haul of our whole global (and globalised) economic system, and evidently none of them could hold that thought in their brains for longer than it took to give an interview to one of the papers whose proprietor's wealth depended on, er, sustaining the existing globalised economic system.

But anyway . . .

We really do need to change, we really do. But – and here's the good bit about this book – we should be moving to Smart Growth now, whether we do decide to move to some sort of better economic future or not. SGA says:

> Although the urgency rises during boom years, Smart Growth never makes more sense than when economic times are tough. Smart, efficient development decisions save taxpayers money and allow governments to stretch their dollars farther, even as they make it possible for households to spend less on expenses such as transportation. And there is mounting evidence that metro areas with Smart Growth attributes – healthy central cities and inner suburbs, excellent transportation networks, vibrant centres and neighbourhoods – have stronger economies.

In 2005, a report[13] was published which showed that American families were paying an increasing amount of their household income to meet their transportation needs. Higher transportation costs hit those on low incomes disproportionately hard, and the problem was most acute where public transport was lacking. In car-dependent Los Angeles families were spending 17.4 per cent of their household income on transportation, and in Kansas City 18.1 per cent, while in New York with its dense public transport network the percentage was just 14.5. The Centers for Disease Control and Prevention produced figures in 2000 showing that road accidents were costing the US $230 billion each year, including the $61 billion in lost productivity they cause. Oh yes, and congestion in urban areas was costing $78 billion every year too. Then, it was calculated, America could save billions by making better use of the existing infrastructure in its cities than by providing new infrastructure for greenfield sprawl – the influential Brookings Institution reckoned it could save hundreds of billions of dollars and millions of hectares of land in a couple of decades this way. Its study,[14] by Rutgers University, worked out that the savings could be achieved simply by channelling development into towns. SGA again:

> Instead of letting the recession extinguish the debate about growth, many communities are taking advantage of today's conditions to gain an upper hand over sprawl. They're investing in sensible economic development, preparing for future growth, and properly accounting for and deploying the scarce resources they possess. When rapid growth returns, they'll be ready.

By the look of things, however, we won't.

Our government might respond that, since 1999, Britain has channelled a lot of development into towns, and this is true – up to a point. We've also gone on building low-density suburbs on both brownfield and greenfield sites. But perhaps the real challenge for the UK is to get growth moved around to the places that need it, instead of trying to build on success in the places that have been achieving it. For the most part these lie in the south and east of England, and a great deal of their growth is based on the flaky and wholly unsustainable growth in financial services. This could disappear almost overnight, and the hysteria in the City after the 2008-9 crash every time a few jobs went to Frankfurt or Singapore or wherever demonstrates this very well. A sustainable industry this is not.

Attempts to reverse the south-eastward flow of economic activity in Britain predate the Second World War, and in the post-war period governments pursued them with vigour and, occasionally, success. But the collapse of British industry that followed the surrender to globalised free marketism under successive governments after 1979 was pretty much the kiss of death, although feeble attempts have continued.

This must change. An economy that writes off three-quarters of the country and encourages its population to crowd into one quarter on the basis of some mad theory, the surrender to globalised free marketism, is not a sound or sustainable one. We have demanded efficiencies of our economy – but what we need is effectiveness.

Consumers or citizens?

Perhaps the most pernicious aspect of the economics of the last 30 years or so has been the growing belief that we can't change things. 'You can't buck the market.' Oh yes we can.

The first step on this journey must be the decision we all need to start taking that we want some power over our destiny. We've put too much power in the hands of currency traders, hedge fund managers, investment institutions and the rest of them and we'd like some back now please. We've been terrified into silence by the threat that if we upset them or interfere with their games for whatever good reason, they will take the money away and give it to someone else.

Well, the bad news is that we've been jolly nice to them and they're still taking the money away. They aren't interested any more. Our oil and gas are running out. Our workforce demands slightly more than starvation wages. Our financial institutions are mired in debt. Our competitors have lower environmental standards than we do. Our competitors have lower wages than we do. Our competitors impose even less financial regulation than we do. We've lowered all these standards as far as we dare and still we can't get them low enough. In a total globalised free-for-all there will always be someone prepared to lower themselves further than we are. It's no good frightening us any more; all the threats are coming true.

Oh yes, and the planet is dying thanks to our addiction to fossil fuels. Let's not forget that before we get back to more pressing matters like the economy. In doing so we might remind ourselves that the 2008-9 crash hit the Western economies like Britain and America, which had most enthusiastically embraced the globalised free market the hardest. The two least affected were France and Canada, with their highly conservative banking systems.

So we have to say boo to these geese and start rebuilding on our terms, not the World Trade Organization's. Exactly how we do that is beyond the scope of this book, but the new economics foundation's *The Great Transition*[15] isn't a bad place to start for those who are interested.

Plainly we need to find better ways of housing 60 million people without destroying our food supply, our water supply and our main carbon sink. But we will also need an economy that benefits people across the whole land, not just south-east England, and we need one resilient to the effects of climate change and which helps us move to a low-carbon economy. Recognising that your actions can have an impact on things is the first step on the path to becoming an active citizen.

So, it's time to climb out of the comfortable but malodorous swamp of consumerism and plunge into the cold but invigorating waters of citizenship. Terrifying, isn't it?

How can we get there?

The general election of May 2010 was a strange affair, with politicians vying to convince electors they alone had the magic elixir to restore the key instrument of national well-being – economic growth. The problem was, the economy had stopped growing for more than a year, wealth was still ebbing out of the country and international political power was following. The sceptics who had spent decades warning that shifting manufacturing to Asia because it was cheap would eventually prompt wealth and power to follow it were suddenly being proved right. The 'Western industrial world' was waking up to the fact that simply controlling the wealth that finances industry wasn't enough; sooner or later the capital will follow the machines. And when that happens all the cosy, arrogant assumptions about the economic, military and political dominance of the West will metaphorically 'go west' just as the economic, military and political power actually goes east.

The trouble with our current fixation with GDP growth is that it's very simple and easy to understand. It goes up or it goes down. When it goes down, most of us become worse off. When it goes up some of us become better off. But – and here's the really dangerous bit – when it goes up, most people imagine they're getting better off even if they're not. It's like income tax: poor people imagine that if income tax rises they will necessarily be worse off. Real life is different, but the basic level of income tax has become a no-go area for chancellors of the exchequer of any political stripe, apart from their occasional irresponsible decisions to bring it down.

We need to develop other measures of well-being that are simple and obvious and don't involve making the world a worse place. One idea, the new economics foundation's Five Ways to Well-being, was commissioned by the government's Foresight Programme (the same people who commissioned *Land Use Futures*, mentioned in Chapter 6, funnily enough) – see box.

Beyond that there's a lot we can do. There's the Transition movement, for instance, which for those unaware of it provides a model for communities who want to react positively to the challenges of peak oil and climate change. Hundreds of communities are now designated Transition Towns, many of them not actually towns but districts, suburbs, villages and at least one forest, so an increasing number of people will be unable to claim they are unaware of what they could do to begin making the transition towards a low-carbon and lower-environmental-impact community. So many communities want to get on board that the movement has now introduced a list of criteria for initiatives wanting to join, to ensure they join only when they are ready to move to the awareness-raising stage.

Five Ways to Well-being

The Government's Foresight Programme's Mental Capital and Well-being project was created to examine current international thinking on improving everyone's mental capital and mental well-being through life. "Evidence suggests that a small improvement in well-being can help to decrease mental health problems and also help people to flourish," it said. Foresight commissioned the new economics foundation to develop 'five ways to well-being' as a set of evidence-based actions to improve personal well-being. It came up with the following.

Connect with the people around you. With family, friends, colleagues and neighbours. At home, work, school or in your local community. Think of these as the corner of your life and invest time in developing them. Building these connections will support and enrich you every day.

Be active. Go for a walk or a run. Step outside. Cycle. Play a game. Garden. Dance. Exercising makes you feel good. Most importantly, discover a physical activity you enjoy and one that suits your level of mobility and fitness.

Take notice. Be curious. Catch sight of the beautiful. Remark on the usual. Notice the changing seasons. Savour the moment, whether you are walking to work, eating lunch or talking to friends. Be aware of the world around you and what you are feeling.

Keep learning. Try something new. Rediscover an old interest. Sign up for that course. Take on a different responsibility at work. Fix a bike. Learn to play an instrument or how to cook your favourite food. Set a challenge you will enjoy achieving. Learning new things will make you more confident as well as being fun.

Give. Do something nice for a friend, or a stranger. Thank someone. Smile. Volunteer your time. Join a community group. Look out, as well as in. Seeing yourself, and your happiness, linked to the wider community can be incredibly rewarding and creates connections with the people around you.

Well, go on then . . .

There's an opportunity here. Communities in the United States and Canada are starting to adopt the Transition Initiative model and many of these are enthusiastic devotees of Smart Growth. In the UK, many communities are starting to adopt the Transition Initiative model too, but none is currently a devotee of Smart Growth. The two ideas are not the same but they are, to a great extent, complementary. A Smart Growth approach to spatial and transport planning and community development is completely in line with the idea of responding to peak oil and climate change. It simply addresses different aspects from the usual early targets of Transition Initiatives, although there are obvious overlaps. In the UK we like to believe we invented the wheel and everything else. Sometimes it's time to listen to other people's ideas. Smart Growth won't solve on its own the problems that peak oil and climate change will cause, but we won't be able to solve them without it.

How can we get there (without cars)?

In the depths of the Second World War, that inveterate motoring pioneer H. V. Morton was able to observe a country getting by without so many of the things that consumerism had begun to offer it, notably cars.

> Confined to our parishes by responsibility, lack of petrol, and also, let us hope, by the knowledge there is no better place to be in war-time, we have without realising it tapped wells of satisfaction which had begun to dry up when the world became restless and irresponsible.[16]

The various Transition movements, etc. offer us a clear path to a more sustainable society, one that's certainly less "restless and irresponsible". But, as things stand, most people aren't thinking like that. They have 'rising expectations' and that means material expectations. Many of these expectations are not actually rising ones, but they do, however, involve continuing to enjoy many of the fruits of consumerism that one currently enjoys – the perceived freedom (however illusory) to drive where you want, when you want, as far as you want. The freedom to fly away almost anywhere in the world on holiday, perhaps several times a year. The freedom to visit a large supermarket or shopping mall even if it involves a long drive. The freedom to 'go and live in the country', even if it's just a newly built suburb where the country once stood.

The number of people who realise things have to change is growing, but it is still a minority. Most of the others probably prefer to read the press telling them they don't have to change, it's all made up by environmentalists, scientists, NIMBY conservationists, socialists, communists, anarchists, loonies, busybodies or, worst of all, do-gooders.

Smart Growth and all that

The beauty of Smart Growth, however, is that it's something we can begin to implement now. It doesn't need root-and-branch reform of the national or international economic system. It doesn't even need root-and-branch reform of the planning and transport planning professions. It certainly needs some pretty radical new government policy and guidance in both these (and other) fields, and might benefit too from a few bits of primary legislation. It also needs some big reordering of public investment, especially in transport. But it doesn't need us all to become better people, at least not in the short term.

Some of the changes, such as sustainable urban transportation, building sustainable housing layouts or reviving traditional shopping centres, are things that are going to take decades to implement, so it's a good idea to start now. Other things, such as not approving more urban sprawl, rejigging local plans to a genuine sustainability approach, dropping the trunk-road building programme and much else, could be done now.

Rebuilding our ailing communities will take longer. All too often environmentalists look forward to building an ideal world. But human beings, unfortunately, don't do ideal worlds; we have a million ways of messing things up. However, the basic material is there and we can do a lot better than we are doing. We can start working together on things that aren't simply focused on making ourselves (or, worse still, a small stratum of very rich people) richer. It doesn't mean we have to be poorer or to abandon material well-being for ourselves, our families and our communities. It's just that we need to look at what well-being entails. And that requires a shift in attitudes – far harder perhaps than merely rebuilding the physical infrastructure of our land. We need some vision.

Principles of Smart Growth community planning

- Mixed-use development.
- Protection of the fabric of functioning communities.
- Affordable housing.
- Densification of some low-density sprawl.
- Protection and enhancement of traditional shopping centres.
- Avoidance of out-of-town shopping and over-large shopping facilities.
- Promotion of citizenship rather than consumerism.
- Promotion of individual well-being.
- Support for Transition Initiatives.

Chapter 13

News from Somewhere: a Smart Growth vision

*If others can see it as I have seen it, then it may be called
a vision rather than a dream.*

William Morris, *News from Nowhere*

Looking forward

Travel writers down the centuries have so often become absorbed with the challenges of flea-ridden inns, blistered feet, creaking bicycles, skittish horses, leaking punts or Punch & Judy shows, it's a miracle they ever found time to observe their surroundings. Any of these hazards could face our future travel writers, of course, plus the hazards of climate change, economic collapse and whatever else the future holds, but, assuming anyone is still recording their journeys 20, 30 or 40 years hence, what would they see?

Books about travel around Britain in the future are pretty scarce. There's a vast science fiction literature, of course, but it throws little light on spatial planning, transport or community development. How the Daleks cope with our shattered, overheated world when they eventually get a successful invasion past Dr Who is not something we need to worry too much about.

"Exterminate! – Oh, they've done it for us."

George Orwell's *1984* and Aldous Huxley's *Brave New World* gave us different future dystopias, while Richard Jefferies' strange 1885 novel, *After London – Wild England*[1] foresees civilisation destroyed by a cataclysm and the few survivors struggling to survive. William Morris I's *News from Nowhere*,[2] however, presents a vision of twenty-first-century society where the old order has been overturned by civil conflict and a utopian civilisation has replaced it. Along with Morris's other writings, it must have had a strong influence on the garden cities movement, though I'm not sure it was a beneficial one.

Morris's utopia is a kind and cosy one, but I really can't bring myself to try to recount my own series of meetings with happy Stepford wives and their equally placid and contented husbands, quietly tending their hand-looms. His twenty-first-century characters are certainly chirpy and creative but, frankly, they aren't really human beings. Humans will always be humans, capable of mixing the highest qualities of altruism and endeavour in the arts, humanities and sciences with the quarrelsome and destructive traits of a band of monkeys. So this won't be *News from Nowhere* but news from right here, just a bit further down the line.

What would a traveller in, say, the 2030s or 2040s record in his or her notebook (or, almost certainly by then, some kind of electronic device) had robust Smart Growth policies been applied? Well, let's not get carried away like Morris and assume everything will be different (he was, to be fair, thinking 12 decades rather than three). Think back 25 years (if you've lived that long) and, physically speaking, the country doesn't look that different, yet profound changes in direction can occur in that sort of span. A vast amount of house building and sprawl happened in the 21 years between the wars – a third of the houses in 1939 hadn't existed in 1918. By 1939 there had been a huge explosion of mass motoring; by the end of 1940 this had wholly ceased. In 1950 the country was wholly dependent on public transport to move people and largely dependent on the railways to move goods; by 1970 we were largely dependent on roads for both. The ten years from 1980 to 1990 saw the country change from being a badly run mixed economy to a badly run free-market economy, while greenfield house building and motorway construction mushroomed. At the time of writing we have another period of massive uncertainty, with politicians of all parties floundering around in a sea of new politics. They are finally talking the talk about the environment and climate change, but they are yet to walk the walk.

Why we need some vision

We need to face the fact that we live in a desperately overcrowded country and fix the way we live in it by dropping some of the cosy fantasies that many of us, environmentalists in particular, have been guilty of. How often have we dreamed of creating some rural idyll, oblivious to the fact that it would be a completely unsustainable way of living for the 50 million people the country had then, the 60 million it has now or anything up to the 70 million it might have in 20 or 30 years? Like it, or like it not, the only sustainable future for the vast majority of us is an urban one.

The aching nostalgia for their rural past felt by Victorians who moved to the towns runs through *News from Nowhere* and has passed down through the generations. In itself, it's not a bad thing at all: that vision of our countryside – that 6,000-year work of collective genius – is part of our identity and a major wellspring of environmentalism, but it has generated a level of contempt for urban life and the delusion that moving to low-density suburbs is country living. In reality, the half-century before the First World War gave us great, compact, permeable, functional, mobile, communities. They weren't perfect of course (what is?), but they were plainly heading in the direction of sustainability. So our points of departure must be, firstly, recognition that the late-Victorians and Edwardians bequeathed us superbly functional and sustainable towns and cities and, secondly, protection of the countryside that lifts our souls and sustains our existence with food, water, timber, flood control, carbon sequestration, amenity, etc.

This is a vision, and like most visionaries we can let ourselves be angry about the forces that undermine progress; that same half-century gave us the sprawl lobby and the roads lobby. The garden cities movement urged us to destroy compact sustainable cities and move to low-density suburbs of one kind or another. Thanks to this woolly minded muddle, tens of millions of us spent the next 100 years moving as far away from our neighbours as we could and living lives wholly dependent on long commuter journeys. As the twentieth century wore on, that was increasingly by car, allowing the sprawl to spread ever further and ensuring the countryside the people sought was ever-more-effectively destroyed. Heading the other way on this road to hell were those intent on destroying our cities under the well-intentioned flag of slum clearance and the ego-sodden flag of modern architecture. And we spent the whole century ripping apart our sustainable transport system in favour of one designed to exacerbate climate change. It would be nice to say all these destructive forces have now ended. Nice, but delusional.

By now we've gained a sobering idea of where we might be headed if we don't get a grip on this, but let's look at where we could be headed if we did.

A Smart Growth vision

Traveller, then, step with me into a Britain where the calendar says twenty-forty-something. It is a Britain which has spent the last three decades vigorously pursuing its own version of Smart Growth policies, adapted from those in North America and elsewhere.

So let's step down cautiously from H. G. Wells's time machine, or Morris's bed of dreams, if you prefer, and look around. Compare the world in the century's fourth or fifth decade with the world at the beginning of its second and permit yourself a small snigger. For, superficially at any rate, much of it looks the same. Those houses over there are the same houses although their brickwork has darkened a little. That clump of trees is the same clump of trees, although they've grown a bit. It's the same road too, although there are fewer cars and they look fairly different. The seasons come and go and the British weather remains changeable too, but the climate has changed, even though that's not obvious on first impressions. The people we see still go to work, fall in love, have families, grow sick and die; the politicians still squabble, the world is still a highly dangerous place and, underneath their slightly more functional clothes, individual members of *Homo sapiens* are pretty much the same.

But look more closely and you will see things are being done very differently. Some of the changes we expected in the early twenty-first century have come to pass and others have not. In this vision, the people of the century's second quarter have been vigorously applying Smart Growth policies and generating outcomes far better adapted to the challenges of their time. The economic shocks that followed the great crash of 2008; the environmental challenges of climate change, resource depletion, biodegradation and over-population have finally driven home the painful messages we spent so long denying. Many of the old twentieth-century prejudices – the freedom to build where you like, to drive where you like, the freedom to develop greenfield areas, etc. have finally broken down and people now widely accept that we must rebuild our cities, towns and villages as sustainable communities for a more challenging age.

The Smart Growth UK principles (see page 19), agreed in 2008, are as applicable here as America's Smart Growth principles are over there. The way we apply Smart Growth may be a bit different, but the principle of compact, communitarian development is even more relevant in a small, overcrowded country.

What do our towns look like?

Our time machine seems to have dropped us in a small city, around 30 years hence. We're near the centre, beside the main railway station and it's pleasing to see that the main line through this town has finally been electrified, a mere 80 years after it was first suggested. Outside the station is a modern transport interchange, with tram routes radiating to most parts of the city and buses to any parts that aren't served – and to the countryside beyond.

We are a short walk from the centre but it isn't the hazardous obstacle course of roads and traffic it would have been 30 years ago. There is still some vehicular traffic – delivery vans, a few electric cars, service vehicles, etc. – but they occupy a great deal less of the road space. That doesn't mean we can walk around with our eyes shut, however; there are clearly delineated parts of the streets for cyclists and they can move around without fear of striking pedestrians or being struck by vehicles. And we pedestrians too can move around safely and easily, for as well as enjoying good footways the town has been designed to be as permeable as possible and we can walk in roughly straight lines. That new road with a flyover cut through part of the town in the 1960s has vanished without trace and its course is now marked by a tramway and new buildings.

Walking, cycling, riding – the mobile town of the future.

It takes us a few minutes to realise something else striking about this town – that many of its buildings are old ones and that most of the pre-1939 buildings in the town centre that we knew from our time are still there. They may have been cleaned and modernised, but they provide a sense of continuity and community that post-war buildings never managed and we haven't wasted the vast amount of embodied energy from their construction.

But plainly the citizens have faced up to the need to lose the energy embodied in some buildings, for many of the modernist structures from the 1960s and thereabouts have gone, as they were beyond redemption in sustainability terms, inflexible, unpopular and ugly. And we have plainly relearned the arts of low-rise, high-density; their replacements are mostly low- or medium-rise and designed to blend harmoniously with the traditional fabric of the town while embodying the highest standards of sustainability – a philosophy widely applied to the existing stock.

The place where a shopping mall used to stand is now a street again, with shop frontages, and only part is an enclosed pedestrian arcade. Life has returned to the streets, with a range of small shops to complement the large multiples, which have plainly become less dominant. People are out and about, exchanging gossip and debating the issues of the day such as the weather, the hopeless political muddle at Westminster and why England's bid for the 2050 football world cup has come so spectacularly unstuck.

Plainly the citizens have become more concerned about their changing and increasingly unpredictable climate, coping as they now do with long periods of great heat and drought or of intense storminess and deluge and, occasionally, bitterly cold winters. Everywhere, even in the centre, there are more trees, their cultivation made possible by restrictions on high buildings, freeing up of road space no longer needed to accommodate traffic congestion, and acceptance of the need to include at least small areas of open space. The trees provide shelter from storms and mitigate the summer heat with their shade. Everywhere opportunities to introduce greenery have been seized, even on roofs of the newer buildings, and open spaces are fiercely protected and planted.

Now let's hop on a tram to the suburbs and see what's happening there.

Alighting at a stop towards the edge of the city, which was just a vast area of inter-war sprawl, we see changes are afoot there too. The small suburban shopping centre here, which was being murdered by out-of-town shopping competition, is reviving and new buildings for employment and shopping have gone up because it's near a tram stop. Some of the run-down streets of inter-war semis close to the tram stop have gone too; in their place have been built streets of high-density terraced houses. Evidently the moans about 'garden grabbing' have ceased, for all these houses, most of them three-storeyed, have

Let's hop on a tram to the suburbs . . .

. . . just like our grandparents did. *Image: National Tramway Museum*

small gardens, while the footprint of the houses themselves is much smaller. Hardly any flats seem to be going up, although some of the many blocks built in the early twenty-first century are being retrofitted for sustainability. The houses plainly include the very latest energy-efficiency measures, but already it's clear that there has been a return to a coherent architectural language for minor domestic architecture, and none creates a discordant note.

There's a tram every few minutes, so we can hop on one to the last stop before the open country beyond. Here the suburbia is having some very radical measures applied, as it's being remodelled as an urban village predominantly for older people, and the economies of scale in providing the facilities they need collectively is substantially reducing the strain on the economy.

Many of its homes were bungalows, and these are gradually being adapted to make them suitable for sustainable living for those in early retirement who wish to garden. But there is a range of new developments too for those who do not, or cannot, run homes with gardens and those who need various levels of care. Most of the new apartments have access to communal gardens and are close to health-care facilities and shops. Many are adaptable to various levels of care and, where their inhabitants' needs can no longer be met, it's easy for them to move to somewhere where they can. And it's pleasing to note that the trauma felt by old people at the loss of the value of their homes to pay for residential care has been obviated by new legislation.

What does the countryside look like?

Let's now take a bus or train out of town and see what the countryside looks like.

Much of it, of course, looks approximately like it does today, though there seem to be more trees and hedges. In fact its familiarity is a striking feature – had we gone on with the dumb growth of the 2000s much of it wouldn't look at all like it does today, in fact it wouldn't look like countryside at all, it would look like low-density suburbia.

Close to the city boundary some of the fields have become allotments for the city dwellers, but they soon give way to a countryside that is still farmed. There are villages too, which look much like they did, although their communities seem to have revived somewhat. The pub that shut in 2008 has reopened. The small shop and sub-post office that shut a few years earlier haven't, however, but where the village hall used to stand is a multi-functional outlet run by the local community with a shop and post office, community hall, cafe and surgeries for the peripatetic GPs and dentists, who provide a service two days a week. There are actually people about too. Some things will never change, of course; they are discussing the peculiar weather, while the farmers are complaining they're being hard done by.

Travelling onwards, however, there are some spots where something striking seems to have happened. The motorway that cut this stretch of countryside in half has been reduced to a single carriageway and works are under way to convert the other to a high-speed railway. Where an out-of-town shopping complex used to stand is – nothing. Just fields. And other things have gone too. Where a speculative post-war housing development was built on a floodplain close to a major river, the inhabitants have finally given up the struggle against ever-more regular floods as their calls for vastly expensive flood controls fell on deaf ears. So their homes now are also fields – it is possible. Lots of industrial sites have been turned back into country, so the same can be done even with shopping or housing centres, and the addition to our productive land is most welcome.

Of course, all undeveloped land now enjoys strong protection under the planning system. Taking a train on a railway recently reopened more than half a century after it was shut, then changing to a bus service, enables us to venture further into a more remote area, where we find areas of moorland have had their drainage reduced to enable them to fulfil the really useful function of peat formation for carbon sequestration and biodiversity purposes. This will also reduce flooding downstream and improve water supplies during droughts. On parts of the non-peat upland soils, trees are being planted as part of rewilding schemes and to enable them to play their part in carbon sequestration too.

The sprawl of our time has been halted. *Image: Henry Oliver*

Without the cheap and abundant road transport of former times, inhabitants and visitors to such areas do face greater challenges. Some road transport is still available for those who live there, using electric vehicles, but mileages are much reduced. Some railway lines have reopened and bus services have improved. Visitors have to find more sustainable ways of reaching remote areas, ways which respect the environment. Meanwhile, pressure for rural leisure in areas near towns and cities has increased – but this too has increased pressure to improve their environmental protection. As ever, there are no simple answers to rural protection.

Where do we live?

The surge of house building sought by the government in the 2000s was comprehensively undermined by the economic recession that followed and never really took off again despite the damage done to the planning system by political meddling from all sides around that time, which set off a surge of low-density greenfield building, leaving the country with an even bigger surplus of poorly located 'family' homes than it had before. It took substantially improved and strengthened planning policies to put that genie back in the bottle.

The raw numbers of new houses proposed for England – three million between 2008 and 2020 and another two million by 2030 – were never achieved, even after the green economic recovery took effect. Builders were deterred by a weakening market for greenfield homes and the planning changes made when the 'household projections' used to justify them proved to be demonstrably misapplied. Finally, it was recognised that the great growth in household numbers would overwhelmingly be single people and childless couples and the majority would be over-55s.

As a result, little of the house building has been family homes with gardens. The extra demand for such homes has been met with fiscal and other measures to encourage those who live in such homes but don't actually need them to move somewhere more suitable. The initial opposition to this idea eventually declined as people came to realise this was an environmental issue and ways were found to meet older people's objectives for family visits, gardening and storage of family treasures.

Substantial numbers of homes have continued to be built, but the development pattern has changed radically. The old way of building low-density homes on greenfield sites ceased early on; it may have been profitable but the real needs were very different and we found better ways of housing ourselves. There was intense pressure too to implement restrictions on soil sealing once Europe finally got its act together on soil protection.

The ordinary homes we're now building are mostly in towns and cities and often on the site of lower-density homes in areas newly linked by rail-based transit. They look strongly like those of an earlier age of house building, with higher-density terraced and semi-detached houses with small footprints and some garden space to the fore.

A huge percentage of our new housing, however, is aimed at older people and some of the lower-density suburbs are being retrofitted to cope with their needs, creating economies of scale. Rather than complaining about the 'Costa Geriatrica', we are happily creating 'grey ghettoes' in most of our towns. Here we find a range of housing to suit older people's changing needs and the services they require to help them with independent, or indeed dependent, living. With access to road vehicles so expensive and restricted, most older people are glad to live within close reach of public transport and services, and find that the chance to meet each other on the street and in shopping centres enriches their lives in a way that low-density bungaloid sprawl never did. But they still complain things aren't done the way they used to be.

Moving house and selling homes has been made very much simpler and, as a result, home builders are no longer able to peddle their 'one size fits all' homes to an increasingly sophisticated public. Buy-to-let has been hit by taxation, freeing up more homes to those who want to buy, and restrictions on motoring have hit second-home occupation, freeing up more housing in rural areas. And it's finally been accepted across the spectrum that those who cannot afford to buy still need adequate socially rented housing.

Greenfield development of any kind is now rare and all development pro-posals are subject to sophisticated sustainability tests on transport, flooding, water supply, proximity to services, etc. Developing land that has not been previously used also attracts a requirement to finance remediation or reclama-tion of brownfield land, and the price rises according to the sustainability of the location. The new rules also restrict development on some brownfield sites, particularly those at remote rural locations, but elsewhere the brownfield chal-lenge is being robustly addressed with a fully operational contaminated land regime and a wide array of incentives and technologies for remediating 300 years of industrial contamination.

All this is facilitated by comprehensive spatial, transport and economic policy at national, regional and local level, all of which enjoy substantial, democratic input.

How do we get about?

As we walk the streets of the future, the most obvious change is the decline in the mentality that demanded complete freedom to drive motor vehicles. We will never again see the attitudes that produced the fuel protests in 2000, although people still use cars and many of their goods are delivered by van or lorry. But we have started to live much nearer the places we work and shop in, and most of the vehicles we see are relatively short-range electric vehicles, small and energy-efficient and capable of driving shorter distances than today, mostly powered by our (relatively expensive) renewable energy. All the big conurbations have now brought in powerful traffic restraint and/or congestion charging and most medium-sized and some smaller towns are now following suit. There is national road pricing for lorries too. Some towns are closing some of the most damaging post-war urban roads altogether; it's a process some US cities started in the first decade of the century but which took longer to take root here (although in 2009 Chatham demolished a town-centre fly-over), and many cities are finding such routes are good places to redevelop or to run light rail schemes along.

Private motoring is now something one thinks twice about before attempt-ing. Outside the towns, major road construction has come to a halt.

Our dependence on the motor lorry is much reduced too. The revival of rail, water and short-sea freight has helped, but the cost of fuel and road-use charging for lorries has finally reversed the decades of expansion of this envi-ronmentally destructive technology. No longer can they secure distribution sites near motorway interchanges and many of these are falling into disuse, though new rail-based distribution centres in towns are proliferating.

Airport expansion has long been a thing of the past, as the rapid decline in flying as fuel became more expansive and the total dependence of the sector on vast consumption of fossil fuel had made it more and more politically unacceptable. Some flying still takes place, mostly long-haul, but it is extremely expensive and fast becoming the luxury it was long ago. Meanwhile, development of passenger shipping has continued.

In the circumstances, a surprising survival has been the Mediterranean holiday, sustained by the development of high-speed rail links from northern to southern Europe and completion of the second Channel Tunnel. But few venture there in high summer, however, for it is far too hot; most such trips are now made in spring and autumn, facilitated by reform of the school term structure.

But there is a big upside to the transport changes too. All major conurbations now have significant light rail or metro systems and those that had them at the beginning of the century have greatly expanded their systems. Now medium-sized towns are following suit and the first light rail systems are under construction in small cities and large towns. The realisation that our first transport need was to fix city transport delayed the development of high-speed inter-urban railways, despite the politicians' talk, but it is happening now, sometimes using one carriageway or even both of old motorway routes. Better connections are also being secured to Europe via the second Channel Tunnel, which links to high-speed routes all across the continent.

Nor are local rail or rail freight services being neglected. The desperate bottlenecks that many city rail networks represent are being addressed with investment, which has also freed up capacity for rail freight expansion. Planning for employment space is now much more geared to siting it near railway lines or major waterways, and the sharply rising cost of diesel fuel means a distribution system based on vast lorry mileage has had to face radical adaptation, helped by the localist agenda.

How do we earn a living?

The Smart Growth philosophy is basically centred on spatial, transport and community planning, but planning has always aimed to be an holistic philosophy and Smart Growth particularly so. For this reason it's not possible to wholly ignore economics, for it's closely related to these things.

By the time of our future journey, some very uncomfortable truths have finally been addressed. We've twigged that our planning system must address more than 100 years' south-eastwards drift of the economy because it has been environmentally, economically and socially destructive and the water resources of south and east England are plainly unable to support so many people. Both the feeble and ineffective regional policy efforts of our politicians at the beginning of the twenty-first century and the contempt for, and destruction of, regional planning that followed have long been recognised as dangerous failures to reverse the drift. Finally, it was realised that unbalancing our economy so seriously, and necessitating construction of so much new infrastructure in the south-east while wasting it in other regions, was destroying our economy and its environmental and social consequences were dire.

By the time of our vision, peak food and increasing world food prices have necessitated strong protection for our agricultural economy and made destruction of agricultural land for anything so worthless as low-density sprawl a matter of outrage. Meanwhile, robust regional policy has facilitated at least some rebuilding of our manufacturing capacity, assisted by the new philosophy of localism and the need to minimise energy spent transporting goods. The process was encouraged too by realisation that many of the cheap-as-dirt manufactured goods we enjoyed in the early twenty-first century, made in foreign countries, were produced so cheaply by the exploitation of the labour force, by ignoring environmental controls and by burning coal as if it were going out of fashion (which it is of course). Some unpleasant political and military developments finally persuaded us that moving our industrial production to large, powerful dictatorships turns them into industrial superpowers – and into dangerous military ones too. (Perhaps we should have realised that in the first decade of the twenty-first century, as Europe's money followed its factories eastwards.)

Given these trends, the pattern of our work has changed too. The revival of our agriculture and manufacturing has been prompted by the increasing turbulence of the world economy, which has finally exposed the dangers of over-reliance on financial services. And we've come to realise the point has been reached where we don't have room to mitigate our labour shortages and low wages by importing the brightest and best young people from poorer countries, for this is a society that has finally come to celebrate diversity and has finally uncoupled the immigration debate from its racist aspects.

Our economy has become significantly more 'localist' – local agricultural and manufacturing production for local needs, more local shops and more local businesses, keen to keep local money in the local economy. We are still very much part of the world's economic system of course, but we have learned it isn't wholly the free lunch many believed it to be at the end of the twentieth century and the beginning of the twenty-first.

Where do we shop?

Policies on town-centre shopping, such as the sequential test and a revised retail needs test, sustained in the face of intense pressure from multiple retailers, held the line against out-of-town shopping and were eventually superseded by much tougher action against it. Meanwhile the increasing cost of motoring and restrictions on it, together with robust and ramped-up parking controls on out-of-town shops, are now driving those out-of-town shopping centres that still exist into a spiral of decline against which investment in their modernisation is seldom deemed worthwhile.

While chain stores continue to dominate the market for in-town shopping, the new localist philosophy and sympathetic planning and fiscal policies are finally seeing some renaissance in smaller local shops. This is at last undoing the years of decline and the damage done by the economic depression that followed 2008.

A vision rather than a dream

No one likes to be proven wrong, so it's maybe just as well I probably won't still be alive in the 2040s. Will our country look anything like this 30 or 40

The economy has become more localist.

A renaissance in smaller shops.

years hence? I have no idea, but I do know it would be a very much better place if it did. We can go on with the kind of dumb growth that has done so much harm and which is so spectacularly ill-suited to the challenges ahead, and undoubtedly we will continue with many of these destructive trends in the short, or the medium, or the long term. But the sort of changes urged here are not some pie-in-the-sky romanticism; all of them are within our reach if only we make the effort. To do that we will surely have to slaughter some of our current idols, but some will be slaughtered by time anyway, and now would be a good time to change.

Whether this vision becomes a reality or remains just a dream will depend on many things, including our decisions – yours and mine.

Chapter 14

Conclusions: urban rides

It is not little books that can make a people good; that can make them moral; that can restrain them from committing crimes. I believe that books, of any sort, never yet had that tendency.

William Cobbett, *Rural Rides*

Loving our country

When William Cobbett took his *Rural Rides*[1] in the 1820s through an English countryside whose economy had been shattered by the end of the protection the Napoleonic Wars had brought and whose society was being shattered by the enclosure acts, the process of changing a rural people into an urban one had already begun. The public health reforms and rising wealth the nineteenth century were to bring would inevitably give us a population that was far too large to live on the land, however assiduously we exported people to the colonies and elsewhere. We became an urban people inspired by the memory of a rural past.

The countryside has thus remained the wellspring from which both the conservation and environmental movements have risen, and it must remain so, but the disjunct in environmental politics between the two has been a source of division and weakness the movement can ill afford; both dangerous and completely unnecessary.

But the countryside has also, funnily enough, been the inspiration for one of the environmental movement's most destructive offshoots, the garden cities/suburbs movement and the vast area of low-density urban sprawl it generated over the last century or so. No doubt many of those who have moved out of our towns and cities in pursuit of the 'good life' really did believe they were moving to the country, encouraged by the bogus rural names developers apply to sprawl. If ever a thing was loved to death, it has been our countryside.

It is a luxury we cannot afford. If our economic prosperity really has demanded squeezing 60 million of us into this congested space then we need to accept the proximity principle. For the sake of the environment, for the sake of our society and for the protection of our communities, most of us must be urban dwellers. Even Cobbett was forced to accept this, concluding *Rural*

Rides with: "For the present, however, farewell to the country, and now for the Wen and its various corruptions."

Cobbett was many things in his life – farmer, political prisoner and refugee, writer and politician. This book hasn't aimed to be about politics, but all through the past, present and future of our story, politicians and their policies have inevitably intruded for good and for ill, and if we are to remain a democracy over the decades to come, they must play a significant role if we are to secure change.

We have met political villains and heroes, and probably the villains outnumber the heroes by a fairly substantial margin – not because there are more of them, but because this has been a story of environmental villainy and the heroes have mostly fought and died in obscurity.

But if it is a political book, it certainly isn't intended to be a party-political one. Heroes and villains are found in all the main political parties – that's politicians for you – but we will need them. John Prescott's unsuccessful urban renaissance and John Gummer's neglected policy commission support for Smart Growth show there is potential, even if the system is against them.

Why should this be? Well, for a long time, both the sprawl and roads lobbies held the intellectual and political high ground so successfully that it was a very rash or very brave politician who dared to question them. Since the birth of the modern environmental movement in the early 1970s (if not before), that high ground should have been challenged intellectually and politically, but this has seldom been the case. Most of the opposition has concentrated on road building and, despite extraordinary individual successes by those heroic individuals who fight road schemes or strive to protect public transport, the roads lobby has held sway over public policy and politicians, succeeding in devoting tens of billions of pounds of public money to destroying the environment and giving us an unsustainable and obsolete transport system.

Comprehensive critiques of the sprawl lobby have been so much rarer. Many people have fought, with some success, to protect rural areas from development, to the point where we increasingly have a two-tier countryside of relatively pristine protected areas and non-protected areas under attack from suburban sprawl and other forms of decay. But few indeed are those prepared to stand up to a lobby which claims the moral and environmental high ground so loudly.

But there, politics can change. Who, in the mid-1970s would have predicted the sea change in British politics that took place in 1979 and held sway for the next 30 years, two changes of government notwithstanding? And that, of course, is one of the key challenges. Throughout the first three-quarters of the twentieth century a change of government from Conservative to Liberal, from Labour to Conservative or vice versa produced a genuine change in policy. But since the mid-1970s and the growth of what might loosely be called the global free market and Chicago School economics, politicians have become increasingly marginalised, to the point where all the mainstream parties see their role as tinkering with the market to make it work 'efficiently'.

It's been a subtle and insidious process. The surrender to the market took over the Conservatives via Thatcherism in the 1970s, Labour via New Labour in the 1990s and the Liberal Democrats via the 'orange bookers' in the 2000s. Significant figures in all the parties stood – and stand – out against this process, but the triumph of free marketism really didn't mark 'the end of history', far from it. It marked the end of effective democratic control; we stopped being citizens and became consumers, or customers, or just plain mugs. We became greedy and selfish and stopped doing the things to support our communities that we used to do, and it's time this phase in our history came to a close. Many of us lived high on the hog on the back of North Sea oil and financial gambling in the City for 30 years, but the oil and gas are running out and the gas about our dependence on financial services still coming out of the City is really no substitute.

How are we going to throw off this tyrant? It isn't going to be easy, for it has its own weapons of mass corruption in the media, in business and, above all, in our own loss of confidence in alternatives. The failure of the left in the post-war world to run a viable economy is still held up as a reason why no other alternative is possible, but we need to move on.

I mentioned the media, and it's depressing to admit that my own profession is the main obstacle to the change this country so urgently needs. Woe betide any politician, Conservative, Labour or Liberal Democrat, who questions the unfettered freedom of the market, ultra-low taxes, the cheapest possible public services, the freedom to drive anywhere you like, for nothing, as fast as you like, the freedom to stuff your dustbin with whatever you like, the freedom to fly where you like, etc. The nutter press will be let out of its kennel snarling and clawing and will tear you to pieces. They write what their proprietors want them to write – and whether that is prompted by deeply held ideological views or just a simple desire to avoid tax and cross-media restrictions doesn't matter; the end result is the same. Any politics outside the narrow band of free marketism they support is ruthlessly ripped to shreds. In this way half a dozen men control our destiny, and we are too powerless or stupid to gainsay them.

Striving hopefully

So, is any progress possible or was this book just a cheap way of making you feel bad and then dashing your hopes of progress? Was this just an attempt to get you reading my own entry for the Most Depressing Environmental Read of the Year Award? Actually, I think not – and anyway, no one would enter that in case they found out how horrific the prize was – a drive up the M1 perhaps, or a weekend in Milton Keynes.

But look once again across the ocean to America, and look at their media. They not only have an extreme press (perhaps a little less powerful than ours, given the lack of truly national newspapers, but not to be trifled with) but they also have absolutely rabid TV and radio stations. Yet, despite this, a curious thing has happened. The Smart Growth movement has grown and prospered. It cuts across the political divide. It survives despite the occasional foray by press attack dogs. It is supported in town and city halls, in state buildings, in Congress and in the White House. It has, to borrow another Americanism, 'real traction'.

I really don't want to analyse why – no doubt someone in some US university is already hard at work on the PhD – what we need to realise is that something truly amazing has happened over there of all places, which we really need to replicate, suitably adapted, over here. Yes, Smart Growth can work in a country where the media is rabidly supportive of the political forces that have undermined the effectiveness of our politics.

That simple fact astonished me too when I first realised it. Here is a way to work towards improving our environment, massively reducing our reliance on fossil fuels, protecting our countryside and heritage, regenerating our towns and restoring our sense of community. And it's just possible we could be allowed to practise it.

The elephant outside the room

Throughout this book there hasn't been so much an 'elephant in the room' as an elephant outside it. Gardens, I mean. 'Garden cities', 'garden suburbs', 'garden grabbing' and so on – it's been a recurring theme. We love our gardens and live in a climate that's conducive to gardening. Whether or not you believe the old proverb that we are closer to God in a garden than anywhere else on Earth will probably depend on your religious beliefs, but gardens have formed an important part of the culture of these islands for hundreds of years. From the cottage gardens of the poor to the formal gardens of the rich, they have framed much of our traditional way of life.

Now I'd be the first to admit that few things make the time pass as pleasantly as a gentle spring sunshine on your back and the feel of a spade in your hand. It's good for your mental and physical health, but, from the beginning of the twentieth century, gardens began to exercise an unhealthy fascination over those who planned our world.

Despite this, one of the curious things about Ebenezer Howard's *Garden Cities of Tomorrow* is just how little mention of gardens it contains. To be sure, he named his ideal vision 'Garden City' and it was certainly to be laid out on the grand, land-hungry scale beloved of visionaries and dictators. Within Garden City's 6,000 acres would be a 1,000-acre town a mile-and-a-half across. Six 120-feet-wide boulevards run outwards from the centre while in the centre is a five-and-a-half-acre municipal garden; around that are the municipal buildings and around that a wide, circular 'Crystal Palace', part shopping mall, part winter garden. Concentric circular roads run around this central core, accommodating housing plots of at least 20x100 feet and averaging 20x130 feet, and we notice "the very varied architecture and design which the houses and groups of houses display – some having common gardens and cooperative kitchens". Towards the edge of town, Howard even worked in a modern ring road, no less than 420 feet wide, called Grand Avenue, although he rather piously predicted that this would be an additional park of 115 acres, dotted with schools and churches. Well, it sounds like a dual-carriageway ring road to me, especially as he expected the industrial and commercial buildings to lie just beyond it.

Beyond all this municipal parkland, there is actually very little about domestic gardens – the city, he says, will be the work of many minds – engineers, architects, surveyors, landscape gardeners and electricians. There's a mention of "six-roomed cottages with a nice little garden" and that's more or less it. The gardens of Garden City that most interested Howard were public gardens, not domestic ones.

Most of Howard's book has actually nothing to do with planning, but is a near-unreadable treatise on his proposals for the economic management of Garden City, an idealistic balloon that pretty soon popped on the spike of reality. His followers seem to have taken the gardening bit to heart, however, even if Howard plainly wasn't very interested, and much grief has been expended on ensuring that as many as possible of us have gardens, even those who lack either the time or the inclination to garden. Today we have a long-hours culture which grudges us the time to garden, cars that need parking where the front garden once stood and an urge to put decking or concrete down in the back garden to save ourselves the toil and sweat of gardening. Yet this still forms a central thread of policy – a home with a garden is, after all, what politicians like to call a 'family home'.

Please don't imagine this is an attack on gardening. I've always liked gardening and I admire the people who find the time to do it well. It's a healthy exercise with an unhealthy influence on planning. Maybe, just maybe, we shall eventually row back from our long-hours culture and stop building Mondeo hutches on allotments and start converting some of those vast, empty, expanses

of grassland so beloved of garden city and modernist architects alike that sur-
round urban flats and occupy much of the surface area of urban parks to allotments. Perhaps.

And personally, I think we're nearer to God in a library than a garden but,
sadly, I don't suppose we shall see 'library cities' any time soon.

The two Williams' legacy

I venture to suggest that William Morris I – doughty fighter for the Society for
the Protection of Ancient Buildings and the Commons Preservation Society
that he was – would have been appalled by the way his ideas have been misused. I don't suppose we would have seen eye to eye on what should have
happened, but I really can't see Morris wanting to see the countryside he loved
covered in badly designed houses. Nor would he have wanted to see the old
buildings he loved in towns left to decay as their inhabitants were herded out
to garden cities (*News from Nowhere* sees dispersal as a voluntary business).
I'm sure William Morris II would have been delighted to think there were 30
million cars in the country, although he would have been shocked to discover
they were all built by foreign companies, often in foreign countries and that
much of our domestic manufacture was little more than assembling foreign-
made parts. That would have been politically and economically unthinkable in
1963, when he died, and for that to happen to British manufacturing in less
than 40 years would have appalled him, as perhaps it should still appal us.

Throughout this book I've taken the view that part of William Morris I's
legacy was the twentieth-century sprawl movement and I believe that to be the
case. How much of that was Morris's fault I leave to the reader to decide; I
admire his work hugely and I wonder if people just make of his work what
they will. Certainly *News from Nowhere* points in the direction of low-density
dispersal beloved of the sprawl lobby, but it's also clear that Morris was never
the passionate ruralist some make him out to be, and he would no doubt have
been appalled by the tidal wave of sprawl unleashed in his name after 1918.
As his biographer Fiona MacCarthy notes:

> The image of Morris as exclusively the ruralist is mistaken, sentimental.
> After his years at Red House in the early 1860s he never spent the bulk
> of his time in the country. Kelmscott Manor was a house he visited only
> occasionally, for long weekends and holidays. He did not even own it.
> Most of his adult life was taken up in the town and not just in any town
> but in London, 'the Great Wen' whose Victorian expansiveness alter-
> nately stimulated Morris – it provided the basis for his business – and
> drove him to terrible despair. Morris was indeed involved in the formation,

in the late 1870s, of the Commons Preservation Society. But at the same period he was also a prime mover in the Society for the Protection of Ancient Buildings and the Kyrle Society, whose remits were much broader, embattled against environmental carelessness, ugliness and squalor generally.[2]

Morris lectured to the Decorative Branch of the Kyrle Society, and perhaps we need to revive something like it today. Long forgotten, it was founded in the 1870s by a number of Victorian philanthropists including Octavia Hill's sister Miranda for "the diffusion of beauty, to bring colour and interest into the lives of people living in dull, drab surroundings. Bright colour to walls and decoration, good singing, open spaces, nature, literature and art". It aimed to bring colour and artistic taste to "the poorer classes" but, stripped of its patronising Victorian condescension, isn't it time we started to think about the sheer demoralising squalor we have come to accept around us? Why have we

---

John Kyrle and the Kyrle Society

The philanthropist John Kyrle (1637-1724) lived in Ross-on-Wye and is remembered there for his extensive public works. These included planting trees in and around the town, mediating disputes and heading off expensive law suits, help for the poor and the creation of The Prospect, an early public garden in 1700.

His life and work inspired Miranda Hill, helped by her sister Octavia and others, to found the Kyrle Society in 1876, a body set up to "bring beauty home to the poor". Its foundation followed a talk Miranda Hill gave to the National Health Society suggesting that the poor needed beauty in their lives once the basic requirements of food, warmth and shelter had been met.

The Society had a number of objectives, including artistic decoration of hospitals, schools and working men's clubs, an endeavour in which William Morris took part. As well as its decorative committee, it also had committees on music, literature and open space – which was influential in saving numerous areas of open land near London, including Burnham Beeches, Marble Hill, Vauxhall Park, etc. It also campaigned to improve churchyards and other areas as public open space.

The Society was active locally through its branches in protecting beauty and fighting damaging sprawl, and provided the inspiration for many of today's local amenity societies. But the Kyrle Society, like the Commons Preservation Society, was not constituted to manage land, and this was one of the inspirations for forming the National Trust in 1895.

With the Hill sisters devoting their efforts to the new body, the Kyrle Society went into a decline and closed down in 1917, but its work lives on in the national and local bodies it inspired.

Have we lost our ability to judge townscape beautiful?
Image: National Tramway Museum

allowed a tide of cynicism and self-interested commercialism to engulf our sense of urban and rural beauty – and our perception of squalor and ugliness? We have become terrified of raising our voices lest we damage the economy or provoke ridicule.

William Morris I spent his life raising his voice against things that brought accusations of damaging the economy or ridicule and he didn't, frankly, give a monkey's. It's time we too had the courage to face down those who are making a bomb out of wrecking the environment (often at great future financial cost to us all, of course) and to those who ridicule us on their behalf.

And, despite his legacy of car-dependent transport, we can learn from William Morris II as well. He came from a most humble background and never let that get in the way of building his business and engineering empire. His business success would today put him at the very pinnacle of our plutocratic society, yet, unlike so many of today's wealthy and successful people, he never forgot that his good fortune had, to a great extent, been built by others and that he had responsibilities to society as well as the right to enjoy his wealth, much of which he gave away during his lifetime (over £30 million at the time, which would be vastly more today) and the remainder of which he left to good causes.

He was a man of simple tastes, hated waste, hated (ahem) journalists and, on being asked about the benefit of wealth, replied: "Well, you can only wear one suit at a time."

... Or ugly?

He lived in an age when Britain made things and it was our own ability to invent things, or to inspire those such as Marc Brunel, Guglielmo Marconi or, indeed, his own designer Alec Issigonis, who came to our shores to invent things, that created the wealth we now seem content to gamble on the world's money markets. This isn't a book about economics, but, as politicians keep telling us, we need to 'rebalance' our economy. Indeed we do – as already noted, times are changing. As we look to the future, we need to rediscover our genius for making things.

Howard's end

I wonder what Ebenezer Howard would make of the modern Britain he helped to shape? What would he even make of Letchworth Garden City or Welwyn Garden City, which he founded? Both towns pay ample respect to their founder and the rest of the garden sprawl movement pioneers, remembered on street names, on public buildings and even, bizarrely, on shopping centres or car parks.

Howard obviously liked Letchworth's traditional cottage-lined streets (the model for a whole generation of council housing) and would not be too uncomfortable with its growth today. He would probably have liked its town centre, although it fell woefully short of his vision in *Garden Cities of Tomorrow*.

But what would he have made of the traffic choking its wide streets (apart from its pedestrianised area)? What would he have made of its growth? Letchworth hasn't grown as large as some – but it would still have virtually run into Baldock if the A1 weren't in the way. Welwyn has grown still more – garden city, new town, expanded town, growth area, growth point. Between them lies the massive sprawl that is Stevenage, to the west Luton-Dunstable-Houghton Regis, and so on and so on. But then Howard foresaw a country where traditional towns and cities died and were replaced by an endless sprawl of new settlements separated by agricultural belts.

The town centres at both Letchworth and Welwyn today look pretty much like any other inter-war suburban centre, which is not surprising given that these towns were taken as the model followed by others. Howard might even have approved of the massive Howard Centre shopping complex in Welwyn – he did envisage a central 'Crystal Palace' shopping arcade for Garden City, after all – though I think he would have been appalled by the naked big-business capitalism of the clone-town chain stores that occupy it. But what on Earth would he have made of the massive multi-storey car park that is part of the Howard Centre? Or even the big surface-level car park that adjoins it? What would he have made of the A1(M) and the other traffic-choked roads around – and even within – the towns? For here is part of Howard's legacy. Letch-

Welwyn Garden City honours its founding fathers.

worth and Welwyn and the thousands of sprawl towns and suburbs that followed them have left themselves barely able to support a poor bus service in straightforward commercial terms, let alone sustainable transport. We should remember with respect Howard's influence in creating the planning profession. We should draw a veil over his attempts to create a communitarian form of economy, not because this would have been a bad thing but because, although they failed, they gave his spatial planning ideas a false veneer of moral authority. We must face the fact that the vast explosion of suburban sprawl that followed the First World War was inspired by the garden suburbs movement, itself an unloved but altogether more successful spin-off from Howard's garden city ideal, however short of garden suburb principles most of the suburbs fell. And we must finally accept that his vision of low-density sprawl wasn't a model of environmental living for an overpopulated country, it was an environmental disaster. His legacy wasn't garden cities, it was car-dependent suburbs.

Look both ways

In his introduction to *Garden Cities of Tomorrow*, Howard quoted the historian John Richard Green's *Short History of the English People* as saying "new forces, new cravings, new aims, which had been silently gathering beneath the crust of reaction, burst suddenly into view."

His new forces had hardly been gathering silently when his book appeared, as Howard and his followers seem to have spent much of their lives haranguing public meetings about the virtues of sprawl. But perhaps it's time for a new craving, a new aim to burst into view. We are happy enough to absorb vast amounts of American culture – so long, it seems, as we don't identify it as such. When we do, we tend toward responses like "there's nothing the Yanks can teach us", with which, as we saw at the beginning of this book, some planners greeted the possibility of a Smart Growth initiative in the UK.

But there *are* things the Yanks can teach us, although Britain and America are divided by much more than a common language. We are very different countries, but I believe very strongly that the ideals and principles developed by America's Smart Growth movement have a huge relevance to our own disorder, albeit requiring substantial adaptation to what is a very different spatial and transport environment. Very different it may be, but in some ways the need for Smart-Growth-type principles is stronger in many respects in this country: we have less space than America, fewer resources and suffer far worse traffic congestion.

A "new force" it might be, but many of the lessons that Smart Growth can teach us are old lessons. Indeed, much of this book has been dedicated to looking at the mistakes of the past hundred years or so for the very good reason that we need to unlearn some of those mistakes and, sometimes, learn older lessons about how we should live; how we should manage our cities, towns and villages; and how we should get about.

We need to recall that the half-century before the First World War produced not Victorian slums but a robust and amazing answer to them. The bye-law homes, the schools, the electric tramways, the compact town and city centres, the parks, the local shops, the sense of common purpose, the belief that all citizens had duties to society as well as to themselves – this is that era's legacy. What have the Victorians ever done for us? Well, they gave us compact, walkable, low-rise, communitarian, transit-oriented towns and cities. Smart Growth, in fact, a century before the term was coined.

We need to relearn many of the lessons of that era. That high-density urban dwellers usually prefer houses to flats. That cities can function perfectly well without cars so long as people can get around on foot, on a bike or on a tram, train or bus. That local shops sustain communities in a way that huge, car-dependent supermarkets or malls don't. That inter-urban transport is best done on a train. That citizens have civic responsibilities as well as rights. That consumers who merely consume end up with nothing left to consume. None of these things would have surprised anyone at all 100 years ago.

We need to divest ourselves of 100 years of cosy assumptions about plan-

Edwardian cities had beaten a path to Smart Growth nearly a century before the term was coined. *Image: National Tramway Museum*

ning and transport planning too. We must nail the myth that the garden cities movement and the new towns movement did anything to put an end to the building of slums. What it did was put an end to the building of sustainable cities and provide a rationale for the creation of the sprawl that has destroyed so much of our island's environment and left us fatally dependent on unsustainable ways of living. We need to end the myth that 'slum clearance' was all about destroying slums: to be sure, much of the buildings it knocked down, at least in its early decades, were indeed slums, but for the most part it just knocked down sustainable urban development that had become slums through overcrowding, poverty and disrepair. We need to put aside the view that Edwardian cities were smoky, sunless slums. Some were and some weren't. But the suburban sprawl that took their place was all unsustainable, however leafy it may have been before we ripped out the front gardens and turned them into car parks.

We need to put an end too to 90 years of unsustainable transport policies, pursued both at the highest level in central government and at the lowest level of our own decisions to drive to work, to the shops, to the school, to anywhere that takes our fancy. We need to discover that trams aren't an expensive luxury we can't afford, they're the core urban transport in our cities that we can't afford not to reintroduce. We need to get away from our dependence on cars and reduce our dependence on lorries and vans. We need to find ways of moving around town and country that don't destroy the planet.

Then we need to look forward to a world where the oil is running out, where the food is running out, where the water is running out, where patience is running out. A world where we may be trying to cram even more people into our hopelessly overcrowded land. A world where climate change is raising sea levels and inundating low-lying land; where it's forcing us to adapt our agriculture to new practices; where storminess, flooding and drought are all becoming more of a threat that requires serious public investment and action.

And finally, perhaps, we need to find ways of getting on with each other better. We need to stop hiding behind privet hedges, behind leylandii hedges, behind larch-lap panels and behind carports. We need to accept that our neighbours aren't necessarily a pain in the neck and that, sometimes, we are. We need to make our communities into communities. We need to stop being consumers and become citizens again.

A contempt for urban life

Deep in environmentalists' psyche is a belief that an environmental lifestyle belongs in the country and an unspoken but clear contempt for urban life. This might be all very well if the UK had six or seven million people, but it doesn't;

it has 60 or 70 million. That being the case, the sustainable future for most of us means living in towns and cities. For like it or not, urban dwellers' environmental footprint is much smaller than rural dwellers' thanks to their transport needs and much else besides. And that's as things stand. If we work at it, urban dwellers' footprints can be much smaller, but country folk's – well that's going to be more difficult.

With this in mind we need to fix the cities. We need to start fixing our transport system by abandoning road and airport expansion schemes, by deferring high-speed inter-urban rail schemes and by building light railways and metros in towns and at least safeguarding abandoned rail alignments everywhere.

Then we need to start fixing how we live in towns – the type of houses, the type of shops, the type of public buildings, etc. We need to ensure our towns enjoy low-carbon mobility and low-carbon living. We need to stop providing new suburban homes for 'families', as we have more than enough such homes, and we need to start providing (or adapting) more homes for the over-55s in a variety of flexible ways of living.

Next we need to start fixing the suburbs. We must provide them with rail-based public transit and we must densify them around transit stops. Densification should go so far, but no further; we don't need lots of mini-Manhattans. And where suburbs are built at hopelessly unsustainable locations – remote from anywhere people need to be, or in floodplains, etc. – we must accept that some may wither and die.

And we need to stop sprawling, altogether. The years to come are going to be challenging enough without destroying our main source of food, water and carbon sequestration, as well as much else. The countryside needs to become a symbol of our identity once again, not a vacant lot for house building.

Then, of course, we need to be better people, but we could do that anyway.

Smart Growth nation

This book has been about our physical environment, but it's also been about power and where it lies. We live in a democracy, of course, but it's one that is fragile and where politicians believe they have little power to change things. The nineteenth century and the first part of the twentieth saw the growth of universal suffrage and the use of democracy to shift power away from the oligarchy of wealth and inheritance that thousands of years of history had created. Democracy was used (and sometimes misused) to promote protection of society and a fairer distribution of our wealth. But the last couple of hundred years have also seen the growth of government power and civil service power at the expense of Parliament. The Edwardian age saw the flowering of lobbies – in this case the sprawl and roads lobbies – and the bodies created a century ago and their successors have flourished and succeeded, perhaps far beyond the dreams of their founders. Then, as the twentieth century grew old, a counter-reformation to democracy was launched by the financial services industry: a very successful counter-revolution that saw power drain away from elected politicians, local and national, and pass into the hands of wealth once again. How far this has been justified and how far it hasn't is outside the scope of this book, but its effect has been to disempower us and, perhaps worse, to make us believe we would be wrong to change anything. Environmentalists dream of really radical change, but it hasn't happened in 40 years and unless we regain a huge measure of lost political courage, of lost environmental courage and the courage sometimes to face down our own material aspirations, we will need to find ways to change things, which work with the grain of the system.

We need the professions – notably planning and transport planning – to come to terms with some different principles of sustainability. This book has included criticism of the planning profession and some criticisms of transport planning too, but both will be utterly essential if we are to tackle these challenges. The planning profession has its roots in the sprawl lobby and it will have to address this continuing strand of its DNA if it is to play a full part in sustainability. It is crazy, for instance, that misuse of the planning system to promote housing sprawl was used to justify completely scrapping regional planning, but that's just what happened in 2010. We are going to need a planning system that's healthy, powerful and sustainable and has local, regional and national components. Transport planning, perhaps, is less influenced by its twentieth-century roots, which lie to some extent in trying to cope with the mess the roads lobby was creating. Again, it will be a vital weapon.

Meanwhile, however, across the Atlantic, in a democracy heavily influenced by wealth and lobbying, the Smart Growth movement has grown and prospered. In their less positive moments, our American Smart Growth cousins call traditional, car-dependent sprawl 'dumb growth', although the term tends not to appear in their official literature. Dumb growth is something America pursued with its usual energy and organisation for nearly a century, and the Americans went a lot further down the path than we did, protected as we were by a great deal of traditional townscape that resisted the worst efforts of those who wished to destroy it.

But the hypersprawl, the 18-lane freeways, the town centres with no sidewalks and a population that took the car to visit their next-door neighbours is not something we can get all superior about, because America, with equal energy, is now starting to address these things while we continue to amble incompetently in the wrong direction.

For dumb growth is certainly something you can find lots of in the UK. I believe that we need to learn from North America's Smart Growth movement and from those European countries where such policies are second nature, but are unlikely to be called Smart Growth. I don't imagine for a minute that we should simply adopt everything the Smart Growth movement says and apply it blindly over here, because our two countries are very different. But we can learn from the Smart Growth principles, adapt them to our purposes and apply them.

We have, so far, taken only the most cautious and hesitant steps down this route. But now is not the time for hesitant steps. It's time to get smart.

References

Introduction

1   Andrew Gilligan: 'Thousands of Gardens "Stolen" by Developers' (*Sunday Telegraph*, 19 December 2009)
2   Sarah Sayce et al.: *Garden Developments: Understanding the Issues – an Investigation into Residential Development on Gardens in England* (London: Communities and Local Government Publications, 2010)
3   'John Healey Calls on Councils to Use Their Powers to Stop "Garden Grabbing"' (Department for Communities and Local Government press release, 19 January 2010)
4   'Government Could Be Risking Environmental Disaster' (Campaign to Protect Rural England press release, 9 June 2010)
5   'Clark – New Powers to Prevent Unwanted "Garden Grabbing"' (Department for Communities and Local Government press release, 9 June 2010)
6   Cecilia Wong & Andreas Schulze-Bäing: *Brownfield Residential Redevelopment in England* (York: The Joseph Rowntree Foundation, 2010)
7   Raymond Unwin & Barry Parker: *The Art of Building a Home* (London: Longmans, 1901)
8   Raymond Unwin: *Cottage Plans and Common Sense* (London: Fabian Society, 1902)

Chapter 1

1   Walter Wilkinson: *The Peep Show* (London: Geoffrey Bles, 1927)
2   Iain Sinclair: *London Orbital* (London: Granta Books, 2002)
3   Ray LaHood, Lisa P. Jackson & Shaun Donovan: 'Federal Partnership Promises a Smarter, Cleaner Way to Create Jobs' (*The Seattle Times*, 3 February 2010)

Chapter 2

1   Ebenezer Howard: *To-morrow: A Peaceful Path to Real Reform* (London: Swan Sonnenschein, 1898)
2   The Hon. John Byng: *Byng's Tours – the Journals of the Hon. John Byng 1781-1792* (London: Century edition, 1991)
3   Friedrich Engels: *The Condition of the Working Class in England* (*Die Lage der arbeitenden Klasse in England* (Leipzig: 1845)
4   F. J. Osborn: 'Sir Ebenezer Howard, The Evolution of His Ideas' (*Town Planning Review*, vol. 21, no. 3, October 1950)
5   Ebenezer Howard: *Garden Cities of Tomorrow* (London: Swan Sonnenschein, 1902)
6   Kenneth Grahame: *The Wind in the Willows* (London: Methuen, 1908)
7   Robbie Coltrane: *B-Road Britain* (London: Bantam Press, 2008)
8   'Northern Distributor and Postwick Decisions "Great News for Norwich and Norfolk"' (Norfolk County Council press release, 16 December 2009)

9 See Paul Tritton: *John Montagu of Beaulieu, Motoring Pioneer and Prophet* (London: Golden Eagle/George Hart, 1985)

10 See Robert Beevers: *The Garden City Utopia – A Critical Biography of Ebenezer Howard* (Abingdon: The Olivia Press, 2002)

11 Ibid.

12 Raymond Unwin: *Nothing Gained by Overcrowding!* (London: P. S. King & Son / Garden Cities & Town Planning Association, 1912)

Chapter 3

1 The New Townsmen: *New Towns After the War* (London: J. M. Dent, 1918)

2 Walter Wilkinson: *A Sussex Peep-Show* (London: Geoffrey Bles, 1933)

3 Stephen V. Ward: *Planning and Urban Change* (London: Paul Chapman Publishing, 1994)

4 Gilbert & Elizabeth Glen McAllister (eds): *Homes, Towns and Countryside* (London: B. T. Batsford, 1945)

5 Patrick Abercrombie: 'Towns in the National Pattern' in Gilbert & Elizabeth Glen McAllister (eds): *Homes, Towns and Countryside* (London: B. T. Batsford, 1945)

6 Cyril Garbett: 'Planning for Human Needs' in Gilbert & Elizabeth Glen McAllister (eds): *Homes, Towns and Countryside* (London: B. T. Batsford, 1945)

7 See William Houghton-Evans: *Planning Cities* (London: Lawrence and Wishart, 1975)

8 F. J. Osborn: Letter to Lewis Mumford, 2 March 1953, in Michael Hughes (ed.): *The Letters of Lewis Mumford and Frederic J. Osborn* (Bath: Adams & Dart, 1971)

9 See J. Barry Cullingworth & Vincent Nadin: *Town and Country Planning in the UK* (12th edn) (London and New York: Routledge, 1997)

10 Colin Buchanan et al.: *Traffic in Towns* (London: HMSO, 1963)

11 F. J. Osborn: Letter to Lewis Mumford, 7 November 1964, in Michael Hughes (ed.): *The Letters of Lewis Mumford and Frederic J. Osborn* (Bath: Adams & Dart, 1971)

12 See Peter Hall: *Urban and Regional Planning* (London: Routledge, 1992)

13 Ibid.

14 Roger Higham: *The South Country* (London, J. M. Dent & Sons, 1972)

15 Paul Balchin: 'Housing' in Barry Cullingworth (ed.): *British Planning* (London: The Athlone Press, 1999)

16 J. Barry Cullingworth & Vincent Nadin: *Town and Country Planning in the UK* (12th edn) (London: Routledge, 1997)

17 See Lord Eversley: *Commons, Forests and Footpaths – the Story of the Battle During the Last Forty-five Years for Public Rights over the Commons, Forests and Footpaths of England and Wales* (London: Cassell, 1910)

18 Ibid.

19 Patrick Abercrombie: *The Preservation of Rural England* (London: Hodder and Stoughton, 1926)

20 Clough Williams-Ellis: *England and the Octopus* (London, Geoffrey Bles, 1928)

21 Clough Williams-Ellis (ed.): *Britain and the Beast* (London, J. M. Dent and Sons, 1937)

Chapter 4

1 Ebenezer Howard: *Garden Cities of Tomorrow* (London: Swan Sonnenschein, 1902)
2 Tom Fort: *Downstream* (London: Random House, 2008)
3 Ralph Tubbs: *Living in Cities* (Harmondsworth: Penguin Books, 1942)
4 Patrick Abercrombie: 'Towns in the National Pattern' in Gilbert & Elizabeth Glen McAllister (eds): *Homes, Towns and Countryside* (London: B. T. Batsford, 1945)
5 F. J. Osborn: Letter to Lewis Mumford, 16 July 1951, in Michael Hughes (ed.): *The Letters of Lewis Mumford and Frederic J. Osborn* (Bath: Adams & Dart, 1971)
6 F. J. Osborn: Letter to Lewis Mumford, 29 January 1952, in Michael Hughes (ed): *The Letters of Lewis Mumford and Frederic J. Osborn* (Bath: Adams & Dart, 1971)
7 Bill Bryson: *Notes from a Small Island* (London: Doubleday, 1995)
8 Joe Bennett: *Mustn't Grumble* (London: Simon & Schuster, 2006)
9 Rebecca O'Connor: 'Cities Face Wrecking Ball to Meet Carbon Targets' *(The Times*, 25 January 2010)
10 Bill Bryson, op. cit.
11 Nik Cohn: *Yes We Have No – Adventures in Other England* (London: Secker & Warburg, 1999)
12 Stuart Maconie: *Adventures on the High Teas* (London: Ebury Press, 2009)
13 The Local Data Company: *End of Year Report 2009* (London: The Local Data Company Ltd, 2010)
14 Andrew Simms, Julian Oram, Alex MacGillivray & Joe Drury: *Ghost Town Britain* (London: new economics foundation, 2002)
15 Campaign to Protect Rural England: *The Lie of the Land* (London: CPRE, 2003)
16 Molly Conisbee, Petra Kjell, Julian Oram, Jessica Bridges-Palmer, Andrew Simms & John Taylor: *Clone Town Britain – The Loss of Local Identity on the Nation's High Streets* (London: new economics foundation, 2004)
17 Brigadier T. I. Lloyd: *Twilight of the Railways – What Roads They'll Make!* (London: Foster Groom, 1957)
18 *Traffic in Towns: A Study of the Long Term Problems of Traffic in Urban Areas. Reports of the Steering Group and Working Group appointed by the Ministry of Transport* (London: HMSO, 1963)

Chapter 5

1 Karl Moritz: *Travels in England in 1782* (London: Cassell and Company, 1886)
2 Joe Bennett: *Mustn't Grumble* (London: Simon & Schuster, 2006)
3 Mick Hamer: *Wheels Within Wheels* (London: Routledge & Kegan Paul, 1987)
4 The Labour Party Policy Commission on the Environment: *In Trust for Tomorrow* (London: The Labour Party, 1994)
5 Ibid.
6 Chris Mullin: *A View from the Foothills* (London: Profile Books, 2009)
7 H. V. Morton: *In Search of England* (London: Methuen, 1927)
8 Walter Wilkinson: *Vagabonds and Puppets* (London: Geoffrey Bles, 1930)
9 H. V. Morton: *I Saw Two Englands* (London: Methuen, 1942)
10 Walter Wilkinson: *A Sussex Peep-Show* (London: Geoffrey Bles, 1933)
11 Mick Hamer: *Wheels Within Wheels* (London: Routledge & Kegan Paul, 1987)

12 Brigadier T. I. Lloyd: *Twilight of the Railways – What Roads They'll Make!* (London: Forster Groom, 1957)
13 Ian Marchant: *Parallel Lines* (London: Bloomsbury Publishing, 2003)
14 J. B. Priestley: *English Journey* (London: William Heinemann / Victor Gollancz, 1934)
15 Ian Marchant, op. cit.

Chapter 6

1 The Labour Party Policy Commission on the Environment: *In Trust for Tomorrow* (London: The Labour Party, 1994)
2 Chris Mullin: *A View from the Foothills* (London: Profile Books, 2009)
3 *Sustainable Communities: Building for the Future* (London: Office of the Deputy Prime Minister, 2003)
4 Kate Barker: *Barker Review of Housing Supply: Securing Our Future Housing Needs: Interim Report* (London: HMSO, 2003)
5 Barker Steering Group minutes, 22 April 2005
6 Barker Steering Group minutes, 22 March 2005
7 Barker Steering Group minutes, 22 April 2005
8 Barker Steering Group key points, 26 October 2005
9 Barker Steering Group minutes, 21 October 2004
10 Barker Steering Group minutes, 13 December 2004
11 Ibid.
12 Ibid.
13 National Housing and Planning Advice Unit: *Developing a Target Range for the Supply of New Homes in England* (Fareham: National Housing and Planning Advice Unit, 2007)
14 Barker Steering Group minutes, 22 April 2005
15 Barker Steering Group minutes, 29 June 2005
16 Barker Steering Group key points, 2 September 2005
17 Barker Steering Group key points, 15 September 2005
18 Barker Steering Group minutes, 13 December 2004
19 Barker Steering Group minutes, 14 June 2005
20 Barker Steering Group key points, 2 September 2005
21 Barker Steering Group key points, 15 September 2005
22 Barker Steering Group key points, 26 October 2005
23 'New Eco Towns Could Help Tackle Climate Change' (Department for Communities and Local Government press release, 7 March 2007)
24 '15 Locations Shortlisted for Next Stage of Eco Towns Programme' (Department for Communities and Local Government press release, 3 April 2008)
25 'New Research Reveals Public Support for the Development of Eco Towns by a Ratio of 5:1' (Department for Communities and Local Government press release, 30 June 2008)
26 'John Healey adds Essex to the Eco-Town Map' (Department for Communities and Local Government press release, 1 April 2010)
27 'Competition Commission Risks Failing Statutory Duty in Supermarket Inquiry, Says nef' (new economics foundation press release, 12 April 2007)
28 'The Competition Commission Enquiry Has Been Hijacked in the Interests of the Supermarkets it Was Set Up to Investigate, Says nef' (new economics foundation press release, 31 October 2007)

29 '"Monotony Commission" Fails Local Communities and the High Street' (Campaign to Protect Rural England press release, 31 October 2007)
30 The Government Office for Science: *Land Use Futures: Making the Most of Land in the 21st Century* (London: Government Office for Science, 2010)
31 *Labour's Plan for Housing* (London: Labour Party, 2010)

Chapter 7

1 Donella H. Meadows, Dennis L Meadows, Jørgen Randers & William W Behrens III: *The Limits to Growth* (New York: Universe Books. Washington: Potomac Associates. Rome: The Club of Rome. 1972)
2 *A Blueprint for Survival* (*The Ecologist*, January 1972. Subsequently published by Penguin: Harmondsworth, 1973)
3 *World Population Prospects: The 2008 Revision* (New York: UN Department of Economic and Social Affairs Population Division, 2009)
4 Peter Madden, James Goodman, Joy Green & Clare Jenkinson: *Growing Pains – Population and Stability in the UK* (London: Forum for the Future, 2010)
5 'Recession Hits SW Population Growth – A Little Less Pressure on Housing but not Good for Growth' (South West Regional Development Agency press release, 24 June 2010)

Chapter 8

1 Walter Wilkinson: *Puppets Through America* (London: Geoffrey Bles, 1938)
2 Bill Bryson: *Notes from a Big Country* (London: Doubleday, 1998)
3 W. Houghton-Evans: *Planning Cities* (London: Lawrence and Wishart, 1975)
4 Oldham and Rochdale Borough Councils: *Residential Design Guide – Supplementary Planning Document* (2007)
5 Bill Bryson, op. cit.
6 Reid Ewing, Rolf Pendall & Don Chen: *Measuring Sprawl and Its Impact* (Washington: Smart Growth America, 2002)
7 Jane Jacobs: *The Death and Life of Great American Cities* (New York: Random House, 1961)
8 Ibid.
9 Ibid.
10 Bill Bryson, op. cit.
11 Ibid.
12 Bruce Katz: *Smart Growth: The Future of the American Metropolis? CASE Paper 58* (London: Centre for Analysis of Social Exclusion, London School of Economics, 2002)
13 Neil Pierce: *Maryland's Smart Growth Law: A National Model?* (Washington: National Academy of Public Administration, 1999)
14 Jenny Sullivan: 'HUD's Shelley Poticha Discusses Sustainable Development' (*Builder*, 18 February 2010)

Chapter 9

1 H. V. Morton: *In Search of England* (London: Methuen, 1927)
2 Celia Fiennes: *Through England on a Side Saddle in the Time of William and Mary* (London: Penguin Classics edition, 2009)

3 Daniel Defoe: *A Tour Thro' the Whole Island of Great Britain, Divided into Circuits or Journies* (London: 1724-1727; Penguin Classics edition, 1978)
4 John Wesley: *The Journal of John Wesley* (London: Kelly, 1903)
5 Bill Bryson: *Notes from a Small Island* (London: Doubleday, 1995)
6 Stuart Maconie: *Pies and Prejudice – In Search of the North* (London: Ebury Press, 2007)
7 George Orwell: *The Road to Wigan Pier* (London: Victor Gollancz, 1937)
8 Walter Wilkinson: *Puppets Through Lancashire* (London: Geoffrey Bles, 1936)
9 Ibid.
10 Rebecca Willis: *The Proximity Principle* (London: Campaign to Protect Rural England, 2008)
11 'Statistical Release: Revised Projection of Households for the English Regions to 2026' (Department for Communities and Local Government statistical release, 28 February 2008)
12 Karen Croucher, Alan Holmans & Steve Wilcox: *An Examination of the Housing Needs and Supply for an Ageing Society* (London: Royal Institution of Chartered Surveyors, 2009)
13 Jenny Sullivan: 'HUD's Shelley Poticha Discusses Sustainable Development' (*Builder*, 18 February 2010)
14 Ibid.
15 Royal Town Planning Institute et al.: Letter to the Rt. Hon. Eric Pickles MP, 5 August 2010
16 Welsh Assembly Government: *Planning Policy Wales* (Cardiff: Welsh Assembly Government, 2010)
17 Raymond Unwin: *Town Planning in Practice: An Introduction to the Art of Designing Cities and Suburbs* (London: T. Fisher Unwin, 1909)
18 Stuart Maconie: *Adventures on the High Teas* (London: Ebury Press, 2009)
19 Lisa Sanfilippo & Pauline Ngan: *Value Added: the Economic, Social and Environmental Benefits from Creating Incentives for the Repair, Maintenance and Use of Historic Buildings* (London: The new economics foundation, 2007)
20 Joe Bennett: *Mustn't Grumble* (London: Simon & Schuster, 2006)
21 *Realizing the Potential: Expanding Housing Opportunities near Transit* (Washington: Reconnecting America's Center for Transit Oriented Development, 2007)
22 Ian Taylor & Lynn Sloman, Transport for Quality of Life: *Masterplanning Checklist for Sustainable Transport in New Developments* (London: Campaign for Better Transport, 2008)

Chapter 10

1 J. B. Priestley, *English Journey* (London: William Heinemann / Victor Gollancz, 1934)
2 H. V. Morton: *In Search of England* (London: Methuen, 1927)
3 Robbie Coltrane: *B-Road Britain* (London: Bantam Press, 2008)
4 William Cobbett: *Rural Rides* (London: William Cobbett, 1830)
5 L. Dudley Stamp: *Applied Geography* (Harmondsworth: Penguin Books, 1960)
6 See M. L. Parry in R. J. Johnson & Vince Gardiner (eds*): The Changing Geography of the United Kingdom* (London: Routledge, 1991)
7 L. Dudley Stamp, op. cit.
8 F. J. Osborn: Letter to Lewis Mumford, 4 October 1956, in Michael Hughes (ed.): *The Letters of Lewis Mumford and Frederic J. Osborn* (Bath: Adams & Dart, 1971)

9   Ibid.
10 L. Dudley Stamp, op. cit.
11 Ibid.
12 DEFRA: *Food 2030 Strategy* (London, DEFRA, 2010)
13 Sustainable Development Commission: *Food Security and Sustainability* (London: Sustainable Development Commission, 2009)
14 Department for Environment, Food and Rural Affairs: *Safeguarding Our Soils – a Strategy for England* (London: DEFRA, 2009)
15 William Cobbett: *Rural Rides* (London: William Cobbett, 1830)
16 H. V. Morton: *I Saw Two Englands* (London: Methuen, 1942)
17 Natural England: *Towards a Future Designations Strategy (NEB PU16 04)* (Natural England Board report, 20 May 2009)
18 Natural England Board minutes, 20 May 2009
19 Paul Gogarty: *The Water Road* (London: Robson Books, 2002)
20 Wynford Vaughan-Thomas: *The Countryside Companion* (London: Bloomsbury Books, 1979)
21 Nadejda Mishkovsky, Matthew Dalbey, Stephanie Bertiana, Anna Read & Tad McGalliard: *Putting Smart Growth to Work in Rural Communities* (Washington: International City/County Management Association, 2010)

Chapter 11

1   H. V. Morton: *I Saw Two Englands* (London: Methuen, 1942)
2   J. B. Priestley: *English Journey* (London: William Heinemann / Victor Gollancz, 1934)
3   Joe Bennett: *Mustn't Grumble* (London: Simon & Schuster, 2006)
4   'Government Delivers £170 million Transport Funding for New Housing' (Department for Communities and Local Government press release, 27 March 2009)
5   *Transport at a Crossroads* (Copenhagen: European Environment Agency, 2009)
6   *Transit Oriented Development and the Potential for VMT-Related Greenhouse Gas Emissions Reductions* (Chicago: Center for Neighborhood Technology, 2010)
7   Keith Buchan: *A Low Carbon Transport Policy for the UK* (London: Campaign for Better Transport, 2008)
8   Department for Transport: *Towards a Sustainable Transport System – Supporting Economic Growth in a Low Carbon World (Cm 7226)* (The Stationery Office, 2007)
9   Phil Goodwin: *The Strategic Road Network Needs Strategic Policy Appraisal* (London: Campaign for Better Transport, 2009)
10 *Connecting Communities – Expanding Access to the Rail Network* (London: Association of Train Operating Companies, 2009)
11 'Motorists Get up to £5,000 Towards the Cost of an Ultra-Low Carbon Car' (Department for Transport press release, 25 February 2010)

Chapter 12

1   *YouGov / Elizabeth Finn Care Survey* (London: YouGov, 2010)
2   Walter Wilkinson: *The Peep Show* (London; Geoffrey Bles, 1927)
3   Walter Wilkinson: *Vagabonds and Puppets* (London: Geoffrey Bles, 1930)
4   Ibid.
5   Iain Sinclair: *London Orbital* (London: Granta Books, 2002)

6   Paul Gogarty: *The Water Road* (London: Robson Books, 2002)
7   John Hillaby: *Journey Through Britain* (London: Constable, 1968)
8   Jane Jacobs: *The Death and Life of Great American Cities* (New York: Random House, 1961)
9   Robbie Coltrane: *B-Road Britain* (London: Bantam Press, 2008)
10 Nik Cohn: *Yes We Have No* (London: Secker & Warburg, 1999)
11 Jane Jacobs, op. cit.
12 www.smartgrowthamerica.org
13 The Surface Transportation Policy Project and the Center for Neighborhood Technology: *Driven to Spend* (Washington, 2005)
14 Robert W. Burchell et al.: *Costs of Sprawl 2000: TCRP Report 74* (Washington: The National Academies Press, 2002)
15 Stephen Spratt, Andrew Simms, Eva Neitzert & Josh Ryan-Collins: *The Great Transition* (London: new economics foundation, 2009)
16 H. V. Morton: *I Saw Two Englands* (London: Methuen, 1942)

Chapter 13
1   Richard Jefferies: *After London – Wild England* (London: Cassell, 1885)
2   William Morris: *News from Nowhere* (London: Reeves and Turner, 1891)

Chapter 14
1   Willaim Cobbett: *Rural Rides* (London: William Cobbett, 1830)
2   Fiona MacCarthy: *William Morris – A Life for our Time* (London: Faber and Faber, 1994)

Index

Abercombie, Patrick 63, 64, 65, 75, 76, 87, 99
Aberdare 114
Adams, Thomas 43, 53, 150, 151
affordability goal 126, 127, 128, 130, 195
agricultural land
　loss of 140, 141-2, 200-2, 203-4, 210-11
　protection for 209-10, 211, 262
air travel 104, 224, 228, 261
airport expansion 10, 224, 261
allotments 190
America see United States
antisocial behaviour 32-3, 231-3
architectural language 186, 189, 241
　see also local vernacular styles; Modern
　　movement
areas of outstanding natural beauty (AONBs)
　77, 206
Arlington, Virginia 161
Arts and Crafts movement 14, 22, 24, 44,
　45, 63
Ashford 70
Atlanta, Georgia 170-1
Automobile Association 49
Automobile Club of Great Britain (RAC) 47, 48
Aylesbury 70

Baltimore, Maryland 164, 217-18
Barker, Kate 124-5, 126, 127
Barker Steering Group 126-8, 129-30
Barnett, Dame Henrietta 45, 54, 236-7
Basildon 66
Bath 94-5
Bathgate 114
Beckett, Margaret 122, 216
Bedford Park 44
Beeching Plan 107, 113, 114
Belfast 119
Bennett, Joe 92, 103, 188, 214
biodegradation 138, 253
biofuels 141
Birmingham 44, 52, 67, 81, 101, 115, 222
Bishop's Stortford 70
Blackburn 232-3
Blackpool 222
Blair, Tony 126, 129, 220

Boone, Daniel 149
Boreham Wood 67
Bournemouth 70
Bracknell 66
Bradford 96
Brentford 242
Bristol 96, 116, 119
British Road Federation (BRF) 105, 106
Brown, Gordon 10, 18, 109, 116, 121-2, 124,
　125, 131, 137, 182
brownfield development 10, 13, 14, 131, 132,
　182
　United States 165, 167, 169
brutalism 87, 90
Bryson, Bill 91-2, 93-4, 147, 148, 149, 153,
　159, 161, 172, 173, 230
Buchan, Keith 218, 220, 221
Buchanan, Sir Colin 69, 95, 99
Burns, John 53, 75
Bury St Edmunds 79
buses 117-19, 223
　bus rapid transit 119, 215-16
　guided busways 118-19, 215
Buxton, Sir Edward 75
buy-to-let 259
bye-law houses 40, 41-2, 65, 82, 84, 133,
　184, 239
Byers, Stephen 122
Byng, Hon. John 27, 38

Cadbury, George 14, 43
California 159, 169
Calthorpe, Birmingham 44
Calthorpe, Peter 159, 162
Cambridge 79, 118-19
Campaign to Protect Rural England (CPRE)
　13, 97, 131, 176
　see also Council for the Preservation of
　　Rural England
Canada 150-1
car dependency 9, 10, 18, 90, 109, 152, 161,
　208, 214, 226
car ownership 49, 108, 110-11
carbon emissions see greenhouse gas
　emissions

carbon sequestration 145, 200, 257
Cardiff 116
Casson, Sir Hugh 95
Castle, Barbara 107
Chamberlain, Neville 61
Channel Tunnel 114, 228
Chelmsford 70, 79
Churchill, Winston 66, 67
climate change 15-16, 27, 138, 139, 140,
  144-6, 248, 253, 277
The Climate Group 220
coalition government policies 12, 13, 31, 137,
  137-8, 182
Cobbett, William 27, 197, 198, 199, 204,
  265-6
Cohn, Nik 80, 232, 238
Colchester 79
Coltrane, Robbie 50, 198, 235
Commons Preservation Society 24, 74-5, 271
community 32, 234, 235, 277
  Ahwahnee principles 162-3
  community spirit 235-6
  compact communities 18, 19, 40, 176
  cynicism about 235
  destruction of 45, 64, 65, 81, 88, 236-7,
    238
  fostering 19, 237-9
  inclusive communities 19
  proximity principle 176, 265
  rural 208-9, 210, 257-8
  Smart Growth communities 239-43, 248-9
  Transition movement 246
community infrastructure fund 215
congestion charging 117, 119
Congestion Transport Innovation Fund 117
conservation areas 192
Conservative Party and governments 10, 11,
  12, 64, 66-7, 73, 93, 104, 109, 137
  see also coalition government
consumerism 70, 245, 248, 276
Cooper, Yvette 130, 131
Corbett, Michael 162
Corby 66
Council for the Preservation of Rural England
  (CPRE) 75, 76
  see also Campaign to Protect Rural
    England
council housing 47, 59, 66, 73, 83-4
  garden suburb model 47, 59
  outer estates 32, 59, 67, 102, 133, 192
countryside
  protection of 19, 65, 74-7, 200-12, 252, 266
  rural beauty 197-8, 210

rural nostalgia 9, 251
rural planning policies 198, 211-12, 226-7
  Smart Growth vision 257-8
  see also agricultural land
Crawley 65
Croydon 97, 116, 117, 222
Cwmbran 66
cyclists, cycle routes 187, 225-6

Darling, Alistair 72, 104, 116, 117, 122
Dartford 232
Dawley 69
Defoe, Daniel 21, 27, 173
demographic time bomb 180
densification 14, 188, 191, 192-3, 195, 218,
  224, 278
Denver, Colorado 218
Department for Communities and Local
  Government (DCLG) 128, 132, 133
Derwenthorpe 14
Dewsbury 235-6
Dickens, Charles 39, 147
distribution depots 78, 111, 260
DoCoMoMo (DOcumentation and
  COnservation of buildings, sites and
  neighbourhoods of the MOdern
  MOvement) 87
Donovan, Shaun 167
Duany, Andrés 156, 158, 162
Dudley Committee 64
dumb growth and planning policies 20, 30,
  32, 227, 236, 264, 279
Dunstable 231
dysfunctional society 232-3, 235

East Kilbride 66
Eastbourne 70
Ebbw Vale 114
eco towns 130-2
economy 243-6, 261-2
  growth fixation 246
  low-carbon economy 245, 246
Edinburgh 116, 117, 222
elderly people
  downsizing 179, 182
  financial disincentive to moving 180-1
  home adaptation 179
  housing 178-9, 181-2, 191, 256, 259
  residential care 180, 181
electric vehicles 10, 141, 208-9, 226-7, 260
Engels, Friedrich 38
environmentalism 9, 139-40, 141, 195, 251,
  277, 279

Fiennes, Celia 27, 173
financial crash (2008) 136-7, 245
First World War 55
Five Ways to Well-being 246, 247
flats *see* high-rise developments
floodplains 13, 190-1
flyovers 90
food production, UK 202, 203
food security 26, 203-4
Foresight Programme 135
Forshaw, J. H. 64
Fort, Tom 84
fossil fuel consumption 15, 29, 31, 117, 138,
    141, 208, 213, 228, 245, 261, 268
free marketism 38, 133, 139, 244, 267
fuel costs, rising 191, 208, 224, 226, 260, 261
fuel protest (2000) 78, 109

Garden Cities and Town Planning Association
    52, 57
garden cities movement 30, 35-7, 40, 43-7,
    52, 53, 55-6, 58-9, 76, 252, 269, 277
Garden City Association 35-6, 43, 45, 51
garden suburbs 44, 45, 47, 52, 55, 59, 76
gardens 12, 268-9
    garden grabbing 11-12, 13, 182
Gateshead 96, 101
generational diversity in housing 180, 182
gentrification 83, 102
Germany, road building 105-6
Giraldus Cambrensis 26
Glasgow 81, 93, 101, 116, 222
Glenrothes 66
global warming *see* climate change
Gogarty, Paul 208, 232-3
Goodwin, Phil 219-20, 221
Gosport 114
Grantham 183
Greater London Regional Planning
    Committee 61, 63
green belt 10, 61-2, 67, 68, 206-7
green wedges 31
greenfield sprawl 13, 31, 51, 53, 60-1, 67, 130,
    131, 190, 194, 195, 205, 207, 208, 214
    controls on 183-4, 207
greenhouse gas emissions 92, 104, 130-1,
    153, 169, 216, 217, 218-21
grey ghettoes 182, 259
growth area sprawl 30, 62, 70, 71, 79, 123,
    129, 206, 215
Gruen, Victor 98
Gummer, John 266

Hall, Peter 36
Hampshire 71-2
Hampstead Garden Suburb 45, 47, 63, 236-7
Harlow 65, 70, 79
Harmsworth, Alfred (Lord Northcliffe) 51
Harmsworth, Cecil (1st Baron Harmsworth)
    51
Hastings 70
Hatfield 66, 78-9
Hatfield, Mark 154
Hawick 114
Healey, John 132
Hemel Hempstead 65-6, 79
Hertfordshire 28-30, 78-9
High Street UK programme 242
high-rise developments 85, 88, 89, 93, 184,
    186, 188, 193
Higham, Roger 28, 55, 71
Hillaby, John 28, 103, 232
historic building restoration 184
house building
    affordability goal 126, 127, 128, 130
    brownfield development 10, 13, 31
    family homes 12, 178, 180, 181
    government targets 30-1, 125, 128, 137, 177
    inter-war 58-9, 60
    post-financial crash (2008) 136
    post-war 64, 66, 67, 70
    Smart Growth vision 258-60
houshold growth projections 177, 178
housing density standards 12-13, 15, 40, 121,
    184
    brownfield 40
    garden suburbs 45, 65
    greenfield 31, 40
    inter-war 58-9
    Victorian 12, 14, 40
housing market renewal 85, 132-3, 192, 239
Howard Cottage Society 57
Howard, Ebenezer 24, 35, 42-3, 44, 47, 51,
    54, 55, 56, 58, 65, 80-1, 150, 155, 237,
    269, 273-5
Hull 214
Hunter, Sir Robert 75

Idris, Thomas 43
immigration 143, 175
industrial and employment location 77, 78, 261
industrialisation 38
inner-city problem 32-3, 64, 101-2
    United States 153, 166, 218
Inverness 93-4
Ipswich 79

Jacobs, Jane 155-6, 157, 167, 233-4, 239
Jeffries, Richard 250
Johnson, Boris 117, 119
Joseph Rowntree Foundation (JRF) 13-14
Joseph Rowntree Housing Trust 14
just-in-time system 31, 78

Kinder Scout mass trespass 76
Kropotkin, Peter 43
Kyoto Protocol 219
Kyrle, John 271
Kyrle Society 24, 271

Labour Party and governments 10, 12, 64,
    66, 69, 72, 93, 102, 104, 106-8, 116,
    120-33, 135-6, 137
land designations 205-8
land use and management 135-6, 204
    see also agricultural land; mixed-use
        development
land value increases, taxing 102
Le Corbusier 88, 156
Leeds 101, 116, 117, 233
Leland, John 26
Letchworth Garden City 44, 46-7, 54, 63,
    273-5
Lever, W. H. 43
light rail systems 15, 32, 72, 109, 115-17,
    191, 222-4
listed buildings 184
Liverpool 68, 116
Lloyd George, David 58, 105
Lloyd, T. I. 98, 113
local vernacular styles 44-5, 63, 189
localism 261, 262, 263
London
    congestion charging 119
    green belt 61-2, 67, 68
    light rail system 117, 222
    overspill estates 67, 68
    ring city 68, 69, 206
    road building 99, 100-1, 105
London County Council 64, 67-8, 88
low-carbon economy 245, 246
low-density sprawl 9, 14, 15, 31, 32, 39,
    43, 62, 63, 81, 83, 118, 121, 150-1, 191,
    191-5, 195, 214, 262, 275
    see also garden cities movement; garden
        suburbs
low-emission vehicles 141
    see also electric vehicles
Luton 79
Lymm 67

Macdonald, Gus 109
Macmillan, Harold 66, 67
Maconie, Stuart 94-5, 173, 183
Maidstone 70
Malvern 242
Manchester 38, 116, 117, 131, 222, 232, 239
Mandelson, Peter 104
manufacturing 262
Margate 96
Marples, Ernest 106, 114
Maryland 163, 164
Matthews, Shannon 235-6
Mean, Geoff 127
Merton Park 44
metro systems 32, 222, 223
Metroland 60
Middlesborough 96, 116
Miliband, David 130
Milton Keynes 69, 79, 193-5, 216
mixed-use development 11, 19, 153, 156,
    159, 161, 169, 193
Mobberley 67
Modern movement 57, 85, 86-96, 155, 156,
    157, 186, 188, 190
Montagu, John Scott (Lord Montagu of
    Beaulieu) 48
Montague-Barlow, Sir Anderson 63
Moritz, Karl 103
Morrell, Paul 92-3
Morris, William 21-3, 24, 39, 43, 45, 63,
    74-5, 189, 250, 270-2
Morris, William (Viscount Nuffield) 21-3, 25,
    270, 272-3
Morton, H. V. 27, 28, 109-10, 172-3, 197-8,
    204-5, 213, 248
Moses, Robert 156
motor racing 48, 54
Mottram, Sir Richard 121-2
Moule, Elizabeth 162
Muir, John 154
Mullin, Chris 109, 121
Mumford, Lewis 63, 64, 157, 201
municipal housing see council housing

'naked streets' concept 187
National Housing Reform Council (NHRC)
    53
national parks 76, 77, 148, 154
neighbourliness, decline in 230, 236-7, 277
Nettlefold, John 52
Network Rail 122
New Addington 67
New Earswick 14, 45, 54, 63

new economics foundation (nef) 97, 135, 236, 242, 247
new towns movement 57, 64, 70, 76, 152, 277
new urbanism 40, 155-9, 162, 188
Newbury 101
Newcastle 92, 93, 94, 101, 116
Newcastle-under-Lyme 114
News from Nowhere (Morris) 24, 250-1
Newton Aycliffe 65
Northampton 69
Northern Ireland Executive planning policies 182
Norwich 50-1, 79, 101
Nottingham 84, 116, 222

Oakington Barracks 131
Obama, Barack 167
oil crisis (1974) 114
Okehampton 114
Old Oak Estate 47
Oliver, Tom 135
Open Source Planning 10
open space 189-90
Orwell, George 9, 27, 82, 83-4, 173, 250
Osborn, F. J. 55, 57, 63, 65, 88, 201-2
out-of-town retailing 77, 96-7, 133-5, 185-6, 263
outer estates 32, 59, 67, 102, 133, 192
overpopulation 139, 142-4, 253
Oxford 91-2

Parker, Barry 14, 45, 46, 54, 63, 152
parks 190
  see also national parks
peak food 16, 140, 141-2, 262
peak oil 16, 140-1, 248
peak water 16, 142
Pearsall, Howard 54
Pease, Edward 43
pedestrianisation 185-6
Peeler, Joe 111-12
permeable town development 187, 213-14
Perry, Clarence 151-2
Peterborough 69
Peterlee 66
Phillips, Jane 95-6
Pickles, Eric 137
place making 186
planning gain supplement 126, 129
planning profession 53, 58, 63
planning system 36, 52-3
  appeal process 73
  plans-led system 74, 77

post-war planning 64-6
process planning 72
roots in the sprawl lobby 279
Whitehall control of 73, 74, 125-6
see also regional planning
Plater-Zyberk, Elizabeth 156, 158, 162
Plymouth 92, 216
Polyzoides, Stefanos 162
Poole 70
population densities 14-15
population growth 26, 27, 28, 68, 139, 142-4, 175
Portsmouth 69
post-modernism 91
Poticha, Shelley 168-9, 180, 181
Poulson, John 93
Poundbury 188
Prescott, John 10, 109, 121, 122, 123, 124, 130, 266
Preston Bypass 106
Priestley, J. B. 27, 105, 115, 120, 197, 214
Prince's Regeneration Trust 184
protected area system 10, 206, 208, 212, 266
proximity principle 176, 265
Purdom, Charles 55, 57, 59

Radburn principle 152
Railtrack 122
Railway Conversion League 114
railways 11, 104, 113-14
  abandoned rail alignments 118, 224-6
  Beeching closures 107, 113, 114
  inter-urban transport 224-6
  nationalisation 113
  privatisation 114
  protected lines 225
  rail freight 31, 105, 114, 216, 224, 261
  rail passenger transport, UK 216, 225
  rail-based urban transit 18, 34, 218, 222-4
  see also light rail systems; metro systems
Reconnecting America 159, 195
red lining 102
Redditch 69
Rees Jeffreys, William 48, 49, 54
regional planning 10, 69-72, 123, 182
  scrapping of 31, 126, 137, 279
Reith, Lord 63, 64, 65
residential care 180, 181
resource depletion 138, 140, 253
retail industry 77, 96-7, 133-5, 241
  small-shop closures 133, 134
  Smart Growth vision 185-6, 263
  see also out-of-town retailing

retirement housing 178-9, 181-2, 191, 256, 259
retrofitting 191, 256, 259
ribbon development 61, 76
Ridley, Nicholas 104, 107
right to buy 59
road building 10, 31, 69, 70, 97-101, 104, 105-9, 215, 266
road haulage 31-2, 77-8, 105, 111-12, 216, 227, 260
road pricing 117, 119, 260
road safety 112-13
Roads Improvement Association (RIA) 48
roads lobby 15, 17, 47-51, 53, 54, 61, 75, 98, 104, 105, 106, 112, 113, 117, 118, 119, 214
Ronan Point 93
Rowntree, Sir Joseph 14, 43
Rowntree, Seebohm 14
Runcorn 69
Ruskin, John 39, 43, 63

St Albans 79
Salford 238
Sandys, Duncan 67
Scott Committee 64
Second World War 62-4
second-home occupation 259
'shared space' concept 187
Shaw, George Bernard 43, 56
Shaw, Norman 44
Sheffield 96, 101, 116, 222
Shenley 29, 30
Sinclair, Iain 28, 29, 232
single households 178, 181
Skelmersdale 68
Slough 94-5, 195
slum clearance 40, 68, 81, 82-5, 132, 277
Smart Growth America (SGA) 166, 183, 240-1, 243, 244
Smart Growth movement
  coalition working 165, 166
  community planning 248-9
  holistic philosophy 165, 228, 261
  principles 19, 165
  rural planning policies 204, 205, 211-12
  Smart Growth vision 252-64
  transport policies 221-9
  UK initiative 18-20
  urban planning policies 194
  see also under United States
Smith, T. Dan 93, 95, 99
social networking 195
social reforms, Victorian 37, 39, 236
social renting sector 181

Society for the Protection of Ancient Buildings 24, 271
soil degradation 16, 138, 203
soil sealing 145, 200, 203, 204, 205, 259
soil strategy 204, 205
soil-carbon challenge 145
Solomon, Daniel 162
South Mimms 28-9, 30
South West Regional Development Agency (SWRDA) 143-4
south-eastward flow of economic activity 175, 182, 244, 261-2
Southampton 69
spatial planning 30, 33, 34, 43, 123, 126, 130, 137, 165, 211, 234, 247, 250, 260, 261
speed limits 48, 54, 61
speed traps 48, 49
sprawl elimination 183-4, 191-2
sprawl lobby 17, 37, 50, 53, 54, 59, 61, 62-4, 65, 70, 75, 214, 266
  see also greenfield sprawl; growth area sprawl; low-density sprawl; urban sprawl
Stamp, Sir Laurence Dudley 200-1, 202
Standing Advisory Committee on Trunk Road Assessment (SACTRA) 108-9
Stanley, Sir Arthur 48
Stein, Clarence 152
Stevenage 65, 66, 79
Stoke-on-Trent 232
strip malls 97
Stukeley, William 27
suburban exodus 32-3, 81, 166, 183
supermarkets 96, 97, 133-5
  see also out-of-town retailing
Sustainable Communities Plan 79, 85, 123-33, 137, 174-5, 215
Sustainable Development Commission (SDC) 203

Tavistock 114
Taylor, W. G. 57
Thatcher, Margaret 73, 77
thermohaline circulation breakdown 146
Thomasson, Franklin 43
Todt, Fritz 106
Town & Country Planning Association (TCPA) 13, 57, 69, 88, 131
town centre revival 184-6, 241, 242, 253-5
town cramming 12, 13, 192
Town Planning Institute 53, 150
traffic management 30, 220, 224
trams 10, 98, 115, 185-6, 277
transit-oriented development 9, 18, 31,

159-61, 195, 217, 218, 224
Transition movement 246-7, 248
transport 213-29, 277
  carbon footprint 31
  Edwardian 105
  inter-urban 34, 153, 213, 218, 222, 224-5,
    262, 276, 278
  planning 18, 30, 119, 165, 229, 234, 247,
    248, 277, 279
  rural 226-7
  Smart Growth policies and vision 221-9,
    260-1
  sustainable transport 19, 114, 182, 196,
    215, 226, 252, 277
  urban transit policy 10, 11, 18, 222-4
  see also air travel; buses; car dependency;
    electric vehicles; railways; road building;
    road haulage; trams
travel writing 25-8, 60, 84, 91-2, 93-4,
  109-10, 147, 172-4, 197-8, 250
trolley-buses 115
Tubbs, Ralph 86, 87, 88, 89-90
Tudor Walters, Sir John 58
Tudor Walters Committee 58-9, 60, 63
Tunbridge Wells 94
Tysons Corner 170-1

United States 17, 147-71
  anti-sprawl movement 154-5, 156
  brownfield development 165
  car dependency 140, 152, 153, 161
  emission-reduction legislation 169
  garden city ideals 150-1, 156
  hypersprawl 9, 148, 149, 150, 151-3, 240
  LEED (Leadership in Energy and
    Environmental Design) rating systems
    196
  Main Street ethos 164, 187, 241
  neighbourhood model 151-2
  new urbanism 155-9, 162
  Office of Sustainable Housing and
    Communities (OSHC) 167, 180
  population density 149
  property prices 32, 140, 190, 218
  road building 98, 99, 153
  rural planning policies 211-12
  Smart Growth movement 17-18, 33-4, 153,
    162-71, 191, 218, 239-41, 243, 244,
    268, 275, 279
  transit-oriented development 9, 159-61
  transport policies 216-18
  transportation costs 32, 190, 195, 243-4
  UK-US idea exchanges 149-50

zoning laws 151, 153, 158
Unwin, Raymond 14, 24, 45, 46, 53, 54,
  58-9, 61, 63, 76
urban regeneration 10, 12, 15, 102, 121, 166,
  185-6, 215, 234
  see also town centre revival
urban sprawl 9, 10, 16, 35, 36, 53-4, 62, 123,
  137, 140, 144
  United States 9, 148, 149, 150, 151-3, 240
Urban Task Force 121

Vaughan-Thomas, Wynford 210
Victorian and Edwardian towns 39-42, 252,
  276, 277
  see also bye-law houses

Warrington 69
Washington 69, 114
water shortages *see* peak water
well-being 246, 247
Wells, H. G. 43
Welsh Assembly planning policies 182
Welwyn Garden City 57, 58, 59, 66, 76, 79,
  274-5
Wesley, John 173
Wigan 83, 172-4, 232
Wilkinson, Walter 28, 60, 94, 110, 138, 147,
  173-4, 230-1
Williams-Ellis, Clough 76
Willis, Rebecca 176
Wolverhampton 96
Wright, Henry 152
Wythall 67
Wythenshawe 152

Young, Arthur 27